WORKS FOR WORKS, BOOK 1

Before you start to read this book, take this moment to think about making a donation to punctum books, an independent non-profit press,

@ https://punctumbooks.com/support/

If you're reading the e-book, you can click on the image below to go directly to our donations site. Any amount, no matter the size, is appreciated and will help us to keep our ship of fools afloat. Contributions from dedicated readers will also help us to keep our commons open and to cultivate new work that can't find a welcoming port elsewhere. Our adventure is not possible without your support.

Vive la Open Access.

Fig. 1. Detail from Hieronymus Bosch, *Ship of Fools* (1490–1500)

First published in 2022 by punctum books, Earth, Milky Way.
https://punctumbooks.com

ISBN-13: 978-1-68571-032-3 (print)
ISBN-13: 978-1-68571-033-0 (ePDF)

DOI: 10.53288/0375.1.00

LCCN: 2022942793
Library of Congress Cataloging Data is available from the Library of Congress

Book design: Vincent W.J. van Gerven Oei
Cover image: James Mackay, Performance by Derek Jarman and colleagues, during post-production, in the field of the projection of *Blue,* 1993. Photo: Liam Daniel. Image courtesy and © Basilisk Communications Ltd.

ⓟ punctumbooks

spontaneous acts of scholarly combustion

HIC SVNT MONSTRA

Gavin Keeney

Works for Works

Book 1: Useless Beauty

p.

Contents

Acknowledgments

"Works for Works" (2019–) is the follow-up research and publications project to "Lived Law" (2017–2019) and "Knowledge, Spirit, Law" (2015–2017), with all three effectively emerging from the doctoral study, "Visual Agency in Art and Architecture" (2011–2014). An elaboration of a form of scholarship increasingly at risk today due to the colonization of the knowledge commons by neoliberal capitalism, *Works for Works* sets sail for an elsewhere that serves as a site for non-utilitarian works of a conceptual rigor that eschews or resists all forms of commodification.

The literal and figurative origins for several of the essays presented here include post-doctoral fellowships at CEPT University, Ahmedabad, India (2016–2017); the Giorgio Cini Foundation, Venice, Italy (2017); and the Birkbeck Institute for the Humanities, London, England (2017). Additionally, aspects of the Works for Works project were presented in lecture form, in 2019 at Justus Liebig University, Giessen, Germany; the Academy of Visual Arts and ZRC-SAZU, Ljubljana, Slovenia; the Kingston School of Art, Kingston, England; and Arts, Letters and Numbers, Averill Park, New York. Transmedia elements of the study were also developed in 2019 through the performance-based projects "Resting Place," Abhivyakti City Arts Project, Ahmedabad, India and "The Icons of IRWIN," Academy of Visual Arts, Ljubljana, Slovenia. See "Appendix C: A Short History of the Project" for full details of the prior art informing this publication.

Works for Works, as publication, follows upon the two-volume publication, *Knowledge, Spirit, Law* (2015–2017), the latter supported, in part, by lectures at the University of Ljubljana, Ljubljana, Slovenia, sponsored by the US Fulbright Specialist Program, in association with the Faculty of Arts and the Faculty of Architecture, University of Ljubljana and the Igor Zabel Association for Culture and Theory, Ljubljana (2015), and also the Center for Transformative Media, Parsons/The New School for Design, New York City (2014–2015). Interim presentations, in reverse chronological order, include Kochi-Muziris Biennale, Kochi, India (2017); University of St. Joseph, Department of Architecture, Faculty of Creative Industries, Macau, China (2016); and Hong Kong University, Faculty of Law and Faculty of Arts, Hong Kong, China (2016).

Behind many of the essays presented here, and making *Works for Works* a type of report on the globalization of academia and the art world, is a 2017–2019 campaign by the Out of India Collective to position forms of transmedia as direct challenges to the various biases and protocols of academia and the art world. Out of India (OOI), formed at CEPT University in early 2017, sought — across nearly 100 submissions over two years, through polemical and conceptually sophisticated submissions to open calls — to effectively sound both worlds for opportunities to escape socio-culturally determined cultural production. Expecting to fail in almost all instances (and quixotically embracing Beckett's somewhat gruesome "Fail. Fail again. Fail better."), the occasional success suggested a chink in the armor of the art-academic-industrial complex through which such works might slip and take up residence. Utilizing transmedia as its preferred methodology, and assiduously documenting every step along the way, OOI has subsequently ceded its archive to the Metropolitan Transmedia Authority (MTA), as a "historical" resource to be re-deployed and re-performed toward the creation of new forms of artistic scholarship. The concept of scriptoria, as presented here, with its focus on the play between "History" and "No History," is also a direct outcome of the OOI-MTA's experimental studies in the production of useless works for works. In this way, OOI-MTA is the de facto think tank from which *Works for Works* has emerged, and the author has merely served as scribe for the event of these texts and the extensive supporting scholarly apparatus that forms, in effect, a second narrative for the otherwise structuralist arguments of the primary texts.

As such, thanks are due to Ishita Jain, Harsh Bhavsar, and Owen O'Carroll of OOI-MTA for enduring the dance with devils noted above, and for carrying the flame of the scriptoria project into whatever futures the Works for Works project might engender.

Additional thanks are extended to the various interlocutors over the years of the three contiguous research projects noted above, and to those who have provided moral and other forms of material and immaterial support along the way. You all know who you are ....

To put it in "Godardian melodramatic" terms (see Susan Sontag's 1968 seminal essay on Godard in *Styles of Radical Will*), across the arc of the following battles between Capital and citizens (in *Works for Works* denoted as artist-scholars), we see the shadow of something that might be called the originary exception (the foundational concept and precept for works for works or works of useless beauty):

1. The Enlightenment-era exception for works and authors (e.g., via Locke, Diderot, et al.) against patrimonial enclosure;
2. The birth of intellectual property and copyright law (e.g., via the Statute of Anne, the Berne Convention, etc.) and its conversion to forms of industrialized capital, symbolic, spectral, or otherwise;
3. The Marxist critique of alienation, labor (both immaterial and material), and value, inclusive of the Young Hegelians (e.g., Feuerbach, Marx, Engels, Stirner, et al.);
4. The historical-materialist critique of the twentieth-century culture industry and attendant capitalist appropriation of subjective states (e.g., via Adorno, Benjamin, Althusser, Debord, Balibar, Bourdieu, et al.);

5. The structuralist and post-structuralist (phenomenological and post-phenomenological) inquisition of language, authorial rights, and event (e.g., from Saussure and Husserl, to Levinas and Heidegger, to Barthes and Derrida, to Agamben, Badiou, Žižek, Cacciari, et al.);

6. The modern (not modernist) avant-garde and anti-modern (not anti-modernist) nihilist elective postures in art, literature, photography, cinema, etc. (from as early as Mannerism forward, through Neo-classicism, Romanticism, Postromanticism, Symbolism, Expressionism, Suprematicism, Dada, Surrealism, etc.); and

7. The late-modern neoliberalization of the knowledge commons, as integrated spectacle, inclusive of academia and the art world (via the hyper-financialization of the art-academic-industrial complex).

This originary exception (an economy of real and irreal agency, addressing the internal metric of works versus any externally imposed justifications), takes the form of a relation, troubled or otherwise, to the concept of prior art, and reaches its apotheosis in the focus on the "secret" or the "ban" (a messianic silence) of post-structuralist and political-theological critique of law in the 2000s. Any post-Enlightenment re-definition of the exception for works will, therefore, offer a suggestive return to what underwrites and underlies cultural production as form of existentially charged (lived) artistic scholarship in excess of the law — language as law, and vice versa.

Works for works therefore reside in a type of no-where that may or may not be found in academia or in the art world at any given time. Such works will, however, in time and across time, often come to inhabit academia and the art world insofar as both worlds always require signature appropriations to revivify their own often-spent resources. Of primary concern, then, as of 2021, is that both academia and the art world, in their neoliberalized forms (as authorized fields of suspect neo-utilitarian inquiry and capitalist production), are irreducibly and intentionally incapable of the actual production and/or valorization of works for works.

The prospects for works for works reside in a renewed wager (Pascalian or otherwise) on the transcendental or essential (universal) aspects of cultural production, yet by escaping the hothouse of mere existential particulars — careerist or otherwise.

To artist–scholars past, present, and yet to come …

"Noverim me, noverim te."
— Saint Augustine

"If a man could pass through Paradise in a dream, and have a flower presented to him as a pledge that his soul had really been there, and if he found that flower in his hand when he awake — Aye! and what then?"
— Samuel Taylor Coleridge

"We need a new idea. It will probably be a very simple one. Will we be able to recognize it?"
— Susan Sontag

(Ir)real Subsummation

The (ir)real subsummation of culture, as the real subsump-tion of labor, proceeds by theft. Yet subsummation of what by what? Is culture subsumed through appropriation, or is cultural appropriation the act of subsummation? Determinations are elusive in the setting of the terms of engagement. For, (ir)real subsummation also has a Hegelian undercurrent, and subsum-mation — regardless of setting — has a normative negative, not-neutral value in any philosophy of freedom concerning rights of authors or citizens. Therefore the (ir)real of subsummation is the formal theft. In such a case the (ir)real is clearly not the ideal, as with Hegel's conjuring of the real as radical immanency on behalf of universalizing Spirit. What is present, instead, is a vast semi-historical shadow-land of appropriational aspira-tions that underwrites the critical imperative of culture as col-lectively produced tableaux of various otherwise-indeterminate systems of signification — the signs that lead elsewhere, or the representational accord and field reached between immanent and transcendental forms of visionary agency. Such fields are also vineyards, requiring stewardship — for subsummation, *as or by theft,* is almost always authorized, and refusal of the same is almost always a breach of social norms if not law.

The Romantic figure of the artist–scholar has long been as-sociated with the production of works that begin and/or remain outside of this appropriational apparatus — at least as intention, or at least as figment of imaginary intention. The literary work of art of the German Romantics was just such a quest, and Giorgio Agamben's recent *The Adventure* (2018) seems to renew that quest, upon closure of his Homo Sacer program — a series of books surveying the subterranean field of cultural appropriation in association with nearly "sub-atomic" theological structures. Serving as sub-structures then, for modernity and for secular concerns, yet irreducibly inculcated through subtle theological constructs that inhabit representation at the mimetic as well as abstract level, these reserve functions serve as alibi for the systems of mediation to be found in the arts. Strangely, they underwrite the very idea of a cultural commons and the artistic exception. Here, the well-worn distinction between iconology and iconography more or less falls apart when these totemic structures condition entire fields (structuring field effects). Ideation and ideology diverge when the subject of the subject returns, as it always returns in the literary or artistic quest for authenticity within fields of enforced cultural production. Bourdieu's sociological maps produced, notably, a locational logic for these articles of intent (objects of intention) that pass as artworks or intellectual endeavors of one kind of another. The upper-right quadrant of these quadrilateral graphs, connoting *positive reception* amidst conformity, is rightly countered in the visual regime by the apophatic vector transgressing the zero degree, the intersection of the paradigmatic and syntagmatic axes, and heading into negation upon negation — the lower-left quadrant. Ideation frees itself from ideology under duress. This path is agonistic.

Which works today, produced under what circumstances, might counter the creeping determinism of neoliberal capitalist hegemony? What subtending logic of production might serve as justification for new works that serve no ideological, social, cultural, or utilitarian master narrative? Confined to the Arts and Humanities, this question concerns immemorial aspects of the Arts and Humanities, so-called prior art — aspects clearly at risk with the elimination of free subjects in the causal field of technocratic, neoliberal post-humanism. This latest brave new world is no different than any other savage old world where incipient system eclipsed subject, and vision suffered occlusion — with occlusion or blindness serving as the experiential mark for the approach of the hegemon, shadow of the gigantomachy underway.

Such works that attempt to escape capture will also serve as cautionary tales. For they will be, through both indistinct and concrete gestures, de facto maneuvers within the systems of enclosure and closure extant or underway. Yet such works will also pre-figure the re-elaboration of the proto-Romantic quest that edges toward a supernatural realism as it enters into accord with the immemorial figure of works for works and useless beauty. Works for works, occupying a type of null set, arguably open on to temporal uselessness to establish a departure's gate for new forms of speculative inquiry in the Arts and Humanities. Not a simple retro-avant-garde act of recovery, such works are also futural. They have been and will be. They engage time-senses in their gestures toward immanentism and presentism almost in the manner of Orthodox icons. This figure of works for works then carries an older and apparently archaic force-field into the future by way of the present. The conferral of subjective agency upon such works also guarantees that they operate outside of and beyond all determinations enforced from without, yet without falling into false arguments concerning autonomy — whether for disciplines or for works. The immanentism of such works belies autonomy — exposes the modernist project as never-autonomous-in-anyway. This revelation alone is sufficient to reload the purposes of such works — to act as provocations to law, where law constitutes a field of enforced measures to sustain neither justice nor freedom but conformity to the gigantomachy of abstract reason in service to power.

Introduction: The Artist–Scholar

If the artist–scholar seeks a vital universalism through works for works (i.e., works of so-called useless artistic scholarship), versus a universal vitalism, the various artworks, provisional and otherwise, will invariably resemble a *spectral* (*irreal*) camera obscura — or, a walled garden. The monumental or the universal is therefore transferred, inverted, into the internalizing formal operations of the work. The universalism of the Romantic quest (with its primary coordinates in a search for the literary work of art and a quixotic and sometimes exotic form of transpersonalism) is particularized, the universal made concrete and contingent. Whereas cognitive capitalism seeks a seamless unity by which to exploit all particulars, bracketing universals other than as an overarching or transformational quest for conquest, the artist–scholar through works for works restores and nominally safeguards something originary to the very concept of the work of art as a synthesis of universal and contingent orders. From Russian Formalism forward, the de-familiarization and de-formation of the syntagmatic regime in representation and mimesis, or the burrowing into the semantic undercurrents of language, provides the keel for the voyages the artist–scholar undertakes on behalf of works for works. Utility is subverted and specularity (as a form of noetic haunting of and for works) is privileged.

The German Romantic quest for the "literary work of art" may be positioned within the trajectory of modernity, but it is also a compensatory rite or rite of passage for the rights of works that are already then well-incorporated within the modernist quest for synchrony at the provisional or temporal expense of diachrony. Oddly, the reversal given to the effects of the camera obscura (as effect versus apparatus) places synchronic and diachronic time in a topological relation of mirroring one another, the former arguably privileged in the literary work of art, whereas the latter is the very basis of any art-historical or critical history of mnemonic and representational strategies, whether "thick" or "thin," in the Arts and Letters.

Pierre Huyghe's recent works (e.g., the so-called living systems) are a totemic shift toward the unstable artwork incorporating incommensurable "generative" elements of a type of cosmographic universalism that sides with duplicity — the artistic strategy being, in part, to incorporate the shady and high-handed incorporations of the cognitive-capitalist gigantomachy toward unearthing or de-stabilizing the same. The ideological underpinnings of artificial intelligence (AI) and hive mind collide. The term *unearthing* implies hidden, noir-ish elements. The term *de-stabilizing* implies mistrust or disdain. Yet Huyghe's works are first and foremost pulsed as artistic "events," and, as incipient works for works, they are also eminently translatable across variable artistic platforms, the installations being "sets" — both in the logical sense and the theatrical sense. The null set — { } — and the Brechtian theater of the absurd intersect. Eugène Ionesco's "The Chairs," 1952, meets Peter Brook's "The Mahabharata," 1989, in terms of mise en scène. The "drive toward zero" (passing toward the apophatic) occurs within the charmed parameters of the absurdities. These works are staged in many cases to be captured by other means (e.g., filmed), while the inversions of stated intent and the mutability of the time-senses engaged undermine the very premises they set out to investigate. Huyghe has always played a slightly paranoid card within these events (e.g., *This Is Not a Time for Dream-*

ing, 2004, or *A Journey That Wasn't,* 2005) — giving himself a license to subvert his own stated intentions, thus signalling a virtual autonomous something else provided to the works. Yet the works circle the sets, and the sets establish the field. The field of effects becomes the generative inquest; works drop away, Romantic inquiry casts its spell, and the literary element moves from foreground to middle ground (and from middle ground to offstage). Returning to the theatrical-cinematic, the set long gone, duly undermines and subverts all previous intentions, setting in motion the voyage. Kafka meets Borges and "infinity goes up on trial" once again. Part vision, part negation of vision, such works set sail for elsewhere.

Such works favor the non-capture of works — *for works.* Whether produced *within or for* the art world per se, they nonetheless evade capture as incessant transmedia event in/for itself. Art-world spectacle is transgressed. Books are meant to be read and film is meant to be projected. If the artist–scholar, working from literary to cinematic–theatrical antecedents, or working within transpositions of the same, works any ground toward walled garden, it is to be found in the claiming of the subjective conditions of the work as camera obscura. With the generative mysteries of works for works incorporated from the explicit universalism of such forms of inquiry to the implicit, non-consequential interior perspectivism and contingency of works (the inverted worlds, the subverted canons, the evaded diktat, the non-servicing of any external agency whatsoever), something truly magical and utterly of no use may then emerge.

Privilegio in the Venetian Renaissance

Quod opus prefatum per Marcum Antonium prefatum dari
possit alicui diligenti impressori qui opus illud imprimat suis
sumptibus et edat et nemini praeter eum liceat opus illud
imprimi facere.[1]

— The Venetian College

The very first recorded *privilegio* or privilege (an early form
of copyright) was given in Venice to Marc'Antonio Sabellico's
Rerum Venetarum, published in 1487, a book on the history of
Venice.[2] The mise-en-abyme quality deepens… not only did the

---

1   Excerpt from the privilege granted September 1, 1486 by the Venetian
    College to Marc'Antonio Sabellico's *Rerum Venetarum* (1487). Horatio F.
    Brown, "1469–1517: Books before Legislation," in *The Venetian Print-
    ing Press: An Historical Study Based Upon Documents for the Most Part
    Hitherto Unpublished* (London: John C. Nimmo, 1891), 53, with reference
    to Carlo Castellani, *I privilegi di stampa e la proprietà letteraria en Venezia
    dalla introduzione della stampa nella città fin verso la fine del secolo XVIII*
    (Venice: Fratelli Visentini, 1888), 6. See also Giovan Battista Gasparini, "La
    natura giuridica dei privilegi per la stampa in Venezia," in *La Stampa degli
    incunaboli nel Veneto,* eds. Neri Pozza et al. (Vicenza: Neri Pozza, 1984),
    103–20.
2   Marco Antonio Coccio da Vicovaro. Brown, "1469–1517: Books before
    Legislation," 53. One of eight such *privilegi* issued in Venice up to 1500.
    Leonardas Vytautas Gerulaitis, "Privileges and Censorship," in *Printing
    and Publishing in Fifteenth-century Venice* (Chicago: American Library
    Association, 1976), 34.

Venetian Senate grant privilege for this book about the murky origins of Venice, plus its history up to the moment of its publication in 1487, but they granted it to the *author,* not to a publisher. Sabellico subsequently chose the printer, Andrea de' Torresani of Asola, to produce the work. This Early Modern concession to the rights of the author followed upon a continuous tradition from classical times forward that a text belonged to whomever owned its printed form. This breach between physical and intellectual property, operative since the beginning of the production of codices and manuscripts, momentarily closed before it opened once more with the triumph of the printed book trade as industry.[3]

Torresani was, notably, the father of the wife of Aldus Manutius, who would later become the "prince" of Venetian printed books. Printing first arrived in Venice in 1469, when the Collegio of the Senato granted German printer Joannes de Spira monopoly rights for a period of five years to print all books issued in the Republic of Venice. Spira promptly died a year later and the privilege was revoked (not passed on to his business partners). Manutius arrived in Venice in 1489, established his press in 1494, and the "reign of Aldus" lasted for the next 25 years based upon quality of printing, innovation in typography, and re-production of Greek classical literature.[4] As most printer–publishers of the period, Manutius assumed ownership of an author's works (dead or alive) when he applied for *privilegio.* There are exceptions, however, such as when an author-

---

3   "The owner of a book [or manuscript] also possessed legal right to its content." Gerulaitus, *Printing and Publishing in Fifteenth-century Venice,* 32. The author as such did not exist. Gerulaitus notes: "It would be rash to assume that the Venetian solons suddenly hit upon such a remarkable modern idea as the copyright. Instead, it seems more likely that the Signoria considered the privilege another means of remuneration for a semiofficial history of Venice, for at the same time it appointed Sabellico the first librarian of San Marco, with an annual stipend of 200 ducats for the rest of his life" (ibid., 36). Brown describes Sabellico as "historiographer to the Republic." Brown, "1469–1517: Books before Legislation," 53.

4   Manutius established the famed Aldine Academy in 1500 for the study of Greek classics.

publisher held the rights and Manutius merely served as print-er.[5] Such was the case with Sabellico and Torresani. Sabellico is essentially the author-publisher and Torresani is the printer. Yet there is something fascinating hiding out in the 17-year gap between Spira's privilege (literally a monopoly on all book pub-lishing in Venice, no matter if enforced or not) and Sabellico's privilege (an accidental or intentional nod to the author versus the printer). It is as if these two events bracket a space or his-torical interval that is exceptional because of the cultural silence instilled — and it is only discernible in retrospect as interval. Regardless, something was going on that cannot quite be seen or denoted. That fascinating "something" is the total absence of any intervening privileges granted in Venice. The Senate left the book trade to its own devices, having perhaps realized the er-ror of their ways in granting a monopoly. Yet when they sprang back into action in 1486, knowingly or not, they opened Pan-dora's Box and author rights emerged. To mix metaphors, the genie was out of the bottle, the horse had bolted the barn, and there was no looking back….

This powerful acknowledgement of the author, operating just beyond the guarded borders of conventional or official pat-ronism, is the beginning of what is often called "literary propri-etorship," arguably the origin of the moral rights of authors that only formalized centuries later. Notably, *privilegio* only applied to the physical book, not to the written manuscript or to the work, in the abstract, *as* work. No one can own ideas, but you can at least own a book. Thus, the Medieval or Classical rule still held sway in the first instances of *privilegio*. Moreover, the book had to quite literally *appear* (be set in lead type and actu-ally printed and sold) to receive protection from illegal copying and piracy. Book-as-text, text-as-book is a two-way street.

---

5   This includes the deluxe *Hypnerotomachia Poliphili* (1499), one of the most famous books from the Aldine Press. The Verona-based "patron" of the book, Leonardo Crasso, owned the privilege for the book, and he renewed it in 1509. Attributed to Francesco Colonna, a Dominican priest and monk who lived in Venice, the true author of the book is unknown to this day.

The abuse of these privileges was common in the absence of any enforcement by the authorities, and in most cases it was a type of traveler's advisory for authors and presses to cooperate. Yet the concept of literary proprietorship was so vague that as of 1544–1545, following repeated adjustments in the laws of *privilegio,* mostly in favor of the book trade and consumer, Venetian printers were forced to produce "documentary proof of the consent of the author or his nearest heirs" before issuing a book or applying for a privilege.[6] The emergence of a parallel "clandestine book trade" took care of that problem, with fake imprints being sold all over the city, from the Rialto to San Salvadore, from the Frezzeria to the Merceria.[7]

Immediately following this first *privilegio* of 1486, the floodgates opened, and the author-publisher privilege was eclipsed by the printer-publisher privilege. From 1486 to 1517 everything started to unravel, and by the mid-1550s *privilegio* was more or less assigned to the printer-publisher, not to the author-publisher. Notable exceptions were, of course, notable authors of the order of Ariosto et al., with rights being passed with ease to their heirs.[8] Ariosto's *Orlando* actually received a life-time privi-

---

6 Horatio F. Brown, "151/ 13491 Earliest Legislation," in *The Venetian Printing Press,* 79.

7 See Horatio F. Brown, "1500–1600: The Venetian Press in the Sixteenth Century," in *The Venetian Printing Press,* 100, for the centers of book printing and bookselling in the city of Venice.

8 Gerulaitus states: "Some of these latter privileges deserve attention because they either represent novel legal thinking or deal with notable people." Gerulaitus, *Printing and Publishing in Fifteenth-century Venice,* 39. He should have written "making deals with notable people," given the insinuation. He goes on to suggest that deals or favors are, indeed, the case, using Daniele Barbaro's ten-year privilege for his brother's *Castigationes Plinianae* as example. Hermolao Barbaro had been ambassador to the Holy See before his elevation to the Patriarch of Aquileia in 1491 (ibid.). The irony is that even if it was not a case of "novel legal thinking," it still has the effect of being novel legal thinking. Average term of privilege varied, but Brown reports the following: for the first 100 years of book publishing in Venice it was 10 years on average; by 1569 it was 20 years; between 1587 and 1593 it reached 24 years; and in 1596 it went even higher. Brown, "1469–1517: Books before Legislation," 58.

lege — i.e., *his* lifetime, not the life of the book. This was issued in 1515. His heirs subsequently acquired rights to his masterworks upon his death in 1535. Without quite realizing it, the Venetian authorities had now stumbled on to the idea of rewarding the life-work (the *lived* work of the literary and artistic class).

In 1517, due to the abuse of the system by presses "registering" long lists of books in advance of their publication, effectively to tie up books and block anyone else from publishing them, the Venetian Senate cancelled all existing privileges and started from scratch. The College charged with issuing the privilege had apparently been corrupted by the publishing trade. Privileges, not unlike indulgences, were being purchased. The new rules of 1517 also required a two-thirds vote of approval *in the Senate* for all new privileges, effectively overriding the role of the College which would henceforth presumably just record the transaction. Not much later, in 1534, due to further evasive tactics by the book trade, the Senate also re-imposed a one-year deadline on producing the actually existing, physical book or books listed in the privilege, after which, if not published, the privilege for that title was revoked.[9]

The vagaries of privilege had been gamed. It is important to note that not all books were issued a privilege, and that the rules after 1517 stipulated that the work had to be new or pre-

9   The creativity with which the book trade evaded these edicts is almost comical. By 1562, with the fearsome Council of Ten watching over an increasingly unruly and often unscrupulous publishing ecosystem (and in concert with new attempts at moral censorship), tribunals, public readers, etc. were installed to review and judge all works to be submitted for licenses. Previously, the printer-publishers had gamed the Council of Ten's system of requesting *imprimatur* by coercing or buying a *testamur* signed by whomever would sign it. See Horatio F. Brown, "1549–1596: The Government and the Guild," in *The Venetian Printing Press*, 92. Brown's wry prose suggests that the Council of Ten was a sop thrown to the Church by the Republic of Venice, and that the Venetian Senate refused to provide the means of enforcement of the *imprimatur*, or for that matter the *privilegio*, intentionally. The laissez-faire approach was also perfectly consistent with Renaissance humanist values in the Venetian Republic. With the Clementine Index of 1596, however, things grew rather grim and the Republic blinked.

viously unpublished to be granted such status.[10] Much of this had to do with how books came to publishers, how they were editioned, with many being translations from Greek, Latin, and Hebrew — meaning classical works — or edited collections. By the 1550s, privilege was more or less a means of protecting a publisher's financial investment in a project.[11] Thus, the glorious

---

10   Brown reports, as a sample, the following number of privileges issued: none in some years, 82 in 1544, 88 in 1549, 100 or so in 1550, 117 in 1561, with the early years of 1469–1498 showing "a steady increase, followed by a decline" and a bottoming out in 1511. Brown, "1500–1600: The Venetian Press in the Sixteenth Century," 97. Gerulaitus notes both a 1469–1486 hiatus, with zero privileges of any kind being issued, and a notable trend toward the end of the 1400s when privileges began to cover "a greater number of titles." Gerulaitus, *Printing and Publishing in Fifteenth-century Venice*, 39. War, the Plague, and censorship would all take their toll on the book trade in the 1500s — in Venice and elsewhere. A brief revival of a preference for hand-copied manuscripts by collectors was, in turn, responsible for a decline in the high-end of the market. Scholars tend to agree that this return to manuscripts by collectors and connoisseurs was precipitated by a decline in the quality of printing as the book trade took flight and profit-taking trumped artistry. Cheap editions, shoddy production, and books rushed to market became the prevailing tendency. The Venetian Senate repeatedly tried to enforce rules regarding quality of works published in Venice, as a point of honor, but they were generally ignored, as were the rules regarding "immoral content," etc

11   Christopher L.C.E. Witcombe, "Introduction," xix–xxxiii, in Christopher L.C.E. Witcombe, *Copyright in the Renaissance: Prints and the "Privilegio" in Sixteenth-century Venice* (Leiden: Brill, 2004), xxv. Witcombe notes the three-step procedure for the publishing and protection of a book or print in Venice: 1/ license; 2/ approval by censor; and 3/ privilege. "License" went through the Council of Ten (established in 1506), "approval by censor" went through the Riformatori dello Studio di Padova (established in 1545 by the Council of Ten "as the official body to which publishers of books and prints were obliged to submit requests for approval of the material they wished to print"), and "privilege" went through the Venetian Senate and College. Approval by censor involved works being judged on "religious, moral, and political grounds" (ibid., xix–xx). Brown notes that Venice generally restricted its own censorship to material that impacted the "honour or authority" of the State. Brown, "1500–1600: The Venetian Press in the Sixteenth Century," 99. The Venetian Senate was generally lax about "religious and moral" content given that these were covered by the Church. It is important to note that the license was required and the privilege was optional, and that a license, after 1545, required that you have

specter of literary proprietorship arrived and disappeared with the book-publishing industry triumphing over the author…. By the time of the Enlightenment, the moral rights of authors will be catastrophically re-defined in France as *separate* rights — and therefore without any ground to stand on. They will float in the air, wistfully. By the twenty-first century they will be a foot-note in the history of copyright law, though still invoked. In the Venetian Renaissance, moral rights and economic rights were, however vaguely, and however briefly, *one* thing.

A version of this essay was published by Intellectual Property Watch *(February 7, 2018). The essay was written under the auspices of a Vittore Branca Center for the Study of Italian Culture Co-funded Research Residency, Giorgio Cini Foundation, Venice, Italy, May 15–30/July 21–28, 2017.*

---

approval by a censor. You could publish a book without a privilege, but you could not publish a book without a license. The clandestine book trade in Venice ignored both license and privilege.

The Editioning of Works

Mannerism, which discovered the spontaneity of the mind and recognized art as an autonomous creative activity, developed, in accordance with the spirit of that discovery, the totally new idea of fictitious space.[1]

— Arnold Hauser

I. "History" and "No History"

Sooner or later the history of the si is bound to serve in the construction of a new project of resistance. The sooner the better; there is no reason to think the moment will be long

---

1 Arnold Hauser, "The Concept of Space in Mannerist Architecture," in *Mannerism: The Crisis of the Renaissance and the Origin of Modern Art,* trans. Eric Mosbacher (London: Routledge and Kegan Paul, 1965), 279. First published as *Der Manierismus: Die Krise der Renaissance und der Ursprung der modernen Kunst* (Munich: Beck, 1964). See also Arnold Hauser, *Sozialgeschichte der Kunst und Literatur,* 2 vols. (Munich: Beck, 1953). First published as *The Social History of Art,* trans. Arnold Hauser and Stanley Godman, 2 vols. (London: Routledge and Kegan Paul, 1951). Mannerism, as an art-historical phenomenon, was first defined by Max Dvořák in "Über Greco und den Manierismus," *Wiener Jahrbuch für Kunstgeschichte* 1 (1921–1922): 22–42. It is, historically defined, a "transitional state" between Renaissance and Baroque art and architecture. A-historically, it is a conceptual operation in the arts invoking an essential non-mimetic agency for the arts.

coming. What that project will be like is still guesswork. Certainly it will have to struggle to reconceive the tentacular unity of its enemy and articulate the grounds of a unity capable of contesting it. The word "totality" will not put [the project] at panic stations. It will want to know the past. And inevitably it will find itself retelling the stories of those moments of refusal and reorganization — the SI being only one of them — that the dreamwork of the Left at present excludes from consciousness.[2]
— T.J. Clark and Donald Nicholson-Smith

What are non-careerist and free works for works? And who or what constitutes the fugitive figure of the artist–scholar in pursuit of the same?

Two gestures from the early years (1957–1960) of the Situationist International (SI) are sufficient to establish a threshold, even if almost sixty years later Debord's intuitions of an advancing and all-encompassing assimilation to capitalist hegemony of intellectual and cultural labor have proven all too prescient and we see both scholarship and artistic inquiry nearly fully enclosed within what he later termed *integrated spectacle.*

These two gestures are: refusal of contribution to capitalist orders and construction of a new poetic totality.[3] The SI's at-

---

2 T.J. Clark and Donald Nicholson-Smith, "Why Art Can't Kill the Situationist International," *October* 79 (Winter 1997): 31. This essay, essentially an impassioned defense of Debord and the Situationists, was published in response to Régis Debray, "Remarks on the Spectacle," *New Left Review* 214 (November-December 1995): 134–41; first published as "A propos du spectacle: Réponse à un jeune chercheur," *Le débat* 85 (May–August 1995): 3–15. Clark and Nicholson-Smith were part of the "English section" of the SI from 1965 to 1967 — or, 1965 to 1966, depending upon the source. *October* 79, an issue "devoted to the work of the Situationist International," was subsequently re-published in book form. See Tom McDonough, ed., *Guy Debord and the Situationist International: Texts and Documents* (Cambridge: MIT Press, 2002).

3 Guy Debord, *Correspondence: The Foundation of the Situationist International (June 1957–August 1960),* trans. Stuart Kendall and John McHale (Los Angeles: Semiotext(e), 2009). First published in 1999. See McKenzie Wark, "Introduction," in ibid., 23. "Totality" here means "totality of social relations."

titude toward intellectual property is also critical: that the "appropriation and correction of culture" is to proceed only on the basis of culture as "common property."[4] Debord's prescience, premised upon refusal and appropriation as corrective, suggests that non-careerist works today will side with communitarian values, and that the implied ethics is toward a collectivist order for works, whether produced individually or collectively — with the collectivist spirit transferred to works by way of a maneuver yet to be defined in relation to regimes of authorization, commodification, and exploitation.

Scholarship under the spell of the adventure is rare. Most works are created as forms of symbolic capital to be leveraged by individuals and/or by institutions, with Intellectual Property (IP) the signature motive, whether overt or covert. What then of works of artistic scholarship that refuse authorization and commodification? What sense or play in the cultural order do such works employ, or enjoy? And what power might they have or take on to alter the terrain of intellectual inquiry? Now or then (here and now or in past circumstances), the "then" speaking of "now" and the "now" speaking of a future, how might works escape the straightjacket of use value, always reducible to use *as* commodity, personal or otherwise, to signal a future now that inhabits works here and now? The apparent circularity of this question actually contains a trajectory for a type of work that closes down the implied field of capitalist reification of use as property. An illicit something hides there, not unlike the hidden God of Goldmann's reading of Pascal and Racine (where the wager on transcendence is everything), the poetic totality moving inward toward the internal resources of works, with this movement conferring an elemental and generative noninstrumentality to works while simultaneously permitting purpose in/through uselessness.[5] Useless beauty is a not-unworthy

---

4 Wark, "Introduction," 7.
5 Ibid., 23; with reference to Lucien Goldmann, *The Hidden God: A Study of Tragic Vision in the "Pensées" of Pascal and the Tragedies of Racine,* trans. Philip Thody (London: Routledge and Kegan Paul, 1964). First published

classic or all-purpose example. Yet to escape cycles of reification and assimilation to the circuit of Capital, works of another order are required — works of a-historical merit, yes. But what is also indicated in the SI experiment is that the work in/for itself must be freed of all socio-cultural non-sense and baggage en route to becoming capable of the insurrectional power required to escape the gravitational field of historically determined and ideologically orchestrated integrated spectacle.

Transitions then — and rites of passage for works — are self-evident. And quite often they invoke a form of "dark" vitalism for works that signals the strenuous measures required. Artist–scholars can actually become trapped inside their works, then seeking an escape route that is only possible by first being trapped inside of works. Arguably, this is in many respects the precise place from which Kierkegaard wrote some of his most excoriating works — e.g., *Fear and Trembling* and *Either/Or,* both published in 1843. This is both historically and a-historically a propositional and situational compact with the aleatory and the ontic basis of works. The existential crises are inescapable, for artist–scholars and for works — with the latter, in the case of works for works, imbued with autonomous subjective states in excess of the author. This condition is also the basis for the very idea of the work or art as "exception" — for its status as autonomous subject versus object for commodification. As antithesis to commodity status, these subjective states for works also suggest the possible transfer of rights to works as a primary means of exiting the law of IP and the careerist excursions paramount to cancelling any authentic or real communitarian ethos or collectivist spirit for works.

Escaping enforced slavery to metrics (in all of its varied forms) in academia, and exiting subtle forms of appropriation and curatorial hubris in the art world, are two primary maneuvers for the editioning of works, of artistic scholarship, for artist–scholars. Both situational and institutional, these forms of

---

as *Le dieu caché: Étude sur la vision tragique dans les Pensées de Pascal et dans le théâtre de Racine* (Paris: Éditions Gallimard, 1955).

law operate as a means for neutralizing free expression by/for works. They condition works both before and after conception. The academic metric relegates research to institutional prerogatives, while the art-world metric converts works to forms of spectral capital. Both forms of capital are relegated to scales of reification, as escalating games of embodied privilege and commodification, at once — an elective rapport assigned to scholars and artists as a rite of status for scholars and artists. That status constitutes the symbolic capital to be subsequently leveraged. Yet once inside the fold, the game dictates terms. The games of the art world are notably self-serving games, for reputations and for elite networks. Subsummation serves the platform — and the platform is the public relations (PR) value of the vertically organized corporate operation of mediatized culture.[6] Mediatized culture is an integrated spectacle. University or biennale, reification proceeds by appropriation, and appropriation proceeds by law — law, in this case, as both rule and affect.[7] The cultural or knowledge commons is ruled by such forms of law — the law being the rules of engagement, measure, valorization, and exchange.

---

6   The term *subsummation* is used here, versus *subsumption,* to distinguish
    the processes of cultural assimilation from the classic Marxist theory
    of the real subsumption of labor under capitalism. Neoliberal capitalist
    subsummation, arguably, functions primarily as formal effect, producing
    distortions in the field of cultural production and spectral forms of com-
    modity, while it also often has an effect on the valuation and definition of
    labor proper.

7   "The main characteristic of the lawscape is that it can play with its degrees
    of visibilisation, making itself fully visible when needed (e.g., an airport
    control where space, time, and human and non-human bodies operate in
    a heightened lawscaping mode that aims at conveying bodies on the other
    side) and withdrawing from visibility when a softer, less obviously legal
    space is needed (e.g., a café with tables available to sit, provided that one
    orders something). This means that, depending on the degree of visibilisa-
    tion, a body is more or less able to manoeuvre the lawscape, namely to act
    lawfully or unlawfully, to ignore ethical and more strictly legal commands,
    to embark on unscripted lines of flight, excesses, conflicts or revolts."
    Andreas Philippopoulos-Mihalopoulos, "Atmospheric Aestheses: Law as
    Affect," in *Atmosphere and Aesthetics: A Plural Perspective,* eds. Tonino
    Griffero and Marco Tedeschini (Cham: Palgrave Macmillan, 2019), 170–71.

The internal measures of works will determine their placement or refusal of placement in such worlds. The internal prospects are also the means for altering such worlds — and time-senses and verb tenses *for works* are the key. These internalized senses and tenses signal, inter alia, the somewhat preposterous presentism that such works enable. The artist–scholar, on behalf of works, chooses accordingly — and the editioning of works proceeds according to the inner resources of the works as such. Philosophical aesthetics and political economy are nonetheless at play in the maneuvers required — in the nervous systems of works. Again, the si foresaw this. Across forty years, and now well into an additional twenty years, artist–scholars used patrimonial culture and its privileged institutions to position works as provocations. From Chris Marker to Guy Debord to Jean-Luc Godard, we find examples (e.g., Centre Pompidou, Éditions Gallimard, Cannes Film Festival).[8]

If the si's approaches to the law of IP presaged Creative Commons licensing, plus copyleft, there remains the unresolved issue of the moral rights of authors. The cco license (an elective, nominally "No Rights Reserved" status for works) makes this

---

8   Debord used the prestigious Paris-based publisher Gallimard for many of
    his late publications. See Jean-Luc Godard's "Le Studio d'Orphée" (2019)
    "an atelier, a recording and editing studio, a living and working place,"
    Fondazione Prada, Milan, produced in association with the feature film,
    Le Livre d'image (2018). Resembling art-world spectacle, Godard is using
    the Prada Foundation — as Chris Marker used the Centre Pompidou (e.g.,
    "Zapping Zone") and Guy Debord used Gallimard (*La Société du spectacle,*
    etc.) — to launch his provocation from within patrimonial culture. For
    Marker's late strategies for the editioning of works, see Gavin Keeney,
    "Marker's Archive," in *Knowledge, Spirit, Law: Book 2, The Anti-capitalist
    Sublime* (Brooklyn: punctum books, 2017), 35–77. The 1992 Gallimard
    edition of *La Société du spectacle,* the third French edition of the book,
    included a new preface by Debord, notably commenting upon post-1989
    spectacle and "a very simple sign, 'the fall of the Berlin Wall,'" as signal for
    the "striving of the spectacle toward modernization and unification." See
    Clark and Nicholson-Smith, "Why Art Can't Kill the Situationist Interna-
    tional," 31. This comment is made in reference to Thesis 58: "The spectacle
    has its roots in the fertile field of the economy, and it is the produce of this
    field which must in the end come to dominate the spectacular market"
    (ibid).

clear.[9] Yet the category of moral rights is held "holy" in IP law, inalienable and non-transferrable. CC0 cannot touch this set of rights. Such rights are also utterly devoid of value for authors, as they have been overwritten by statutory law and made a subset of monetary rights. This situational abyss suggests that they are safely parked in the non-spaces of prerogative versus proprietary rights, functioning as reserve for authorial privileges long superseded by Capital — by publishers and by institutions.[10] The possibility of transferring moral rights to works, while impossible by IP law, is the first major step in freeing works from proprietary exploitation at all levels. The moral rights regime, much like the exceptional status of the work of art, is a late-modern remainder from the universality employed by Capital to commandeer rights. This category of rights, in/for itself, reduced to useless immateriality by law, requires once again its ontic function.

The ontic function is the artefact, not the conceptualization of the work as supposed product of individual agency and genius. Yet this hypothesis of works attaining moral rights can only concern a class of works that seeks to overturn proprietary rights. The shift, while categorical, is also highly situational or contingent. Works for works suggests that the transfer of moral rights to works is also the transfer of works back to the commons, from whence they came in most cases, as copyleft and CC0 seem to indicate, or to where they belong, as the communitarian ethos of non-careerist artistic scholarship might portend given half a chance.[11]

---

9 See Creative Commons, "CC-0 License," https://creativecommons.org/share-your-work/public-domain/cc0/.

10 See Gavin Keeney, "A Brief Sketch of *Privilegio* in the Venetian Renaissance," *Intellectual Property Watch* (February 7, 2018), https://www.ip-watch.org/2018/02/07/brief-sketch-privilegio-venetian-renaissance/, for the origin of copyright and the immediate maneuvers by the book trade to game the system.

11 A common critique of the knowledge commons is that it is part and parcel of the alienation of labor. "Today, the left is similarly seduced by the communism of affects: the privatization of communism, as a community of synchronized emotions. Very much as Virilio argues: 'Socialism has

What would this maneuver accomplish, for works *and* for authors? Such a question must be answered through experimentation. The only a priori justification would be to re-launch empty
universalist claims, purporting authorial agency for works in
advance of actual works. This elective, aleatory maneuver is
also notably at odds with law. That law supports such an archaic
gesture, rendering the ontic status of works a type of symbolic
capital of no real value in/for itself, which is paradoxical in the
extreme and suggests that moral rights (as a type of politics) is
the Achilles' heel for IP law in all of its forms and in all of its ex-
ceptionalist positions and claims on behalf of exploitation and
monetization of knowledge — i.e., the law of Capital on behalf
of/for itself. With most IP rights transferred to rights holders,
yet another euphemism in IP law (typically benefiting publishers), and with the author rarely being the primary rights holder
(and this pertains to Open Access (OA) as much as it pertains
to CC licensing), the etiolated legacy of moral rights nonetheless
prevents complete enclosure of the commons by fiat, metrics, or
law.[12] These rights sit embedded in law, effectively given a halo

---

not found its relationship to postmodern individuality'. For instance,
resistance to claiming IP on many platforms takes form in the shape of
competing ideological productions, such as the multifarious and easily
cooptable 'commons' and 'platform cooperativism', who end up involun-
tary promoters of their own alienation and exploitation, consolidating the
deterioration of the very digital labor conditions they purportedly seek to
transform." Athina Karatzogianni and Andrew Robinson, "Virilio's Parting
Song: The Administration of Fear and the Privatisation of Communism
through the Communism of Affect," *Media Theory* 3, no. 2 (December 2,
2019): 172.

12 For problems concerning the neoliberalization of the open-access movement, see, for example, Gary Hall, "Anti-bourgeois Theory," *Media Theory*,
February 3, 2020, http://mediatheoryjournal.org/gary-hall-anti-bour-
geois-theory; Martin Paul Eve, "Open Access and Neoliberalism," *Social
Epistemology Review and Reply Collective* 9, no. 1 (2020): 22–26, https://
wp.me/p1Bfg0–4Lv; John Holmwood, "Commercial Enclosure: Whatever
Happened to Open Access?" *Radical Philosophy* 181 (2018): 2–5; and John
Holmwood and Chaime Marcuello Servós, "Challenges to Public Universities: Digitalisation, Commodification and Precarity," *Social Epistemology*
33, no. 4 (2019): 309–20.

and reduced to inoperativity as relic. To make them operative again, on behalf of works and authors, yet authors privileging works for works, proposes the end for IP for a class of works that might then command a new field for works. What are these mysterious works other than "gift versus property"?[13] What is an author in such cases other than witness to the event of the work? And why do these works in turn signal, if not produce, the artist–scholar qua artist–scholar?

To study the path of these works by producing such works will answer all of these questions. The principal gestures are all in place, then and now — and, again, here and now. Certain historical moments suggest that to reverse the machinery of reification requires the restoration of free subjective states for works through the interior of works: through the passage and passageways of non-authorial privilege and aleatory and ontic experimentation in editioning; and toward, then, an only apparently archaic economy of license opposed to license. In such instances "the law disappears…"[14] It is the foremost position

---

13 See Wark, "Introduction," 20, where "gift versus property" in the SI world-view is also applied to love.

14 Of such historical interest, then, is Debord's book *Society of the Spectacle* (1967), as well as Debord's film *Society of the Spectacle* (1973). What Debord seems to get wrong, at that point along the way at least, is that "irreversible time" (what he identifies as the specific "nature," or anti-nature, of capitalist production and spectacular forms of urban design, in particular) is not historical in quite the way he suggests, nor is it what needs to be re-appropriated or taken back by revolutionary praxis. Instead, it would seem that another type of time is at stake, a time that is buried inside of so-called irreversible (teleological) time — or, that which has been termed *eschatological time* by Walter Benjamin and others of a more poetic and perhaps apocalyptic persuasion. For Debord's supposed relationship to/dependence upon Feuerbach, see Debray, "Remarks on the Spectacle." For a response to Debray, see Clark and Nicholson-Smith, "Why Art Can't Kill the Situationist International." The NLR translation is an abridged ("somewhat abbreviated") version of the original article (ibid). Régis Debray is the author of *Revolution within the Revolution? Armed Struggle and Political Struggle in Latin America*, trans. Bobbye Ortiz and Gregory Elliott (London: Verso, 2017). First published as *Révolution dans la révolution* (Paris: Maspéro, 1967).

held yet, against enclosure of—and complete expropriation of—knowledge as free inquiry, by royal fiat, or by law.

"History" and "No History"—as set—is a type of spectralized *topos*. In this case, the scare quotes provide cover for its non-conformity to normative terminologies. This dyad has been appropriated by modernist avant-gardes to justify a year zero for projects—and for manifestos. Works for works assimilates projects past, yet departs from the "No History" position of "beginning anew." Michel Serres has written about the immense background noise of a milieu that must be silenced to begin anew. "New History" follows "No History." This circuit invokes Malevich's plea to Meyerhold to "re-install the footlights," following the insurrectional activities of the Russian avant-garde.[15]

II. Ontic and De-ontic

> The literary text is the "soul and substance of its author," despite "a multiple authorial being of uncertain boundaries."[16]
>
> —Diderot

---

15 See T.J. Clark, "Reinstall the Footlights," *London Review of Books* 39, no. 22 (November 16, 2017): 10–12. Regarding Clark's supposed fixation on the "social history of art," plus his relation to negative dialectics and a historical critique of forms of aesthetic mediation, see Gail Day, "T.J. Clark and the Pain of the Unattainable Beyond," in *Dialectical Passions: Negation in Postwar Art Theory* (New York: Columbia University Press, 2010), 25–69. Clark's interest in the socio-cultural aspects of art history were influenced by the writings of Arnold Hauser. See Hauser, *Sozialgeschichte der Kunst und Literatur*. For Hauser's impact on Anglo-American art history in the 1950s, see Michael R. Orwicz, "Critical Discourse in the Formation of a Social History of Art: Anglo-American Response to Arnold Hauser," *Oxford Art Journal* 8, no. 2 (1985): 52–62.

16 Denis Diderot, "Lettre sur la liberté de la presse." Written in 1763, on behalf of publishers, as "Lettre historique et politique sur le commerce de la librairie," and republished in 1777 as "Lettre sur la liberté de la presse." "Lettre historique et politique sur le commerce de la librairie," in Denis Diderot, *Œuvres complètes*, ed. Roger Lewinter, 15 vols. (Paris: Le Club Français du Livre, 1969–1973), 5:305–81. Regarding the context of this letter, see Roger Chartier, *The Cultural Origins of the French Revolution*, trans. Lydia G. Cochrane (Durham: Duke University Press, 1991), 53–56. First published as *Les origines culturelles de la Révolution française* (Paris:

The most sacred, the most legitimate, the most unassailable, and […] the most personal of all properties, is the work, [which is] the fruit of a writer's thought; yet it is a property of a type totally different from other properties.[17]

— M. Le Chapelier

The rule and the exception, the syntagmatic and the paradigmatic, the ontic and the de-ontic — such is the field of cultural production defined in often-abstract terms, and such too is the shift from pragmatism to idealism, through and beyond works. How this plays out in contemporary art and scholarship, through the thick and the thin of representational orders, and through the rhetoric of entanglement and dissent, defines the rough contours of a paradoxical topology of effects and affects that both haunts and animates artistic scholarship. From the Enlightenment through to the Contemporary, the shadow of moral rights falls across works, defining, re-defining, and re-re-defining the relationship of authors to works and any escape route from a mere utility for works. Contemporary biases toward neo-utilitarianism in art or in so-called scientific scholarship have an incommensurate relationship to the status of scholarship or art as commodity, spectral or otherwise, symbolic or actual. Amidst all claims to art or scholarship as "event" there

---

Éditions du Seuil, 1990). See also the chapter "*Droits d'auteur* and *Approbation* as Cultural Capital: Literary Property, Censorship, and Legitimacy at the Comédie Française, 1760–1780," in Gregory S. Brown, *A Field of Honor: Writers, Court Culture and Public Theater in the French Intellectual Field from Racine to the Revolution* (New York: Columbia University Press, 2005), and Carla Hesse, "Enlightenment Epistemologies and the Laws of Authorship in Revolutionary France, 1777–1793," *Representations* 30 (1990): 114–16. Brown points to Geoffrey Turnovsky, "Modern Authorship and the Rise of the Market: Evolution of the Literary Field in France, 1750–1789," PhD diss., Columbia University, 2000, 103–62, as one source for a reading that positions Diderot's remarks as "an attempt to valorize the author as a creative force."

17 Isaac-René-Guy Le Chapelier, *Rapport fait par M. Le Chapelier, au nom du Comité de Constitution, sur la pétition des auteurs dramatiques, dans la séance du jeudi 13 janvier 1791, avec le décret rendu dans cette séance* (Paris: De l'Imprimerie Nationale, 1791).

is always the trinitarian, theological or a-theological economy of idea, artefact, and social value. Yet value resides most commonly in the conversion of idea and artefact to social or cultural merit, and the exception remains a mostly ghostly affair amidst the commodification of effect and affect. If artistic scholarship is to counter this trend and restore a proper or improper revolutionary ethos to social value, then artistic scholarship will engage the ontic and de-ontic stages of art and scholarship as socially constructed system, with the exception functioning as proverbial wild card. That wild card's place in cultural production will serve as semaphore for escape when the rule otherwise neutralizes, obscures, or defines the exception and the event of art and scholarship is at risk of absolute subsummation by and within systems; i.e., defined downward toward mere utility as sole purpose for Art, Love, and Revolution.[18]

There are three steps in the analytic of works for works that slowly displace the very idea of the author. These are:

1. The author produces the work and transfers it to the public domain as exception;
2. The author produces the work in the public domain and it belongs to the public domain as exception; and

---

18 See Alain Badiou, *Being and Event,* trans. Oliver Feltham (London: Continuum, 2005). First published as *L'être et l'événement* (Paris: Éditions du Seuil, 1988). "Art, Love, and Revolution" is, of course, the trinitarian model Badiou utilizes for describing the fidelity required of the witness in honor of the presence of the Event. See also Alexandros Kioupkiolis, *Freedom after the Critique of Foundations: Marx, Liberalism, Castoriades and Agonistic Autonomy* (New York: Palgrave Macmillan, 2012). "Transformative action is theorized as a procedure that fabricates a new truth in art, science, politics and love by way of disciplined work that pledges allegiance to a situated event of rupture and revelation; an event that contains a fecund statement to be fleshed out and developed in its concrete and diverse consequences" (ibid., n.p). And: "Agents are not considered to be capable of generating evental ruptures and new beginnings in the first place. They wait for these to irrupt as a quasi-messianic miracle, a matter of sheer luck, and then they go on to draw out and specify their various consequences in a certain situation of knowledge, politics or love and art" (ibid., n.p).

3. The work produces itself as exception and it belongs to the public domain as exception.

In the case of the third scenario, a range of questions arises that characterizes the work as exception in advance of it becoming de facto exception to proprietary regimes of cultural production. This third class of works is also the only example possible for a proper investigation of the premise that the transfer of moral rights to works for works secures for such works the status of exception. All three steps remain nonetheless within the law of copyright and the problematic of author and work. Something else altogether different, in the topology of this relational economy, would be required to step outside this circuit.

If defining the exception upward is also to free the exception from its relationship to forms of appropriation and expropriation, to utility and non-utility, to ontic and de-ontic status, as the circuit in which the very idea of the exception has emerged, the primary means of measuring the value of hypothetically value-less works is to be found precisely where moral rights reside for works and what purpose they serve for works.[19] Yet such an undertaking would also require a metaphysic of prior art; i.e., a proper re-affirmation of things given versus things taken, and a properly elective nod toward non-proprietary fields of knowledge that embody the precepts of that metaphysic. This metaphysic would, out of necessity, open or re-open theological and a-theological speculations regarding the rapport of worlds, a rapport Dostoevsky describes in the following manner:

---

19 See Roger Chartier on Kant's "reading" of the position of the book between object and discourse. Ivan Jablonka and Roger Chartier, "The Book: Its Past, Its Future," trans. Eric Rosencrantz, *Books and Ideas,* October 14, 2013, http://www.booksandideas.net/The-Book-Its-Past-Its-Future.html. "Object" connotes property; "discourse" connotes moral rights. The book, for Kant, exists as "indefinite plurality of successive states or simultaneous states of works" (ibid). Kant discusses the status of the book in Part Two of *Groundwork of the Metaphysic of Morals* (1785).

What grows lives and is alive only through the feeling of its contact with other mysterious worlds.[20]

In terms of artistic scholarship and works for works, the university has obviously failed in its measurement of research based on authorship and associated metrics.[21] Even collectively produced works within the university fail to reach the most basic level of exception, as public relations values and institutes and funding regimes automatically compromise free works. They may be in the public domain, but they are also subject to subtle and not-so-subtle forms of commodification. The milieu in which works for works in artistic scholarship are produced then becomes part of the exceptional status for works. This milieu will have to safeguard such works from all forms of appropriation and commodification, both overt and subtle, and also confer upon works the status of exception — from conception.

In the production of artistic scholarship as exception, methodology and "product" count as one.[22] Here, methodology is the de-ontic elemental datum, and the "product" is the ontic elemental datum. While methodology and "product" might take the form of contingent process and eventual work, in the paradigmatic and transcendental order they are the same event — of the same event.[23] The de-ontic, while normally considered to

20 Fyodor Dostoevsky, *The Brothers Karamazov,* trans. Constance Garnett (New York: Modern Library, n.d.), 398.

21 See Anthony J. Stanonis, "No Time for Muses: The Research Excellence Framework and the Pursuit of Mediocrity," in *Why Academic Freedom Matters: A Response to Current Challenges,* eds. Cheryl Hudson and Joanna Williams (London: Civitas, 2016), 128–44.

22 See Henry Laycock, *Words without Objects: Semantics, Ontology, and Logic for Non-singularity* (Oxford: Clarendon Press, 2006), for non-object-based methods of "counting."

23 "For there's a rule and an exception. Culture is the rule, and art is the exception…. Nobody speaks the exception. It isn't spoken, it's written… It's composed… It's painted… It's filmed… Or it's lived, and then it's the art of living…." Jean-Luc Godard, *Je vous salue, Sarajevo* (1993), on Jean-Luc Godard and Anne-Marie Miéville, dirs., *Four Short Films: De l'origine du XXIe siècle* (2000); *The Old Place* (1999); *Liberté et patrie* (2002); *and Je vous salue, Sarajevo* (1993), ECM, 2006, DVD.

ducible to authorial identity, is under other auspices indistin-
guishable from the ontic, nominally the object as commodity. In
the event of Art, Love, or Revolution, it is impossible to separate
out method and object. The transcendental object of Art, Love,
and Revolution is the event of Art, Love, and Revolution — and
in the case of such events there can be no author as such. Moral
rights shade toward the Moral Law, where the author will do
what is right or good even if it is not in his/her best interest.[24]
This best interest is, in most cases concerning art and scholarship, also the authorial presence reified into commodity status — with the careerist agenda of the author placed as primary
concern over and above all other concerns.

This is not a case of the death of the author, as in post-structuralist literary exegesis, nor is it a case of the marginalization
or bracketing of authorial intent as in structuralist criticism. It
is, instead, the transpersonalization of authorial privilege, for
works. While the post-structuralist gambit brought scholarship
to the edge of the abyss, and structuralism sought deep gram-
mars or constitutional agency within language, the valorization
of works for works includes the author, as author, yet transfers
subjective agency to works. It is a process that is transfigurative.
If works of this order produce themselves, an entire regime of
cultural and socio-economic value and valuation vanishes, or
slowly falls away, and in a valedictory manner something departs, as something else arrives.

If milieu becomes critical, what types of milieu are possible
for the production of such works — to allow them to appear?
If de-ontic rights were once locked within guilds, to safeguard
collectivist authorial status for works, and if authorial privilege
since the Enlightenment has held semi-sacred an author's labor
in producing works, present-day circumstances do not permit

---

24 "Moral law grows out of the testimony of conscience, and conscience
    itself is […] developed on its formal and not its material side." Vladimir
    Solovyov, *The Justification of the Good: An Essay on Moral Philosophy*,
    trans. Nathalie A. Doddington (Grand Rapids: Eerdmans, 2005), 405. First
    published as *Opravdanie dobra: Nravstvennaya filosofia* (St. Petersburg:
    Stasjulevič, 1897).

nor secure the perimeter for works that, through an incommensurate operativity, engage inoperativity. The absence of the milieux required, or the marginalization of such milieux, suggests that, much like methodology, the nature of the milieu for works for works will also be "counted as one" — contingent with and within methodology and object. It is the transpersonalization and transpositioning of the work and the attendant status as event that will produce the required milieu for works for works.[25] Neither the lonely tower nor the ivory tower will suffice, as they once did. The collectivist spirit of the operation requires the re-definition of terms, as noted, plus the re-creation ex nihilo of the venues and terms for the appearance and re-appearance of works for works. A re-definition of the knowledge commons is called for, across such works, and it is instrumental reason that generally blocks such a re-definition.

This confluence of interests and incidental or accidental clauses in the production of works, with the risk of reification

---

25 See Gavin Keeney, "Notes on Milieu and Anti-milieu," in *"Else-where":
Essays in Art, Architecture, and Cultural Production, 2002–2011* (Newcastle upon Tyne: Cambridge Scholars Publishing, 2011), 309–15. See especially excerpts from Henri Focillon, *The Life of Forms in Art,* trans. Charles Beecher Hogan and George Kubler (New York: Zone Books, 1989), in ibid., 314. First published as *Vie des forms* (Paris: E. Leroux, 1934). Walter Benjamin closes Convolute N in the Arcades Project with a series of citations from this book. See Walter Benjamin, *The Arcades Project,* trans. Howard Eiland and Kevin McLaughlin (Cambridge: Belknap Press, 1999), 487–88. First published as *Das Passagen-Werk,* ed. Rolf Tiedemann (Frankfurt am Main: Suhrkamp, 1982). "Some theses by Focillon which have appearances on their side. Of course, the materialist theory of art is interested in dispelling such appearance" (ibid., 487, Convolute N19, a1). This observation is then followed by: "We have no right to confuse the state of the life of forms with the state of social life. The time that gives support to a work of art does not give definition either to its principle or to its specific form." Focillon, *Vie des forms,* 93; cited in Benjamin, *The Arcades Project,* 487, Convolute N19, a1. The reflections established in Convolute N may be said to have come to fruition in Benjamin's "On the Concept of History" (1940). See Walter Benjamin, "On the Concept of History," in *Walter Benjamin: Selected Writings,* Vol. 4: *1938–1940,* eds. Howard Eiland and Michael W. Jennings, trans. Edward Jephcott et al. (Cambridge: Belknap Press, 2003), 389–400.

by commodification at each new turn, suggests that the next major issue to be dealt with, tactically, is the editioning of works for works. While this is likely only to be dealt with through the aleatory processes of works as event, the various incidental or accidental recurrences of forms of reified rights likely to be encountered provides a readymade roadmap toward new iterative and generative modalities in artistic scholarship that serve to short circuit the return of proprietary rights and institutional or patrimonial prerogatives.[26] If the work determines its milieu,

---

26 In communications theory, patrimonialism is equated with paternalism: "In his book *Communications*, Raymond Williams […] distinguishes between authoritarian, paternal, commercial and democratic communication systems (communications). The first three communication systems are political, cultural and commercial expressions of instrumental reason. Authoritarian communications involve state control, manipulation and censorship of the media. The 'purpose of communication is to protect, maintain, or advance a social order based on minority power' […]. Paternal communications are authoritarian communications 'with a conscience: that is to say, with values and purposes beyond the maintenance of its own power' […]. In such communication systems, there is ideological control that aims to impose certain moral values on audiences. The controllers of paternal communication systems assume that specific morals are good for citizens and that the latter are too silly to understand the world. In commercial communications, there is commercial control: 'Anything can be said, provided that you can afford to say it and that you can say it profitably' […]. All three forms are instrumental: they instrumentalise communications as tools for control and domination." Christian Fuchs, "Introduction," *tripleC* 18, no. 1 (2020): 23, Special Issue: "Communicative Socialism/Digital Socialism." With reference to Raymond Williams, *Communications* (Harmondsworth: Penguin, 1976), 130–37. Neoliberal academia employs the "paternal communications" model, which is, in turn, enforced by metrics. Neo-utilitarianism or neo-determinism in academia is a form of institutionalized instrumental reason that serves as cover story for the commodification of knowledge. Additionally: "The logic of communicative capitalism and the commodity form favours superficiality, high-speed flows of information and news, the personalisation of politics, tabloidisation, one-dimensionality, and partiality in the interest of the bourgeoisie. Alternatives decelerate information flows (slow media), foster informed political debate and learning through collective creation, and participation in spaces of public communication that are ad-free, non-commercial, and not-for-profit. Such spaces enable both professional media and citizen media as well as the dialectical fusion of both. Socialist

and the methodology determines the object, the editioning of works, dependent upon type, content, form, and intention, will serve as re-formalization of ontic status through appearance, re-appearance, and dis-appearance. In the latter case, ephemerality will substitute for the ontic condition for works, whereas appearance and re-appearance signal the iterative and generative spirit of works for works. Through appearance, re-appearance, and dis-appearance, works for works engage conventional and unconventional forms of editioning, yet always with the condition of moral rights subsumed by works and — most likely — by milieu. Milieu escapes *habitus*; and, as convention, subtends privilege whereby both authorial privilege and institutional conventions are entirely forsaken. While this may only happen incrementally, through engagement with author rights and institutions, artistic scholarship of the order of works for works is — irreducibly — irreconcilable with both. Far from a slow march through institutions, the prospects for such a revolution in scholarship requires testing the limits of institutions.[27]

---

communication politics supports the creation and sustenance of media that have the potential to help to advance critical, anti-ideological thought by fostering engagement with content that stimulates critical, dialectical, anti-ideological thought and debate, and opposes classist, fascist, racist, xenophobic and sexist discourse" (ibid., 28).

27 "Politics, in the form we have it, is nothing without a modernity constantly in the offing, at last about to realize itself: it has no other telos, no other way to imagine things otherwise. The task of the left is to provide one." T.J. Clark, "For a Left with No Future," *New Left Review* 2, no. 74 (March–April 2012): 72. For a summary of Clark's art-historical contribution to the left critique of social relations, beginning in the early 1960s, see Susan Watkins, "Presentism? A Reply to T.J. Clark," *New Left Review* 2, no. 74 (March-April 2012): 77–78. According to Watkins, previous Marxist critique had mostly ignored the arts and focused on literature, as supplement to socio-economic critique. "Historically, the culture of the left, from Marx to Trotsky, Lukács to Sartre, focused overwhelmingly on literature, with far less to say about the visual arts, let alone painting. Clark has brought to it a body of work to match anything in the literary tradition" (ibid., 78). Her remark unfortunately misses the extraordinary privileging of the visual image in left cultural critique in mid-to-late 1940s' Paris — Sartre included, and leading Emmanuel Levinas to question the penchant for the visual at the expense of the verbal and ethical. Emmanuel Levinas, "La réalité et

son ombre," *Les temps modernes* 38 (November 1948): 771–89. Sartre's *Les temps modernes* was, curiously, one model for the *New Left Review* when it was launched in 1960. Levinas questions the truth-telling nature of visual knowledge, with only criticism of the image able to return the necessary ethical content otherwise effaced. "The way in which the closed world of art therefore freezes time within images doubles and immobilizes being: characters suffer an eternal anxiety, imprisoned in an inhuman interval. The disengagement this encourages means that art is an evasion of responsibility, since it offers consolation rather than a challenge. Only criticism relates this irresponsibility to real history once more by measuring the distance between the myth proposed by art, and real being." Séan Hand, "Introduction," Emmanuel Levinas, "Reality and Its Shadow," trans. Alphonso Lingis, in Emmanuel Levinas, *The Levinas Reader,* ed. Séan Hand (Oxford: Blackwell, 1989), 129. This period is the left-critical, existentially charged post-war milieu out of which the "miracle" of Chris Marker emerged. Watkins also makes, in passing, an obligatory affirmation of Clark's unrepentant Situationism. "Clark's art writings have been proof in themselves of Situationism's explanatory power and intellectual vitality" (ibid). This is de rigueur for NLR. Yet, this passage opens a forensic and historical-materialist dissection, by Watkins, editor of NLR, of Clark's literary polemic, "For a Left with No Future," in which he accepts both Watkins's and Perry Anderson's "left pessimism" ("pessimism of the intellect") in the face of unrepentant (2000) and resurgent (2012) neoliberal capitalist hegemony, while countering it with an impassioned argument for moderation in the face of defeat versus a return to empty Marxist rhetoric ("revolutionary stylistics"), empty ideological posturing ("literariness"), and renewed empty promises for an imminent post-revolutionary, post-capitalist socialist utopia. "Left, then, is a term denoting an absence; and this near nonexistence ought to be explicit in a new thinking of politics. But it does not follow that the left should go on exalting its marginality, in the way it is constantly tempted to — exulting in the glamour of the great refusal, and consigning to outer darkness the rest of an unregenerate world. That way literariness lies. The only left politics worth the name is, as always, the one that looks its insignificance in the face, but whose whole interest is in what it might be that could turn the vestige, slowly or suddenly, into the beginning of a 'movement'. Many and bitter will be the things sacrificed — the big ideas, the revolutionary stylistics — in the process" (Clark, "For a Left with No Future," 57). Watkins buries Clark's literary, artistic, and political illustrations for his spirited polemic in a massive socio-cultural reconstitution of context, suggesting, for example, that one cannot have Nietzsche without fascism, even though left orthodoxy permits one to throw out Early Marx for Late Marx. Watkins more or less re-re-historicizes Clark's nominally "creative Marxist" positions into oblivion as a means of dismissing them on behalf of left orthodoxy. Regarding varieties of "Creative Marxism," see Göran Therborn, *From Marxism to Post-Marxism?* (London: Verso, 2008).

4

Lived Law and Works for Works

I am not a Platonist. The material already has the Idea in it.
Novalis: "All materials are connected […]."[1]

— Anselm Kiefer

I. Scriptoria as Milieux

The universal subject of Art is the subject of Art itself. The milieu of artistic scholarship is the iterative transfiguration of that
subjective state. Never static, and never mere abstract or hypostatized state, the subject of Art is the subject of artistic scholarship. Tautologies and forms of presentism in works of art spell
out this complex, while the complex shifts and turns according
to the predicates or statements of the works in question.

The commercium of academia and the spectacular conditions of the art world, if to be negated in works of artistic scholarship and works for works, require a type of milieu that permits
the return of the a-temporal and temporal terms of engagement
for art and scholarship to inherent properties, shedding in the
process the acquired traits of a very different order of reductive
means to ends that connote operativity and, therefore, use and
so-called value. These include all of the historically determined

---

1   Anselm Kiefer, January 23, 2007, The Royal Academy, London, England
(audio recording/RA).

justifications, plus all of the passing socio-cultural concerns of the day, while the antithetical reductive force of the work of art or artistic scholarship as subject only to the internal metrics of art opens successive and indeterminate senses of time, purpose, no purpose, and — critically — a-temporality as form of time for works.[2]

A non-spatial model of scriptoria, for works, and for a-temporality, may be found in all possible spatial scriptoria, as temporality already contains a-temporality. A-temporality is prior to art as Concept, or, a-temporality is the principal immaterial mark of prior art.[3] It is the *dynamis* and the signature.[4] The universalizing traits are the key, while the premise of the universal

---

2   See Krzysztof Ziarek, *The Force of Art* (Stanford: Stanford University Press, 2004). See esp. "Art as Forcework," 19–59. "The work of art, understood as a force field [Adorno], immediately reveals a different internal momentum and a new set of relationships to society. For one thing, the tensions and constellations of forces render the artwork dynamic, disclosing it as an event, a temporalizing occurrence and a transformative rupture, whose features become unrecognizable in the notion of an aesthetic object [...] As a field of forces, the artwork remains irreducible to its socially dictated functions – discrete object of aesthetic experience, and commodity – no matter how strenuously these rules are enforced by cultural commerce" (ibid., 13). Ziarek goes on to describe the force of art by way of the term *aphesis*, "a releasing, a letting be or a letting go, deliverance, and even liberty" (ibid., 22). "The work of art is first and foremost a spatial-temporal and nonviolent play of forces, a play that remains in excess of and, as such, critical of art's function as an aesthetic commodity, the function that brings art in line with the general social economy of power and production" (ibid). "The event is a decisive and radical intervention of the way things have been before, an alteration in the historical force field, which frees up the force of the possible" (ibid., 27).

3   Prior art is the functional equivalent of the "thing-in-itself" of metaphysics. It is also the sponsor of the "secret" of Derrida and the "ban" of Agamben. It is always already contested across contingency as the missed convention of the iterative and the generative. See "Appendix B: Notes on Language and Its Other" regarding Derrida and Agamben's encounters with forms of "messianicity," which are quite often ciphers for prior art or the given.

4   See Giorgio Agamben, *The Signature of All Things: On Method,* trans. Luca D'Isanto and Kevin Attell (New York: Zone Books, 2009). First published as *Signatura rerum: Sul metodo* (Turin: Bollati Boringhieri, 2008).

subject requires a countering force in contingent terms, as *faktum* and *faktura,* to prevent the abstraction serving as excuse for no purchase in actual worlds. This well-established criticism of abstract and ideal conceptual orders — of Idealism proper — is situated in the field of reification that constitutes disciplines, schools, and markets. If this field of reification is also capable of neutralizing anything contrary to its purposes (contrary to its laws), the terms of engagement for artistic scholarship must simultaneously be defined in abstract and concrete particulars. (The Ideal becomes the Real, and the Real becomes the Ideal.[5]) Scriptorium as milieu becomes model and exception (rule and exception negated); or, scriptorium as model and exception becomes universal and a contingent world for works for works.[6]

Scriptorium as milieu is a proscribed world. What does it shut out and what does it shut in? And to what end? If it shuts out rote operativity, it also encloses speculative inoperativity as a form of ultra-operativity. The paradox is telling, though also self-serving for works. To make inoperativity operative is to privilege a set of concerns that are nominally buried or inoperative in the operative fields of art and scholarship as defined by external agency.

Silence as antithesis to noise is an example of an operative field of inoperativity. Per John Cage, Daniel Barenboim, et al., silence underwrites music. In the context of scriptoria for artistic scholarship, silence is the exclusion of discursive noise — in disciplines and in various markets that facilitate the appropriation and expropriation of art and scholarship as form of capital.

---

5   G.W.F. Hegel et al.

6   See Jean Molino's Introduction to Henri Focillon's *The Life of Forms in Art.*
    Form, according to Focillon, "sets up within history an immutable order,"
    a "fourth realm." This fourth realm is superadded to "the three realms
    of the physical world." Focillon, *The Life of Forms in Art,* 11. This fourth
    realm resembles the "medieval voice" Pico della Mirandola defended
    against Renaissance humanist appropriations of the mere surface or
    syntax of the archaic. See Gavin Keeney, "The Origin of the Arts," in *"Elsewhere": Essays in Art, Architecture, and Cultural Production, 2002–2011*
    (Newcastle upon Tyne: Cambridge Scholars Publishing, 2011), 245, for
    Pico's use of this medieval voice against "schools of word-catchers."

Through operative inoperativity, therefore, silence acquires a voice. Notably, it first speaks by omission — by not speaking. It then acquires its own voice, external noise excluded.

Two problems arise that are also incipient paralogisms. Stated in proleptic terms they are: (1) That the space of the scriptoria, whatever form that may take, does not reify artistic and curatorial hubris, re-privileging authorial license,[7] and (2) That the exception, always elective, does not invalidate works that are not of the same class or diminish the value of socio-economic and socio-cultural commentary through works that operate in and through markets. The first proviso establishes a datum for authorial intent and a relationship to the "History" and "No History" paradox of the works-for-works idiom. The second proviso refuses categorical and systemic incorporations of ideology at the expense of complexity and non-uniformity. In some of the more peculiar time-senses associated with the incipient or possible justifications for scriptoria there is a non-ideological wilding or re-wilding for works that is predicated on excluding all forms of ideology that might serve as a Trojan horse for the re-institution or re-introduction of banished forms of conformity, utility, and patrimonialism. The peculiar instance of incipient presentism in works for works is the foremost example of a time-sense that engages the temporal and the a-temporal, the

---

7   See Georges Canguilhem, "The Living and Its Milieu," trans. John Savage, *Grey Room* 3 (Spring 2001): 7–31; first published in *La connaissance de la vie* (Paris: Librairie Hachette, 1952). "Living man takes from his relationship with man the scholar, in whose work ordinary perceptive experience finds itself contradicted and corrected, a sort of unconscious fatuousness that leads him to prefer his own milieu to that of other living things as having not only a different value, but a higher degree of reality" (ibid., 27). Ruskin: "Art is valuable or otherwise, only as it expresses the personality, activity, and living perception of a good and great human soul; that it may express and contain this with little help from execution, and less from science; and that if it have not this, if it show not the vigour, perception, and invention of a mighty human spirit, it is worthless." John Ruskin, *The Stones of Venice*, Vol. 3 (London: George Allen and Unwin, 1925), 169–70. The term *worthless* in this context is relative to what Ruskin is proscribing within the rhetorical ambit of the statement.

historical and the a-historical, and the theological and the a-theological "registers" that inhabit the scriptoria model.

II. Veronese's Presentism and *The Wedding at Cana*

> I felt as if I had been plunged into a sea of wine of thought, and must drink to drowning. But the first distinct impression which fixed itself on one was that of the entire superiority of Painting to Literature as a test, expression, and record of human intellect.[8]
>
> — John Ruskin

Peter Greenaway's 2009 animation of Paolo Veronese's *The Wedding at Cana* (1562–1563) is a tour de force because the painting is a tour de force.[9] Setting aside the fact that the "painting" Greenaway animated at the refectory of the former monastery

---

8   John Ruskin, "Dinner at Simon, the Pharisee's," 1.311; cited in Andrew Tate, "'Archangel' Veronese: Ruskin as Protestant Spectator," in *Ruskin's Artists: Studies in the Victorian Visual Economy*, ed. Robert Hewison (Aldershot: Ashgate, 2000), 134. Here Ruskin is describing his encounter in 1849, at the Louvre, with Veronese's *The Wedding at Cana*. He continues, in similar terms, to describe what "inhabits" the painting: "awful and inconceivable intellect"; "reach of conscience"; "moral feeling"; "kingly imaginative power"; and an "Interpretation of Humanity." Ruskin, "Dinner at Simon, the Pharisee's," 2.437. See also John Ruskin, *Diaries: 1848–1873*, eds. Joan Evans and John Howard Whitehouse (Oxford: Clarendon Press, 1958), 437–38.

9   See Peter Greenaway, *Veronese, The Wedding at Cana: A Vision by Peter Greenaway* (Milan: Charta, 2010). Greenaway's installation at San Giorgio occurred June 6 to September 13, 2009. See also Pasquale Gagliardi, ed., *The Miracle of Cana: The Originality of the Re-production* — The Wedding at Cana *by Paolo Veronese: The Biography of a Painting, the Creation of a Facsimile and Its Theoretical Implications* (Venice/Verona: Fondazione Giorgio Cini/Cierre Edizioni, 2011), a translation and revision of the catalogue of the exhibition held at the Fondazione Giorgio Cini, Venice, Italy, September 15–30 and October 12–December 16, 2007. The painting at the Louvre was scanned in November–December 2006 by Factum Arte. The resulting reproduction was installed in the Palladian refectory in August 2007. This was preceded by a "virtual return" in March 2005 via a high-definition projection (ibid., 8–9).

of San Giorgio Maggiore in Venice is a facsimile created by exacting technical means (the original at the Louvre, taken by Napoleon in 1797 as war reparations), what precisely inhabits this painting and why did it serve to serve notice in 1849 on John Ruskin's former English pietism; i.e., preparing the way for his famous "unconversion" to occur about ten years later, in 1858, in front of yet another Veronese painting, in Turin?[10] Curiously, Greenaway claims that Veronese adopted the schema for the painting from "satirist and pornographer" Pietro Aretino, "who wrote a full devotional transcription of the event as he imagined it, taking his information from the Gospel of St. John."[11] Aretino was effectively Titian's publicist (since c.1540) and Veronese was competing with Tintoretto at the time as "most accomplished" student of Titian.[12] In 1573 the Inquisition inquired as to whether Veronese's *The Last Supper* at the Dominican monastery of Santi Giovanni e Paolo in Venice was licentious or not — no doubt

---

10   "Desertion before disconfirmation" is Jay Fellows's term for Ruskin's leaving naive piety behind. See Jay Fellows, *Ruskin's Maze: Mastery and Madness in His Art* (Princeton: Princeton University Press, 1981), xv–xvi. The full passage is: "If Ruskin is eventually alone (and desertion before disconfirmation informs much of his performance), he is not, in any case, unified in his loneliness. Rather, solipsistically antiphonal, with only himself as company, he is, as if severed by a double axe, either halved or doubled, with his consciousness, like a double tiered labyrinth that is his penultimate Theatre of Blindness, in attempted dialogic discourse with itself, which is, perhaps, Ruskin's ultimate point of failure/success." See also Jay Fellows, *The Failing Distance: The Autobiographical Impulse in John Ruskin* (Baltimore: Johns Hopkins University Press, 1975).

11   Greenaway, *Veronese, The Wedding at Cana*, 10. Greenaway describes Aretino's text as a "certain sort of film-script" (ibid). Aretino died in 1556, well before Veronese's *The Wedding at Cana* was created. But the "thematic" was at large and both Jacopo Tintoretto and Veronese worked from the conventions of Titian, forward. Tintoretto painted *The Wedding at Cana* at Santa Maria della Salute, Venice, in 1561.

12   In the 1540s, rivalries emerged: Pietro Aretino, "Titian's most enthusiastic publicity agent," embraces Tintoretto, then desists (upon Titian's insistence); Veronese develops "more rapidly" than Tintoretto; Tintoretto as anti-Titian; Veronese as Titian's protégé (and pawn). Curatorial gloss, "Titian, Tintoretto, Veronese: Rivals in Renaissance Venice," Museum of Fine Arts, Boston, MA, USA, March 15–August 16, 2009.

given the well-known Aretino-Veronese compact. Nearly a decade earlier had *The Wedding at Cana* at San Giorgio Maggiore alerted the post-Council of Trent (1545-1563) authorities to Veronese's heterodoxy? Apparently, it was then permissible to take liberties with the latter subject but not with the former. Yet it is those liberties taken by Veronese, with both paintings, that warrant a closer look insofar as Veronese's *The Wedding at Cana* encloses a then-prevalent theme of the relationship of sacred space to artistic space, with the main arguments turning on issues regarding the *differences* between sacred time and artistic time.[13] Suffice to say that the presentism of theological time did not then quite mean the same thing as the presentism of artistic time. It was Veronese's relationship to Renaissance illusionism and Renaissance *illuminism* that got him into hot water. He actually departed both conventions, but used them to mix up time-senses in a manner that put him at risk of being accused of heresy and heresies. This relationship to the conventions of the day was troubled. He played at it until it made no sense to him. It is, indeed, a case of artistic anamorphic topologies versus theological heresies. The quibbles by art historians about who is actually in *The Wedding at Cana* are not actually so important. What is important is that Veronese developed a type of historical perspectivalism that was effectively sensationalist. This merely included the inclusion of a wide range of potentates from across Europe and from within Venice (i.e., from hither and yon) in the painting to declare its ultimate non-sensical nature to ration-

---

13 This was but one aspect of the 2009 exhibition at the MFA in Boston. Another was the sheer bravado of the three-way competition across the last half of the 1500s between Titian, Tintoretto, and Veronese. For example, by the early 1550s Titian's "incredible refinement and diligence" gave way to "bold strokes, applied broadly, and with blotches of paint" (Vasari). As a result, in the 1570s and 1580s "both Tintoretto and Veronese responded to Titian's late style by employing their own versions of open brushwork, monochrome palettes, and shadowy and visionary settings." See Tintoretto, "Saint Jerome in the Wilderness," c.1571–1572, "knotted, potentially explosive energy," and Titian, "Saint Jerome in the Wilderness," c.1570–1575, "loose, vibrating, and shadowy late style," and spiritual self-portrait. Tintoretto's death in 1594 closes "the golden age of Venetian painting."

ality proper. He had practiced painterly architectural mischief at Villa Maser (for Daniele Barbaro and his brother, Marcantonio), through a series of frescoes, as early as 1561. He was by 1562–1563, however, practicing historico-mythological mischief at San Giorgio. Both projects were commissions in association with Palladio. Perhaps it is not a stretch to say that Veronese had had quite enough of Palladio's reductive and pristine architecture and his role at San Giorgio required a leap into a type of deconstruction of architectural rationality in service to the client, a fairly wealthy monastery by the standards of the day. At Maser he had practiced this leap in a more mytho-poetic tense and sense, while nonetheless producing absurdist scenarios for his clients (i.e., Venetian notables). Palladio and Veronese were not so much the duet in *both* cases that art history might otherwise then suggest. It was much more like a duel of sensibilities. Often illusionism (perspective, etc.) is also illuminism (an affect of intellect). At some point it no longer registers. Hence, and in terms of what came next, the arrival of "Mannerism" (usually traced to Late Michelangelo).

All of the above, which it may be said is duly embedded in the painting, including the "40 conversations" created by Greenaway, is duly erased by the painting. Ruskin's idea of painting as "an Interpretation of Humanity" comes into play, as do statements by others regarding Veronese's accomplishments. The painting famously incorporates the architecture of the Palladian refectory, as it incorporates the larger field of Venetian Renaissance manners, mores, architecture, and costume. The "stage-like setting" of the painting in the refectory, the completion of the architecture by trompe-l'oeil effect, plus its "irreverent illusionistic extravagance" bely the fact that the accomplishment is most of all to be found in the internal resources of the painting.[14] Veronese jests while something else obtains. Unlike a text, and according to Étienne Gilson, a painting is "inseparable

---

14 Pasquale Gagliardi, "Foreword: The Return of *The Wedding at Cana* to the Monastery of San Giorgio Maggiore," in *The Miracle of Cana*, ed. Gagliardi, 7.

from its matter."[15] For Gilson, painting is "a middle road, lower than metaphysics, higher than phenomenology."[16] It might also be the ideal model for the model of a scriptorium for artistic scholarship.

If presentism elides times and time-senses, what then does it privilege? In turn, what does the presentism of Veronese's *The Wedding at Cana* privilege? Both Ruskin and Dostoevsky suggest an answer. For Dostoevsky, as described in *The Brothers Karamazov,* the miracle of Christ's conversion of water into wine at Cana is a moral tale: "He is calling new ones unceasingly for ever and ever."[17] For Ruskin, and for Veronese, the "wine of thought" in which we might drown concerns the concentration of discursivity that might occur in a painting as opposed to mere words. If this is true for some paintings, it is not true for all paintings. Circumstantially, a book is an object — yet the book is also a model where discursivity is also compressed. Most books are the enclosure of a much larger discourse. They too present a type of "wine of thought" into which the reader may plunge.[18] The larger field condensed into "textuality" is "sociological polymorphism."[19] In favoring the internal metric of works, the polymorphism of discourse contracts. To privilege that contraction or erasure invokes new paralogisms. To favor reduction but to retain *"materia signata"* (Gilson/Aquinas), the act of compression must actually elicit an internal expansion. The

---

15 Étienne Gilson, *Peinture et réalité* (Paris: J. Vrin, 1958), 95–96; cited in Pasquale Gagliardi, Bruno Latour, and Pedro Memelsdorff, eds., *Coping with the Past: Conservation and Restoration* (Florence: Leo S. Olschki, 2010), 134–35. *Coping with the Past* is based on the "Dialoghi di San Giorgio: Inheriting the Past" colloquium.

16 Gilson, *Peinture et réalité*, 12; cited in Gagliardi et al., eds., *Coping with the Past,* 135.

17 Fyodor Dostoevsky, *The Brothers Karamazov,* trans. Constance Garnett (New York: Macmillan, 1922), 386; cited in Gagliardi, "Foreword," 14.

18 For Carlo Ginzburg a book represents "the shift from performance to transcription" as "loss." Carlo Ginzburg, "Invisible Texts, Visible Images," in *Coping with the Past,* eds. Gagliardi et al., 136. This loss includes "gestures, intonations, even words [i.e., from performance to performance]" (ibid., 137–38).

19 Ibid., 137.

fact that neither the book nor the painting is the artefact — or, that both book and painting exceed the artefact — is the initial gesture in restoring moral rights to works. Authorial matters aside, both book and painting are de facto "scriptoria" in which things other than mere text and image appear and *dis*-appear. Veronese's *The Wedding at Cana* is both a painting and a text. As de facto scriptorium, the painting exhibits characteristics of the dynamic fold the scriptoria model offers as respite from "sociological polymorphism." The stillness of the miracle at Cana amidst the clamor of the event is the miracle of the painting. That stillness is present in key works by Rembrandt as well, as Aby Warburg and Georg Simmel admirably detailed, with Simmel (sociologist) notably exiting "sociological polymorphism" via Rembrandt, and Warburg (art historian) exiting "magico-religious" perturbations. Curiously, or not, Greenaway has tackled works by both Rembrandt and Veronese in his "Classic Paintings Revisited Series" (2006–), suggesting that part of his artistic project is to re-create and trouble the very background noise such works have silenced. The series was launched with Rembrandt's *The Nightwatch*. Along the way Greenaway has, indeed, tackled da Vinci's *The Last Supper* (2008–), no doubt well aware of Renaissance-era prohibitions regarding intentional artistic mis-readings or the bawdification of the subject, and will close the project with Michelangelo's *The Last Judgement*.[20]

---

20 Greenaway announced preliminary approval for The Last Judgement project at the "Future Passé" conference sessions at the V&A, London, England, on June 2, 2017. In his presentation, which was entitled "Visual Literacy," Greenaway also announced "cinema is dead." He then went on to denounce "wordsmiths" as the primary problem for cinema. His presentation favored a painter's cinema, not a writer's cinema. Cinema is about "images, images, images," he declared, not "bedtime stories for adults." His embrace of heritage (Leonardo's *Last Supper, Wedding at Cana,* etc.) is, in his words, "to keep *it* alive." The V&A program presented Greenaway as "painter, curator, opera director, and vj." Greenaway noted that his multiscreen, non-narrative projects operate in the present tense — i.e., they are dynamic versus static and premised upon change. As "vj," Greenaway favors stripping down works into loops, plus music, and placing the onus on the audience for making the necessary connections. See the "Future Passé" conference, https://www.vam.ac.uk/event/Mo7OM405/future-passe.

Dialogically, the circumstances of the book and the circumstances of the painting disappear and new circumstances appear. Anti-milieu becomes milieu and presentism suggests sacred or eternal time. There is the suggestion or hint of theosis — as remnant for new works.[21] In this manner, and, as the event of *The Wedding at Cana* signifies, "the law disappears…."[22] As possible models for scriptoria, what appears by way of *dis*-appearance becomes the new dispensation of works for works. Substantial "noise" (e.g., the rules of observance and engagement, the canon, the articles of production and commodification) are eclipsed through the instantiation of an internal law for works that "comes over from" all that has been embedded in works through assimilation of prior art. This confirmation by configuration has also been ill-served by being considered a form of performative closure for works. That such externally defined closure has often served to neutralize the incipient critique that such works convey, directly or indirectly, suggests that the work of art or artistic scholarship has yet to escape the double bind of being either a cultural commodity, defined by utility, or an otherwise-harmless exception or anomaly to market ideology.

III. Coda: Jarman's *Blue*

In the pandemonium of image / I present you with the universal Blue / Blue an open door to soul / An infinite possibility / Becoming tangible.[23]

— Derek Jarman

---

21 St. Paul's concept of the remnant is here transposed or transfigured by the spatial and non-spatial figures of speech and thought given to the very idea of scriptoria. See Giorgio Agamben, *The Time that Remains: A Commentary on the Letter to the Romans,* trans. Patricia Dailey (Stanford: Stanford University Press, 2005). First published as *Il tempo che resta* (Turin: Bollati Boringhieri, 2000).

22 Fausto di Riez, "Discorso 5 sull'Epifania," c.440. In *Patrologiae Latinae, Supplementum 3,* 560–62; cited in Giuseppe Pavanello, "Più vino per la festa," in *The Miracle of Cana,* ed. Gagliardi, 24n1.

23 Derek Jarman, *Blue: Text of a Film by Derek Jarman* (London: Channel 4 Television/BBC Radio 3, 1993), 17. The pamphlet is 30 pages long, including

Derek Jarman's last film, *Blue,* was first shown in the United Kingdom on Channel 4 and simultaneously broadcast on BBC Radio 3 in September 1993.[24] *Blue* is an elegiac swan song by a filmmaker who was also — simultaneously — a painter. Yet the project dates as far back as 1974 with the working titles, "Bliss" and "Blueprint." Along the way Jarman, as wordsmith, kept handmade notebooks with aphoristic commentaries — inclusive of an undated typescript, "Notes on 'Alchemical Blue...,'" all leading to the first filmscript, "Blueprint," composed in 1993.[25]

As of 1990, with the making of *The Garden,* Jarman is slipping — again or for the first time — toward a type of filmmaking that privileges the aleatory and the iterative. It is an alchemical prospect for film that brings much that does not belong to film per se into film. "Making a film with no script you have to be on your toes: visual ideas develop as they run."[26] The visible register and the ambient environment of film are becoming an experimental tableau where the accidental and the intentional collide. The apparent sampling strategy of *Blue* — sampling in the sense that the evolution of the project over years has led to decisions that reduce the discursive content to fragments — suggests that Jarman has reached a plateau with *Blue* where his approach to

---

colophon, and was issued in an edition of 3,000 copies. First impression "printed letterpress by Littlehampton Printing, West Sussex, on Heritage White, acid free paper, and Saunders Waterford mould-made Water colour paper supplied by John Purcell, London (Set in Sabon roman)."

24 Derek Jarman, dir., *Blue* (1993) (Kino Lorber, 2019), DVD. A Basilisk Communications/Uplink production for Channel 4 in association with the Arts Council of Great Britain, Opal and BBC Radio 3. Written and directed by: Derek Jarman. Produced by: James Mackay and Takashi Asai. Composer: Simon Fisher Turner. Associate Director: David Lewis. Sound Design: Marvin Black.

25 These working documents were presented in a vitrine at the Tate Modern's "spotlight" re-presentation of *Blue* in 2017.

26 Derek Jarman, *Modern Nature: The Journals of Derek Jarman* (London: Vintage, 1991), 200; with reference to *The Garden* (1990). "We film a sequence of a glass harmonium. As hands circle over glasses and the studio fills with the unearthly sound, we watch mesmerized. What spirits are they conjuring? Tilda asks to be put into the scene" (ibid., 199–200). The scene is conducted "with extras from *Caravaggio*."

the space of painting and the space of cinema have effectively converged to favor a productive interchange between boundaries and all that lies beyond those boundaries, an evocation of memory and the complex time-senses of the presentism given to the painterly cinematic arts.[27]

A sampling of this sampling of discursive or verbal content that Jarman brings into *Blue,* the visual register famously composed of an unwavering Klein Blue (IKB) screen for the entirety of its 79 minutes, underscores what is at stake.

> Ages and Aeons quit the room exploding into timelessness / No entrances or exits now / No need for obituaries or judgments / We knew that time would end after tomorrow at sunrise / We scrubbed the floors / And did the washing up / It would not catch us unawares.[28]

In a small "untitled notebook" with no date, included amidst notes on blue, is a dedication to Yves Klein and Klein Blue: "Pure existential space (was winking at me)...." The earlier impressions of Klein Blue have survived in *Blue,* the film, but they have been "transcribed" by Jarman's struggle with his own impending end. He will die four months after the film is released. Blue now is a field of vision — a visionary space — that permits or enforces escape. "Pray to be released from image."[29]

---

27 For discursive operations "of and around" the theme of color, see Derek Jarman, *Chroma: A Book of Colour – June '93* (London: Century/Random House, 1994). Somewhere along the trajectory of its development, Blue (as project) was also to become a performance. See Mason Leaver-Yap, "Film without Film: Derek Jarman's *Blue,*" *Walker Art Center,* October 23, 2014, https://walkerart.org/magazine/film-without-film-derek-jarmans-blue; with reference to Tony Peake, *Derek Jarman: A Biography* (London: Little, Brown, 1999).

28 Jarman, *Blue,* 22–23. There is an implicit nod toward Gnosticism in the capitalization of "Aeons" ... Aeons create worlds. In this poetic fragment it would seem that they are exiting the world they have created.

29 Ibid., 12. "The image is a prison of the soul, your heredity, your education, your vices and aspirations, your qualities, your psychological world" (ibid.).

Amidst the fragments of a project long delayed for various reasons, including simply finding sponsorship and enduring the various judgements made along the way by Channel 4, dream imagery piles upon dream imagery: "The dog barks, the caravan passes. Marco Polo stumbles across the Blue Mountain."[30] Blue is now personified in blue people, blue canvases, lapis, labyrinth of mirrors: "Blue walks into the labyrinth."[31] Early on, passages of sublimity and silence are interspersed with "rhetorical gestures" and ethereal music: Gautama's "Walk away from illness" is countered with a type of angelic reply via plainsong: "Fate is the strongest / fate fated fatal…." This is followed by, "How am I going to walk away from this?" And then, "Blue stretches, yawns and is awake…."[32] Jarman has passed into the blue mirror he is conjuring. The associations are half-lucid, intentionally so. The last words of the film and filmscript are: "I place a delphinium, Blue, upon your grave."[33] The 30-page "text of a film" — in being transcribed to film — will be brought, with the voices of Nigel Terry, John Quentin, Derek Jarman, and Tilda Swinton, into indescribable tension with music by Jon Balance, Gini Ball, Marvin Black, Peter Christopherson, Markus Dravius, Brian Eno, Tony Hinnigan, Danny Hyde, Jan Latham Koenig, Marden Hill, The Klug of Luxembourg, Miranda Sex Garden, Momus, Vini Reilly, Kate St. John, Simon Fisher Turner, Richard Watson, and Hugh Webb, plus excerpts from Karol Szymanowski and Erik Satie. This soundscape will serve to effectively further destabilize the already fragmented discursive content and further distance the realization of the film *Blue* from the long-standing project of *Blue*. Again, "History" and "No History" …. Jarman's film — inclusive of the circumstances of its making, however proscribed — constitutes enclosure of the space and the non-space, the iterative and the non-iterative associative magic of the ongoing project. Jarman's long fascination with "Alchemical

---

30 Ibid., 9.
31 Ibid., 10.
32 Ibid., 6–7.
33 Ibid., 30.

Blue" has produced *Blue,* yet it is also notably eclipsed by *Blue. Thus, parataxis and hypotaxis ... yet in literary-cinematic terms.*

The aleatory and the ontic converge in the artefact of the 35mm print — bought, collected, and archived by institutions. Now converted to video, the film has also lost some of its merit as film — as projected, but also by virtue of a loss of tonality in the transfer to video. The long tail of the project, its journey to 35mm print, connotes upon the film proper its status as work. The reduction of the project to the artefact also contains or covers the transfer of rights from author to work. For it is the work (the 35mm film) not the operativity of the long tail as defined by film scholars or by museum curators that speaks of the compression and transfiguration of affects to effect, and vice versa. That *Blue* might have been a performance — and was and is depending on how and where it is shown today — registers all of the mysteries and conturbations regarding possible forms such a project may take, the iterative or so-called transmedial versions nonetheless eclipsed by the film itself. If art criticism reloads the complex tale of the development of the project, that complication belongs to art criticism. If museums are afraid to show the 35mm print for fear of scratching their pristine copy, and thus resort to various transfers to permit screening, that belongs to the museological structure and culture of collection and exhibition.

Jarman's *Blue* is, after all, a film. As film, it withholds its own history, at least in the time of its screening. In screening the film as performance — for various reasons, but including those Jarman orchestrated in 1993 for promotional purposes — *Blue* as proscribed space and non-space for its author's reflections on forms of transcendence (of escaping whatever it is that haunts him) escapes its own archival register as 35mm film and swims against the grain of memorialization as artefact (as Jarman and colleagues swam in the blue field of the projection in 1993 to bring the then-completed film back to life). Amidst the complexities of the positions staked out by film itself and by criticism, the multivalent expression or field otherwise elided by film returns from within the film. This cinematic space is representational space; and this representational space is — as Jarman suggests — a blue distance in the arts and a collapsible or expandable distance that opens onto theological precepts that have nothing or little to do with conventional theology. The appearance, the re-appearance, the play, the re-play, the iterative and the generative, and the incarnational and the entombment associated with the passage of the work is, in effect, the very figure of works for works. The end product, aleatory and ontic at once, is merely the impression left. Yet the impression is where the moral agency resides — for the work, and for the author of the work in question.

If the transfer of moral rights to works confers upon the work itself a certain or uncertain moral imperative, it is because the exceptional status of the work of art returns as autonomous field for works — inoperativity momentarily construed as evasion of utility.[34] Works for works, therefore, are given a prescience and a status that evades any concern for mere commodification. *Blue* is, in many respects, a work that resides beyond the categories defined by film culture and by the regimes of commodification the work undergoes as film. As performance — and as indefin-

34 This reading of inoperativity has little to do with Jean-Luc Nancy's concept of "inoperative community," other than that such a community does seek to collectively resist immanent forms of power. Jean-Luc Nancy, *The Inoperative Community*, ed. Peter Connor, trans. Peter Connor, Lisa Garbus, Michael Holland, and Simona Sawhney (Minneapolis: University of Minnesota Press, 1991). Essentially a compilation, parts of the book were first published in *La communauté désœuvrée* (Paris: Christian Bourgois, 1986). Nancy's readings of power belong to political geography versus works per se. See Nancy's concept of "literary communism" as discussed in Keeney, "The Origin of the Arts," in *"Else-where,"* 246–48. See also Keeney, "The Literary Work of Art," in ibid., 249–59, for Roman Ingarden's pursuit of the key to formalist agency in literature. Ingarden identifies the force-field (or, "literary time-consciousness") that inhabits the literary work of art. Roman Ingarden, *The Literary Work of Art: An Investigation on the Borderlines of Ontology, Logic, and Theory of Literature,* trans. George G. Grabowicz (Evanston: Northwestern University Press, 1973). First published as *Das literarische Kunstwerk: Eine Untesuchung aus dem Grenzgebiet der Ontologie, Logik und Literaturwissenschaft* (Halle/Saale: M. Niemeyer, 1931).

able transmedial project — *Blue* is altogether a different type of commodity. Its instances, its re-play, its metamorphoses under the aegis of performance or event closes down the exceptional for the contingent, with inoperativity transferred to the non-space of event. The contingent exists in such a play of outtakes as an otherwise conventional dance with the unconventional.[35] Transmedia eclipses and transforms works across a spectrum of instances and possible venues, further troubling the ontic nature of the work while also freeing the moral imperative from the peculiar non-operative operativity of work as an exception defined within the structure of modernist cultural production. In such a strained milieu, where film is also not-film, the internal resources of *Blue* are the primary means of and for its hypothetical or fugitive moral imperative — its incarnational merit as work of art. That echoing field, as illuminated tableau established by Jarman, but by no means exhausted by Jarman, is illustrative of why a works-for-works idiom in artistic scholarship must also, at times, leave aside both backstory and mediatized myth, mere contingent agency and mere critical agency, hyper-valorization and hyper-canonization by markets as hyper-commodity, for the exacting and austere ground its actual appearance in time has demarcated and enclosed. This moral imperative for *Blue* is reducible to tautology. It is what it is. Jarman's "Aeons" have slipped into the film, left their mark there, and vanished.

Research on Jarman's Blue *was conducted under the auspices of a Visiting Research Fellowship, Birkbeck Institute for the Humanities, Birkbeck, University of London, London, England, June 2017.*

---

35   See any of the attempts by major art institutions to re-screen *Blue,* since its release, including the Tate Modern, the Getty, and the Walker. Each time there is a struggle with the fact that the film does not seem to want to remain merely a film, in part due to its legendary status, and the curators respond by mounting all manner of interpretive gloss and socio-cultural commentary to re-constitute the implied dynamic that has somehow gone missing from the artefact itself. Always in part a multimedia event, the Radio 3 broadcast of *Blue* in 1993 was supplemented by a blue card mailed to listeners in advance of the actual broadcast.

5

Prior Art and Things Given

But what if I had to speak and this compulsion to speak were the sign of the inspiration of language, of a vitality of language within me? And what if my will also wished only what I were compelled to do? Then might not this, after all, without my knowledge and conviction, be poetry and elucidate a mystery of language? And might I not then be called to be a writer[;] for what is a writer but one who is inspired by language?[1]

— Novalis

I. Prior Art and Universality

What weighs upon me is the conviction which nothing can shake in my soul, that my readers would have been delighted with the same hero, this same Tchitchikov, if the author had not looked too deeply into his soul, had not stirred up in its depths what slips away and hides from the light, had not displayed the most secret thoughts which a man does not trust to any other,

---

1   Novalis, "Monolog"; cited in Ian Balfour, "The Scope and Texture of Romantic Prophecy: Wordsworth and Novalis Among Others," in *The Rhetoric of Romantic Prophecy* (Stanford: Stanford University Press, 2002), 47; from Novalis, *Novalis Schriften: Die Werke Friedrich von Hardenbergs,* Vol. 2: *Das philosophische Werk,* ed. Richard Samuel, in collaboration with Hans-Joachim Mähl and Gerhard Schultz (Stuttgart: W. Kohlhammer, 1968).

but had shown him such as he appeared to all the town, to Manilov and others; then every one would have been delighted with him, and would have welcomed him as an interesting man. It would not have mattered that neither his face nor his whole figure would have moved as though living before their eyes; on the other hand, when they had finished the book, their souls would have been untroubled and they could go back to the card table, which is the solace of all Russia. Yes, my gentle readers, you would rather not see the poverty of human nature exposed.[2]

— Nikolai Gogol

The internal metric of a work of art has no value. Value is the wrong word. The only value comes from prior art. Yet the metric of a work has merit, and it is the difference between value and merit that constitutes the relationship between prior art and work.

This strange concord through dissonance is evident in the long authorial digressions Gogol makes use of in *Dead Souls* (1842) — authorial digressions, or narratological license, staged in the author's voice, often in the first person, where he, the narrator, comments upon the novel, and upon how he has constructed the novel or why he has waited from time to time to fill the reader in on the backstory. Most famously, he waits until very near the end of the novel to tell us the origins of his hero, Tchitchikov, proving that his hero is actually a rascal.

The internal metric or landscape of the work of art is a well-known, long-established form of literary vitalism — and often a form of "dark" vitalism. In the case of *Dead Souls,* this interiority or subjective state for works is in service to so-called literary realism; and it is Part I, ending with the famous scene of the troika rushing across the Russian landscape, scaring or bewitching everyone in its path, that subsequent authors admired most of all, including Dostoevsky, who mimicked and cited it in *The*

2   Nikolai Gogol, *Dead Souls,* trans. Constance Garnett (New York: Barnes and Noble, 2005), 246. First published in 1842.

Brothers Karamazov.[3] Part II, actually an attempt to justify Part I's satiric and bleak portrait of Russia in the early to mid-1800s, and never intended by Gogol to be published, is in effect *another story*. It is a failed sequel. Gogol, somewhat distressed that Part I was so bleak, attempted, post-publication, to re-enter the fray, with Part II. That he failed has as much to say about Part I as it does about Part II. Despite the author supposedly burning the last chapters to prevent their publication, copies were nevertheless found after his death and spliced onto the novel (which Gogol actually referred to as a poem).[4]

————————

3   Gogol is describing Tchitchikov's escape from the provincial town of N. after his plot to buy dead serfs has been exposed. "And, Russia, art not thou too flying onwards like a spirited troika that nothing can overtake? The road is smoking under thee, the bridges rumble, everything falls back and is left behind! The spectator stands still struck dumb by the divine miracle: is it not a flash of lightning from heaven? What is the meaning of this terrifying onrush? What mysterious force is hidden in this troika, never seen before? Ah, horses, horses — what horses! Is the whirlwind hidden under your manes? Is there some delicate sense tingling in every vein? They hear the familiar song over their heads — at once in unison they strain their iron chests and scarcely touching the earth with their hoofs are transformed almost into straight lines flying through the air — and the troika rushes on, full of divine inspiration.... Russia, whither flyest thou? Answer! She gives no answer. The ringing of the bells melts into music; the air, torn to shreds, whirs and rushes like the wind, everything there is on earth is flying by, and the other states and nations, with looks askance, make way for her and draw aside" (ibid., 250–51).

4   In some ways the schism between Part I and Part II resembles the red line in Nietzsche's *The Birth of Tragedy,* with Nietzsche eventually disowning the second part of the book. This disavowal had to do with his eventual disenchantment with Wagner — yet, perhaps the red line was always there. This disavowal is retrospective or, more properly, retroactive. The beauty of the first part of *The Birth of Tragedy* is already marred by the second part and cannot be remedied. See Friedrich Nietzsche, *The Birth of Tragedy, and The Case of Wagner,* trans. Walter Kaufmann (New York: Vintage, 1967). In a slightly different manner, Book IV of *Thus Spoke Zarathustra,* with 40 copies circulated privately by Nietzsche, but later incorporated into the book, suggests that the tautological state of works concerns both the work's voice and the author's conversation with that voice. Regarding Book IV of *Thus Spoke Zarathustra,* see Keeney, "Introduction: The 'History' of Art History," in *"Else-where": Essays in Art, Architecture, and Cultural Production, 2002–2011* (Newcastle upon Tyne: Cambridge

The prior art in this "poem" is, effectively, *all of Russia* — or, at the least, the "all of Russia" that Gogol knew personally or could imagine.[5] It has come into the novel in excruciatingly bizarre descriptive passages and portraits, the latter including that of the hero, Tchitchikov. These renowned passages include exquisite yet blurred or florid descriptions of landscape, architecture, fashion, the culinary arts, rhetoric, manners and mores, and much else that spirals in and out of view until the reader surrenders and lets all of it wash over the mind in theatrical-cinematic splendor. But it has also been transfigured within the spaces of the novel as abject allegory and no longer resembles reality as such.[6] The internal metric of the work has assumed a life of its own, and it may be said that it was that very internal life of the work that resisted Gogol's attempt to redeem the story in the catastrophic and never-completed Part II.[7] The tale does seem to have gotten the better of him, and much has been written, in literary criticism, of his post-publication attempts to "redeem" the story and himself.

This work of literary art had, in and for itself, its benefactors, or partisans, in the form of the literary world Gogol inhabited. Pushkin had first suggested the basic plot lines. Reading passag-

---

Scholars Publishing, 2011), xiii–xvi. Paradoxically, Gogol labored to undo the beauty of Part I of *Dead Souls* by agonistically constructing a mostly didactic corrective in the form of Part II. That he failed has more to do with the emphatic autonomy of Part I than the spiritual crisis he endured in his last years. What he had brought into the world constitutionally defied the intended corrective. That Part II has been spliced onto Part I in later editions is effectively a case of the literary establishment carrying out, in a botched manner, what Gogol could not endure while alive.

5   Set in the years 1815–1833. Jeffrey Meyers, "Introduction," in Gogol, *Dead Souls,* xx; with reference to Richard Pevear, "Introduction," in Nikolai Gogol, *Dead Souls,* trans. Richard Pevear and Larissa Volokhonsky (New York: Pantheon, 1996), xxiii. First published in 1842.

6   Regarding the allegorical nature of *Dead Souls,* plus its relation to the classical epic, see James B. Woodward, *Gogol's "Dead Souls"* (Princeton: Princeton University Press, 1978).

7   Part II was effectively a sequel that threatened to ruin the studied imprecision, dark beauty, and magisterial voice of Part I. See Meyers, "Introduction," in Gogol, *Dead Souls* (2005), xvi–xvii.

es of Part II to his colleagues, after returning from Rome, where Part I of the book was finished, and shortly after Part I was published and widely acclaimed, they were suitably appalled at the author's attempts to justify or re-justify the tale along moral lines.[8] The story is effectively so immoral in its licentiousness and matter-of-fact way of describing the *preposterous* scheme of the anti-hero to purchase dead serfs to then mortgage to the government, that to attach moral significance to the tale after the fact was also to violate the internal coherence and beauty of the literary artwork. It might also be said that the sordid tale was, secretly, a moral tale anyway, and that it did not need the subsequent chapters at all. That is one secret to "dark" vitalism in the Arts and Letters. Part of that internalization and forensic portrait of the Russian soul, as later perfected by Dostoevsky, via what has been called psychological clairvoyance, is clearly the displacements of prior art by literary transfiguration. While normative, and given to literature as such, in the case of Gogol and Dostoevsky the displacement is configured along epic lines — as

---

8   Gogol returned from his travels to Russia in 1839–1840 and again in 1841. *Dead Souls* was published in 1842. By 1845 he was convinced that Part II was a disaster: "I have tortured myself, forced myself to write, suffered severe pains when I saw my impotence … everything came out forced and inferior" (quoted in ibid., xvi). It was in 1845 that Gogol burned the first version of Part II. Ten days before his death in 1852 he burned a second version (ibid., xvii). In-between, in 1848, he made a pilgrimage to the Holy Land where, at Easter service in the Church of the Holy Sepulcher, he hoped Divine Grace might sanctify his mission to "save sinful Russia" (ibid., xvi). How Part II survived is open to speculation, as is much else that Gogol perpetrated in the name of baffling his literary interlocutors. It all resembles the story of Ruskin burning Turner's drawings of nudes, when the Turner Bequest reached the National Gallery in London. The story persisted for decades until debunked. What Gogol was up to, in all probability, was a preternatural wrestling match with his angels, whom he mistook for demons — or vice versa.

in a poem.[9] Lukács's "extensivity of life" is yet present.[10] Whether it died in the late nineteenth century, as Lukács claimed, is immaterial. At the time of Gogol it was yet operative. It is axiomatic that this version of artistic vitalism requires its other — prior art — to sustain its own time-senses, no matter how bizarrely those transpositions and fugitive temporalities transpire. Prior art sustains all such works, and it is prior art that suggests all works owe an inestimable debt to what has been borrowed and to what has been transposed to wholly new terms.

Yet there is also the fact that prior art saves the work of art from implosion. Thus, vitalism and its other as dialectical operation. While transfigured, the "history" that inhabits the work as apparent "no history," or as ghost, in what might be called sublimated form, or through dialectical sublimation, also re-connects the work of art to the world from which it has come.[11] This

---

9   See Victor Shklovsky, "The Literary Genre of *Dead Souls*," in Nikolai Gogol, *"Dead Souls": The Reavey Translation, Backgrounds and Sources, Essays in Criticism*, ed. George Gibian (New York: W.W. Norton, 1985), 564–69.

10 See György Lukács, *The Theory of the Novel: A Historico-philosophical Essay on the Forms of Great Epic Literature*, trans. Anna Bostock (Cambridge: MIT Press, 1971), regarding how the novel, c.1900, supplanted the epic poem of Romanticism. First published as *Die Theorie des Romans: Ein geschichtsphilosophischer Versuch über die Formen der großen Epik* (Berlin: P. Cassirer, 1920). The detail and "grain" of *Dead Souls* is what makes it resemble an epic poem.

11 Regarding dialectical sublimation and Novalis, see Gaston Bachelard, *The Psychoanalysis of Fire*, trans. Alan C.M. Ross, preface by Northrop Frye (Boston: Beacon Press, 1964). First published as *La psychanalyse du feu* (Paris: Éditions Gallimard, 1938). Bachelard describes Novalis's attempts to find a hybrid form of literary-poetic praxis that fuses intentionality and instinct. See also Keeney, "The Origin of the Arts," in Keeney, *"Else-where,"* 227–48. Novalis's quest was subsequently assimilated to the literary-artistic experiments of Surrealism. "I know that Antonin Artaud saw, the way Rimbaud, as well as Novalis and Arnim before him, had spoken of seeing. It is of little consequence, ever since the publication of [Gérard de Nerval's] *Aurélia* [1855], that what was seen this way does not coincide with what is objectively visible. The real tragedy is that the society to which we are less and less honored to belong persists in making it an inexpiable crime to have gone over to the other side of the looking glass." André Breton, "A Tribute to Antonin Artaud," in *Free Rein (La clé des champs),*

internal generativity draws upon external generativity (agency begets agency), even if, in the novel, as in Gogol and Dostoevsky, the epic genre of poetry, as origin, slowly breaks down, mirroring the collapse of Romantic Idealism and the superimpositions of the Late Romanticism of distended and etiolated self for world. The myth of "art for art's sake" is premised upon an aesthetic exception that does not bear close scrutiny. The idea of "exception" is forever linked to a source for that exception. The idealist posture of the exception, while nonetheless a concept in excess of the real of the work, circles back through the work. Vitalism in works retains the trace of the very justifications for the artistic exception — this exception, in turn, justifying artistic expression or license. Perhaps it is that trace that permits a very different level of precocity to works than rote utility. Perhaps that precocity connotes the value of useless beauty and its analogues in art and literature. Perhaps that recursivity is the very point of dialectical sublimation in works?

If Hegel's aesthetics banned any discipline that retained traces of utility from the realm of art (e.g., Architecture), it was because ideality was the ultimate anchor or keel for his aesthetics. Whether anchor or keel depends upon where he was traveling at the time, or where he had found safe harbor for his world-historical analyses. Indeed, Hegel refused the ability of even the arts to encompass "universal spirit" — claiming universality of Spirit incapable of being individualized in the work of art.[12] Regardless of these highest flights of idealist speculation, for Hegel ideality and ideation preclude mere utility, and for art to be freed of determinism and utilitarianism requires that the

---

trans. Michel Parmentier and Jacqueline d'Amboise (Lincoln: University of Nebraska Press, 1995), 77–79; cited in Jacques Derrida and Paule Thévenin, *The Secret Art of Antonin Artaud,* trans. Mary Ann Caws (Cambridge: MIT Press, 1998), v.

12 Spirit, or *Geist,* might only come to full self-knowledge in the collective, not in individuals and not in forms of particularization, including the work of art. Whether Hegel's Pleroma or Parousia is a transposition of Kant's Kingdom of Ends is a matter of speculation, given that Hegel had one eye on Kant's legacy while distancing himself from Kant's legacy.

real of art be strenuously framed by the concept of exception. This discursive operation nonetheless is based on the sleight of hand perpetrated by all aesthetic theory — and that trick is to claim an aesthetic terrain within cultural production that is free of particularity of purpose. Purposeless beauty is also useless beauty, even if claims are made after the fact by the interpretive community for forms of value for works. Criticality, while often knocking the work of art off of its pedestal, can never quite justify its own means to ends, which are effectively reducible to an embarrassment of riches on behalf of criticality. Art itself often knocks art off its pedestal, but for very different reasons.

The critical field in which a work resides is a form of temporality — a time and a place for re-naturalization of the exception. Project-based works that are today situated in a field of cultural inquiry that effectively neutralizes the aesthetic exception are typically justified by making that exception anathema. This is the origin of the critique of the modernist avant-garde (that it did not exist or that it was elitist); and this is also the origin of the contemporary bias of "artistic research," where ideality and ideation are supplanted by socio-cultural and socio-political justifications for works as defined by the paternalism of industry standards. Industry, in such cases, connotes the globalized culture industry, inclusive of academia, which has through assimilation of the rhetoric and the metrics of industry and innovation re-defined all valuable cultural inquiry as "project-based research." In terms of useless beauty, and in terms of prior art, this research constitutes an attempt to produce forms of intellectual property that might be leveraged as cultural property, in pursuit of funding or in pursuit of public-relations value for institutions and for scholars and artists. The re-constitution of research by institute or by platform is the principal sign that academia has accepted the metric of the culture industry, imposed from without, and that research is privileged by report and product versus work per se.[13]

---

13 Work per se, in this configuration of possible justifications for non-utilitarian artistic scholarship, is roughly equivalent to attempts in the

art world to escape forms of censure, patrimonialism, and appropriation — i.e., rote commodification. As in the art world, this form of inquiry
has also been more or less eliminated within academia, and for the same
reasons. For the commodification of modernist art and culture, and the
need for distanced critical reflection, see Theodor W. Adorno, *The Culture
Industry: Selected Essays on Mass Culture,* ed. J.M. Bernstein (London:
Routledge, 1991). For the early use of the term *culture industry,* see Theodor W. Adorno and Max Horkheimer, "The Culture Industry: Enlightenment as Mass Deception" (1944), in *Dialectic of Enlightenment: Philosophical Fragments,* ed. Gunzelin Schmid Noerr, trans. Edmund Jephcott
(Stanford: Stanford University Press, 2002). First published as *Dialektik
der Aufklärung: Philosophische Fragmente* (Amsterdam: Querido, 1947).
For mid- to late-twentieth-century, neo-avant-garde attempts to escape the
commodification of art, see Benjamin H.D. Buchloh, *Neo-avantgarde and
Culture Industry: Essays on European and American Art from 1955 to 1975*
(Cambridge: MIT Press, 2000). For a valedictory dismissal of modernist
avant-garde painting (and avant-garde visual art in general), see Eric Hobsbawm, *Behind the Times: The Decline and Fall of the Twentieth-century
Avant-gardes* (New York: Thames and Hudson, 1998). For Hobsbawm, art
must be collective or popular to be properly social — i.e., of revolutionary value. His polemical embrace of this formula (a variant of Marxist
utilitarianism and historical materialism) also permits him to pronounce
the death of modernist avant-garde exceptionalism, as elitist, which was
nonetheless quite often a direct response to the commodification of art
by the culture industry — viz., the very terms and conditions Adorno and
Horkheimer diagnose, and resign themselves to, in "The Culture Industry:
Enlightenment as Mass Deception." See also T.J. Clark, *Farewell to an Idea:
Episodes from a History of Modernism* (New Haven: Yale University Press,
1999). The fact that left defeatism has been enshrined in academia as the
wound sponsoring the new utilitarianism (roughly equivalent to market
fundamentalism) remains one of the most remarkable turns of fortune
imaginable for left critique after 1989. On modernist, anti-modernist, and
pre-modernist attempts by artists and non-artists to escape the "prison-
house" of language (site of both fossilized conventions and alienated
subjective states), through forays into and toward both silence and its
antithesis, verbosity, see Susan Sontag, "The Aesthetics of Silence," in *Styles
of Radical Will* (New York: Farrar, Straus and Giroux, 1969), 3–34. First
published in *Aspen* 5–6 (Fall–Winter 1967): Section 3, 1–21. Sontag's essay
is suitably dialectical, and her focus on silence is performative, insofar as
what she is really interested in is the perennial need to find a new way of
speaking about the spiritual purpose of art through art. Regarding *Aspen,*
an experimental multimedia "journal" (or "literary-artistic multiple"),
published between the years 1965 and 1971, plus the greater cultural
context of Sontag's "commissioned essay," see Lucy Cotter, "Between the
White Cube and the White Box: Brian O'Doherty's *Aspen* 5+6, an Early

The Achilles' heel for this model is, nothing less than, prior art. The presumptions of the model collapse under the stresses of all that has been assimilated to the model. Prior art in terms of universality is, per Hegel, all that has been eclipsed in the evolution of the work of absolute instantiation. In terms of works for works, this eclipse is what is to be honored, while the very concept or conceptual field of prior art is duly abstracted or re-universalized through the autonomous field of works. Useless beauty tends to act as place holder for a set of values that are not only idiomatic of works for works, as expressions of the internalizing agency or subjective status invoked, but as defining condition for the universal tendencies brought over from the non-utilitarian ethos of the exception. In returning to the exception, the works that evade capture by metric or other means of commodification (as symbolic capital or as intellectual property) are always positioned in relation to prior art and the extensivity that has been eclipsed through the work. This discord, which is also a paradoxical accord, acts to serve notice on all attempts to delimit use as property — to formalize what is otherwise, categorically, only able to be measured by its own internal metric. Prior art is, insubstantially and incorporeally, the Concept, not the content. The Concept of prior art is "the debt that can never be repaid."

II. Metaphysic of Prior Art

History is the object of a construction whose place is formed not in homogeneous and empty time, but in that which is fulfilled by the here-and-now [Jetztzeit]. For Robespierre, Roman antiquity was a past charged with the here-and-now, which he exploded out of the continuum of history. The French revolution thought of itself as a latter day Rome. It cited ancient Rome exactly the way fashion cites a past costume. Fashion

---

Exposition," in *Artistic Research Expositions: Publishing Art in Academia,* eds. Michael Schwab and Henk Borgdorff (Leiden: Leiden University Press, 2014), 220–36.

has an eye for what is up-to-date, wherever it moves in the
jungle [Dickicht: maze, thicket] of what was. It is the tiger's
leap into that which has gone before. Only it takes place in
an arena in which the ruling classes are in control. The same
leap into the open sky of history is the dialectical one, as Marx
conceptualized the revolution.[14]

— Walter Benjamin

A proper recognition of the presence and significance of prior
art and the transfer of moral rights to works suggests the necessity that works for works exist (subsist as exception) beyond the
commercium of both careerist agendas and proprietary regimes
for the editioning of works. Even the enforced rules of citation
for works (the scholarly apparatuses associated with research
publications) and the situational and socio-culturally determined auspices of works of contemporary art might be seen
as evidence of this otherwise hidden accord with a "no rights"
idiom for works that seek to exit the circuit of Capital and the
various forms of capitalization of works for authors and for institutions. In exiting the various systems for the production of
scholarship and the work of art, an opportunity to vacate the
field of received opinions is also self-evident, for authors and for
works. Needless to say, these systems reinforce biases through
an instrumentalized form of prior art as, in the case of research
publications, primary and secondary literature, or, in the case
of works of art, what is permissible or likely to be assimilated
to art-world spectacle as artistic and symbolic capital, for artists
and for the art world. Artistic scholarship, combining the inter-

---

14 Walter Benjamin, "On the Concept of History," trans. Dennis Redmond,
    "Walter Benjamin Archive," *Marxists.org,* 2005, https://www.marxists.org/
    reference/archive/benjamin/1940/history.htm. In Walter Benjamin, *Gesa-
    mmelten Schriften I:2,* eds. Rolf Tiedemann and Hermann Schweppenhäu-
    ser (Frankfurt am Main: Suhrkamp Verlag, 1974). Also published in Walter
    Benjamin, *Illuminations,* ed. Hannah Arendt, trans. Harry Zohn (New
    York: Schocken, 1969), "Theses on the Philosophy of History," 253–64, and
    Benjamin, *Walter Benjamin: Selected Writings,* Vol. 4, *1938–1940,* 389–400,
    under the section entitled "Materialist Theology, 1940."

est of both worlds, exits both worlds for the proverbial hinterlands that underwrite both worlds, re-engaging with — through the necessary austerities — what constitutes a metaphysic of prior art. Negation upon negation, yes. But also — in and out of time — the negation of negation.

The type or class of works that might emerge from a re-engagement with what underwrites normative works — a metaphysic of prior art — reverses the various accretions and forms of orthodoxy applied to cultural production and criticism of cultural production. Works of this order will, under the right circumstances, or through the proper situational tests or iterative measures, disclose what often hides beneath the operative rules of engagement, all the while permitting the foundational concerns of art and scholarship to be re-examined in light of altered circumstances —with these circumstances often enforced, while any escape oddly requires a form of presentism that acknowledges that the rules are constantly shifting *as if* to prevent real change.[15] This suggests that a radical break may not

---

15 "Turgot: 'Before we have learned to deal with things in a given state, they have already changed several times. Thus, we always find out too late about what has happened. And therefore it can be said that politics is obliged to foresee the present." Anne-Robert-Jacques Turgot, "Pensées et fragments [...] sur les progrès et la décadence des sciences et des arts," in Anne-Robert-Jacques Turgot, *Œuvres de Turgot*, Vol. 2, eds. Eugène Daine and Hippolyte Dussard (Paris: Guillaumin, 1844), 673; cited in Clark, "For a Left with No Future," 73; with reference to Walter Benjamin, "Convolute N: On the Theory of Knowledge, Theory of Progress," in *The Arcades Project*, trans. Howard Eiland and Kevin McLaughlin (Cambridge: Belknap Press, 1999), 477–78, Convolute N12a,1. This citation is part of the various "notes to self" Benjamin assembled in loose-leaf form (folded sheets) in support of the Arcades Project, which originally was to take the form of an extended essay. Benjamin cites Turgot's statement as an example of "presence of mind as a political category." It is this time-sense that Clark is referencing, via Turgot and via Benjamin. Preceding this citation by Benjamin, in "Pensées et fragments," Turgot states: "It is not error that prevents the progresses of truth. It is laxity, stubbornness, habit [*esprit de routine*], everything that encourages inaction." Turgot, "Pensées et fragments," 672; cited in David W. Bates, *Enlightenment Aberrations: Error and Revolution in France* (Ithaca: Cornell University Press, 2002), 95. Turgot (the French Adam Smith) was mentor to Condorcet. Benjamin

seems to be mining the French Enlightenment for statements in support
of his philosophy of history, which traverses other works coincidental to
the time-frame of the Arcades Project. He is countering the concept of
progress with the critical theory of history, with the former becoming
an absurd or uncritical hypostatization when it is separated from actual
historical (lived) experience and instead measures the distance between a
mythical origin and a legendary end of history. Notably, he points out that
this neutralization of actual material agency supports regression as often
as it supports progression. By regression, he means romanticizing the past
at the expense of the work of the present — i.e., class struggle. Benjamin, "Convolute N: On the Theory of Knowledge, Theory of Progress,"
478, Convolute N13a,1. This extension of the theory of progress over the
"totality of recorded history," as useless theorization, is characterized by
Benjamin as the purview of a "satiated bourgeoisie" (ibid., 479, Convolute
N13,3). Benjamin's "Über den Begriff der Geschichte" ("On the Concept
of History"), written in 1940, the year of his death, would be published in
1942. *The Arcades Project* was assembled between 1927 and 1940. Along the
way, toward "On the Concept of History," Benjamin's attitude toward the
retrospective view will alter, as typified by the semi-tragic figure of the Angel of History (Klee's *Angelus Novus*). This makes the parenthetical remark
closing Convolute N13a,1 ("Thus Turgot, Jochmann.") all the more curious.
"Jochmann" is Carl Gustav Jochmann. Jochmann's "Die Rückschritte der
Poesie" ("The Regression of Poetry"), published anonymously in *Über
die Sprache* (Heidelberg: C.F. Winter, 1828), will influence Benjamin's
thoughts on the value of retrospection. Benjamin re-published a version
of this essay, with an introduction and curious omissions, in *Zeitschrift
für Sozialforschung* 8 (1939–1940): 92–114. *Zeitschrift für Sozialforschung*
was the Frankfurt School's "inhouse" journal. See Theodor W. Adorno,
Critical Models: Interventions and Catchwords, trans. Henry W. Pickford
(New York: Columbia University Press, 2005), 361n13. For the emergence
of the figure of the Angel of History, across Benjamin's works of this
period, see O.K. Werckmeister, "Walter Benjamin's Angel of History, or
the Transfiguration of the Revolutionary into the Historian," in *Walter
Benjamin: Critical Evaluations in Cultural Theory,* Vol. 2: *Modernity,* ed.
Peter Osborne (London: Routledge, 2005), 425–30. The implied presentism
of Benjamin's appropriation of Turgot, and Clark's appropriation of Turgot
by way of Benjamin, opens onto an eschatological temporality (time-
sense), internal to the work of art, and Benjamin's troubling of revolutionary *Jetztzeit* or "now-time" — i.e., the event of the present-present versus
the retrospective artifact of the present-past. With the Angel of History
we see Benjamin's idealism collide with his often half-hearted historical
materialism. He is looking backward and forward at once, with the figure
of the angel marking the very place of a preposterous presentism. For a
brief history of the Arcades Project, plus Benjamin's troubled relationship
with orthodox Marxism, see J.M. Coetzee, "The Man Who Went Shopping

always require absolute refusal or abject resignation, and that
the event of works for works might occur within any given set of
already punishing systems of paternalistic repression (on the left
or right). Orthodoxy is, after all, its own tautological state, and
the shifting sands of forms of orthodoxy often bury or reveal the
fault lines in ideologically fortified rules of engagement. Lodg-
ing the exception within the existing field of cultural production
is, often, the most radical gesture versus refusal to enter the fray

---

for Truth," *The Guardian,* January 20, 2001, https://www.theguardian.com/
books/2001/jan/20/history.society. For an exhaustive treatment of a work
that Benjamin "regarded as his masterpiece," see Rolf Tiedemann, "Dialectics at a Standstill: Approaches to the Passagen-Werk," trans. Gary Smith
and André Lefevere, in Benjamin, *The Arcades Project,* 929–45. Tiedmann
states that the methodology of "Das Kunstwerk im Zeitalter seiner technischen Reproduzierbarkeit" ("The Work of Art in the Age of Technological
Reproducibility," 1935–1936) came to be embedded in "On the Concept of
History," while it was "On the Concept of History," according to Adorno,
that most closely resembled what was at stake in the Arcades Project (ibid.,
929). The significance of the fragments on an unfinished book on Baude-
laire (1937–1939) is a red herring, insofar as that project was a result of
criticism by Adorno of the Arcades Project. Coetzee: "The man who went
shopping for truth." The Arcades Project was, ironically, a "sponsored research project" of the Institut für Sozialforschung. Benjamin wrote at least
two proposals (1935 and 1939) for funding. Benjamin, a failed academic
(not unlike Nietzsche), was then seeking "habilitation, or re-habilitation,"
via Adorno and Horkheimer and the Frankfurt School in New York. The
school moved to New York, via Geneva, in 1935. It left Frankfurt in 1933.
Horkheimer was, in 1935–1939, shopping the project around, looking for
patrons. This included a New York banker. But, was it not really just a case
of "work for hire"? As peripatetic essayist, Benjamin had also returned to
the long-form work with the Arcades Project. Regarding the construction of the convolutes ("426 loose sheets of yellow paper," and the bulk of
the Arcades Project), a copy of which Benjamin left behind in Paris, with
Georges Bataille, before heading for the South of France (subsequently
found at the Bibliothèque Nationale in 1981), see Tiedemann, "Dialectics at
a Standstill: Approaches to the Passagen-Werk," 958. In some ways each of
the 36 convolutes, organized into two series (A–Z; a, b, d, g, i, k, l, m, p, r),
with gaps in series two, was a road map for an essay. Regarding the large
black briefcase (never found) supposedly containing the manuscript of the
Arcades Project that Benjamin carried across the French–Spanish border
to Port Bou in September 1940, just prior to his suicide (prompted by being refused entry into Spain), see Lisa Fittko, "The Story of Old Benjamin"
(written July 1980), in Benjamin, *The Arcades Project,* 946–54.

and preferring endless class warfare (i.e., in this case, a war between classes of works) or the pursuit of private utopias for the
production of the exception — or, for arguing on behalf of the
exception but without producing it. The metaphysic of prior art
extends across all classes of works, whether it is acknowledged
or unacknowledged, and contains the possibility of a futural
tense for works as works within the pretext of a present tense for
works. Here is the significance, then, of an elective presentism
for works and its often-absurdist attempts to present the metaphysic of the exception as situational exception, whether via
anomie or alienation, or via mediation and constructive engagement as revolutionary gesturalism. This particular fault line is
also where internecine battles on the left usually break out, and
break down, rendering the hoped-for insurgency null and void.

The metaphysic of prior art conditions or mediates the form
of works for works — viz., the form such works might take, and
the location within the field of cultural production that they may
inhabit. Yet, it does also offer no mediation and no conditionality for such works when, in fact, culturally, there is no place
to lodge such works in orders that have wall-to-wall conditions
and rules that preempt any such situational exception. Such an
utterly closed system is possible, but most such systems that appear closed always have holes in the brickwork through which
the exception may slip, from the outside, or through which
those on the inside might observe the exception as constituted
on the outside. Claims that systems have no such holes are those
that purport a "smoothness" to systems, eliminating any outside
and any inside per se. Capitalism repeatedly attempts this condition, via commodification, but almost always fails to achieve
it. Whether technocratic, neoliberal capitalism will succeed is
an open question. Such possible systems are operative totalities
that are, at best, always provisional. They do exist, as incipient
systems, and it is that existence that is the threat to any and all
exceptions. In the case of works for works the breach is internalized. It does not depend upon holes in the wall to exist. That
internalization is reinforced or defined by the transfer of moral
rights to works. Prior art and moral rights converge, as works

(negating first-order abstraction), giving to works for works an agenda (via second-order abstraction) that has next to nothing to do with the systems that this agenda exists within or the systems it stands as exception to. The exception returns repeatedly, across iteration, to its implicit universality, all the while offering (not seeking) full, not-partial contingent expression. This would appear to be the a-historical merit of avant-gardes past, even if the reading of those moments in art-critical or socio-political history tend to historicize into oblivion the exception upon which they are nominally based.

First-, second-, and third-order abstraction brings into view the iterative and generative nature or anti-nature of the metaphysic of prior art as fugitive expressivity given to the exception by way of the conferral of moral status to works. The universality implied undergoes degrees of re-naturalization and sublimation in works. The works display, through overt or implied antipathy or irony, an accord that signals the primary address as moral address. That this extends to works typically dismissed as anarchistic, nihilistic, or merely subversive — implying immorality or amorality — is part of the absurdist gestures of presentism as presentational tactic for works. Most of all, such works cannot bear to carry a merely moralistic charge or current, and strategically devolve to a stance beyond the pale that appears, by default, and defined by detractors, amoral or nihilistic. This amorality, immorality, or nihilism is always in relation to the greater nihilism of the system represented and defended by the detractors. Detractors will, of course, often proclaim such works fully immoral — meaning, regarding forms of artistic scholarship, against the law of art as commerce and scholarship as academic capital. Refusing an overt moral stand, to avert any embarrassment with moralizing or moralistic agendas, such works slip through the cracks of the masonry nonetheless, usually well after the fact, to take up residence in the hall of honors reserved for subversive works. A general rule is that the author should be dead and buried before this occurs. Again, the history of the modernist avant-garde shows this propensity for art-critical assimilation of the avant-garde to the official history of modernist art, even if much of the work assimilated was produced to intentionally subvert the modernist agenda and, later, canon. Retrospection in art-critical matters pays unusual "dividends." Thus, the issue of moral rights for works, and the prioritization of prior art as reserve function for defining the exception, does not devolve to morality as such. Instead, the transfer of moral rights to works, ostensibly part of many anti-modernist works of the modernist era, prepares a path for works that skip the entire moralistic universe of neo-Calvinist utilitarian mores and values for first-order abstraction, as hinterland for works with no interest in the commercium of arguments regarding conventional means to ends that secretly hide a moralistic agenda on behalf of the capitalist commodification of life.

One such venue or hinterland for first-order abstraction is the written or spoken word — in all of its many forms. Whether first-order abstraction can also be found today in works of art and scholarship, in the age of integrated spectacle and the commodification of knowledge and identity (of intellectual inquiry and subjective states), is the task of works for works as class of and for works that privilege the metaphysic of prior art and the elective transfer of authorial rights to such works.

6

In Search of Benevolent Capital

I. No Works For/Before Capital

Benevolent capital is not benevolent capitalism, the latter being a contradiction in terms or an apparent oxymoron. Benevolent capitalism would seem to not exist, as such, even under the auspices of patronage and classical philanthropy, insofar as the latter operates as exception to capitalism while the former has suffered across centuries, if not millennia, the distortions induced in systems held in thrall to Capital — pre-modern forms included. As apparent oxymoron, the term *benevolent capitalism* invokes all of the latent and overt games of capture Capital plays with cultural production and labor (both material and immaterial). In the case of cultural production in the age of neoliberal capitalism, those games include the production of platforms and networks of privilege that are constantly in pursuit of content or data, arguably what neoliberal capitalism has reduced cultural production to.[1]

Works that resist assimilation to Capital do not necessarily need to refuse all forms of capitalization. Non-monetary forms of capital are first-order representations of benevolent capital, whereas monetizing works for works versus for exploitation and

---

1   See Marc James Léger, *Don't Network: The Avant-garde after Networks* (Brooklyn: Minor Compositions/Autonomedia, 2018).

expropriation suggests the representational field where capital may take innumerable inappropriable forms — the term *inappropriable* signalling the presence of an older order of cultural production that has, in most cases, long since been assimilated to Capital. "No works for/before Capital" then suggests forms of cultural production that either resist assimilation and appropriation to markets as content or utilize those markets and delivery systems toward entirely useless ends for Capital per se. To invoke benevolent capital is, therefore, to secure *for works* semi-archaic and immemorial forms of capitalization that do not enter into the self-serving games of Capital. Yet given the present state of hyper-capitalist exploitation, it is highly possible that all future forms of benevolent capital are to be found through the chinks in the armor of Capital.

Such then is the potential for cryptocurrency and blockchain or distributed-ledger technologies *as applied to works.* Works developed in this manner may draw on the latency of forms of semi-archaic benevolent capital buried within the neoliberal capitalist machinery of the world while never being able to fully exit the circuit of Capital.

It is this paradox that introduces the necessity of a full accounting for authors of the vagaries and smokescreens of ecosystems associated with publication and exhibition systems within the twin worlds of the Arts and Humanities (e.g., the art world, the literary world, and the academic world). Both worlds suffer the same indignities today, mined by Capital for value, with the author orphaned in the process, or de-funded by Capital, as judgment visited upon their otherwise useless wares. Vague promises delivered to aspiring authors by both worlds suggest that half the game is the promise of privilege of the order of the privileged (the vectorial class), yet endlessly deferred, privilege always offered, by definition, at the expense of the orphaned (the artistic precariat).[2] The invitation and the temptation, then, is to join the privileged and abandon the abandoned.

---

2   McKenzie Wark uses the term *vectoral* (versus *vectorial*) to describe the operations of spectral capitalist exploitation of the knowledge commons.

Any attempt at a correction to this stilted version of mining cultural production for inherent value (with explicit value hardly the game when the vast majority of works will never produce anything resembling "return on investment" and implicit value is only relevant to exploiting works across platforms) requires a singular re-definition of terms of engagement in the form of the allocation or re-allocation of rights — e.g., via the transfer of author rights *to works,* with such works then transformed to life-works (viz., works for works defined across works). The necessary and hoped-for transformation of rights is stalled today due only to the fact that the vectorial class (and it must be clarified that the privileged include those who are in high positions within the art and academic worlds functioning as self-anointed or self-appointed gatekeepers to platforms) refuses a key article in the history of author rights — moral rights. It is the transfer of moral rights *to works* by and from authors that might correct present-day imbalances, yet only if that elective renunciation of rights by authors is followed by a system that prevents the presumption of such abandoned or transferred rights to exploitation by Capital. The *point of transfer* is the key; for the point of transfer is where the crimes of centuries have historically taken place. This place is the "place of taking-place" of and for

---

See McKenzie Wark, "A Hacker Manifesto (Version 4.0)," ed. Joanne Richardson, *Subsol,* n.d., http://subsol.c3.hu/subsol_2/contributorso/wark-text.html. "Vectoralists try to break capital's monopoly on the production process, and subordinate the production of goods to the circulation of information. The leading corporations divest themselves of their productive capacity, as this is no longer a source of power. Their power lies in monopolising intellectual property — patents and brands — and the means of reproducing their value — the vectors of communication. The privatisation of information becomes the dominant, rather than a subsidiary, aspect of commodified life. As private property advances from land to capital to information, property itself becomes more abstract. As capital frees land from its spatial fixity, information as property frees capital from its fixity in a particular object. [...] Information, once it becomes a form of property, develops beyond a mere support for capital — it becomes the basis of a form of accumulation in its own right. [...] The vectoral class comes into its own once it is in possession of powerful technologies for vectoralising information" (ibid).

Capital, with all of the attendant, twisted Greek–Mallarméan–Heideggerean etymologies and/or lexical mystifications one might wish to muster. It is the theft of "coming into presence" or "birth to presence" (*alētheia, parousia,* etc.) of the "gift of the world" and the Gnostic "sacrifice of aeons."[3]

In such a scenario, where and when benevolent capital steps forth, parasitical or malevolent capital will step back and away — wary of the interloper, and no doubt perplexed in the process. This is far more than mere wishful thinking because, historically, avant-garde or radical works have often had avant-garde or radical patrons, whether individuals or institutions. But this is not an instance of the re-justification or re-substantiation of the non-profit sector of civil society or anarchistic processes of barter. Nor is it indicative of a black market or the dark web. The measures required necessitate an entirely new methodology for exchange, for production, and for re-naturalizing works of an otherwise abstract, universalizing, and often abstruse kind. The key terms in this abstruse political economy become *immemoriality* and *eschatology* (the beginning and the end of and for works that have no home address at the time of their incarnation as works). This de-personalization of the work *for the life work* (the life of the work) brings with it half-forgotten maneuvers and measures buried within capitalist exploitation and partly the presumption of, or basis for, so-called non-profits or confraternal orders. The overriding figure of privilege returns — yet privilege as rights *for works.* Privilege as *privilegio…* De-personalization leads toward transpersonalization; and, notably, the latter term opens up whole new prospects for works to be developed as autonomous subjects — a re-subjectivization process that will also only work for certain kinds of works.

3   See Jacob Rogozinski, "The Gift of the World" (1988), in Jean-François Courtine et al., *Of the Sublime: Presence in Question,* trans. Jeffrey S. Librett (Albany: State University of New York Press, 1993). First published as *Du sublime* (Paris: Belin, 1988).

II. Symbolic Capital as Working Capital

The cryptic terms of engagement for *work as life-work* can only be developed existentially — *en passant* and *in extremis.* The necessity of the aleatory is tell-tale. The abstruse call to works *of a certain kind* is also a call to works that counter practices associated with neoliberalized finance capitalism and its deformations of what constitutes property in pursuit of rent (i.e., extracted tribute). These works-based practices, on behalf of the concept of life-work for works, function on the side of massive indeterminacy, and they take post-modern incommensurability to new heights. The irony and the pain are emblematic of the aleatory processes engaged in negotiating a knowledge commons haunted by traces and intimations of what was and what might be. It is often also a neo-gothic repertoire of vampirism and sadism, insofar as dodging the vampires and sadists is half the game for any new avant-garde.

Therefore, all discursive games fall apart and the pragmatics of neo-realism collapse. There is no realism in the lower circles of Hell. Consigning souls to Hell is a fool's errand — and such is the game of finance capitalism and the vectorial class. Yet there is an inverse relation involved.

From Bourdieu we must launch ships to the proverbial elsewhere. Re-citing and re-citing the authorities of left critique will only favor the propagation of reputations and rhetoric. Rhetoric that is not lived rhetoric is idle and/or gratuitous. What is to be done? The Leninist question returns. Under-funded fellowships for scholars rise and fall like the seas. Revolutionary creditors hover, awaiting the crown jewels in return for financing the latest revolution to fail. Whether it takes ten years or one hundred years to fail is of no concern to creditors. Capitalism has presumed the rights of souls, and then transferred those rights to corporate fiat, which outlives mere subjects anyway, a spectral stamp with congealed blood for wax. Corporate fiat is piracy writ large — transition to enslavement for all. The *work as life-work* is pariah to edict, fiat, and the law of Capital.

The odd thing about parasitical capital is that it does not know how to produce works — it needs to cannibalize those works it can set its claws into. It has long abandoned actual production. This is the role of the vectorial class, previously the managerial class. The odd thing about benevolent capital is that it only exists today as embedded in parasitical capitalism or as a result of parasitical capitalism — as nascent *other state and/or address* for works. Thus, the foremost game for works *of a certain kind* is to redeem forms of parasitical capitalism by converting them to forms of benevolent capital. What else is possible? This can only proceed incrementally, inexorably in some parallel transhistorical dimension, where the Arts and Humanities hit a primordial re-set button and everything turns golden, not unlike the evening in Venice, Italy — otherwise known as "Titian's Hour."

Valorous souls drop one by one, seduced by privilege. One by one becomes the thousands and the tens of thousands. Academia eats souls alive, consigning them to pits where they are enslaved in service to research or teaching metrics.[4] A few escape to alt-academia — as, for example, librarians. The art world devours works, one by one. The author is left as a few bones on the desert of what used to be called the Real. Most are never heard from again, after accimilation to the carnivorous machine. Biennale, bespoke exhibition, art book, catalogue, festival — it matters not. The refuse pile at the end of the affair is almost always

---

4   For the origin of metrics in UK academia, see Charles Petersen, "Serfs of Academe," *New York Review of Books,* March 12, 2020, https://www.nybooks.com/articles/2020/03/12/adjuncts-serfs-of-academe/. "For a fearful example of what this can look like, one need only consider the United Kingdom, which from Margaret Thatcher to Tony Blair to David Cameron raised tuition, lowered the academic quality of its universities, and further ratcheted up the demands on teachers by quantifying every element of education in the most reductive ways possible, whether the total number of times other scholars cite an article or the measurable economic impact of research" (ibid.). The "this" of "what this can look like" is so-called reform in the name of accountability. Petersen's article is a round-up of ten books, plus one database, on higher education in the US. These range from Geoff Cebula's *Adjunct* (2017), a self-published "gothic" novel on the perils of precarious employment in academia, to otherwise well-meaning bromides on what went wrong or what constitutes a "good" university.

human refuse. Publishers devour souls, inhaling works across myriad platforms to extract data and rent, the book hardly mattering, the meta-data extremely valuable. Writing becomes a contract, the contract dictates terms, the terms are salubrious for the vectorial class. Physical book becomes electronic data, publicity machine manufactures reputations, vertical integration extrapolates maximum value across media and platforms, and celebrity status beckons or vanishes. Book returns to dust, dust breeds phantom regrets, and authors dust themselves off and rise again — reborn in another place, in another time, and in another work looking for a publisher.

III. Personal Capital and Return

> To the end that suitable habits of thought on certain heads may be conserved in the incoming generation, a scholastic discipline is sanctioned by the common sense of the community and incorporated into the accredited scheme of life. The habits of thought which are so formed under the guidance of teachers and scholastic traditions have an economic value — a value as affecting the serviceability of the individual — no less real than the similar economic value of the habits of thought formed without such guidance under the discipline of everyday life. […] It is in learning proper, and more particularly in the higher learning, that the influence of leisure-class ideals is most patent; and since the purpose here is not to make an exhaustive collation of data showing the effect of the pecuniary culture upon education, but rather to illustrate the method and trend of the leisure-class influence in education, a survey of certain salient features of the higher learning, such as may serve this purpose, is all that will be attempted.[5]
>
> — Thorstein Veblen

---

5   Thorstein Veblen, "The Higher Learning as an Expression of the Pecuniary Culture," in *The Theory of the Leisure Class: An Economic Study in the Evolution of Institutions* (New York: The Macmillan Company, 1899), 363–64.

When a project is "before" Capital, seeking forms of benevolent capital, which by definition only exist buried within capitalist exploitation (across platforms and across institutions), and then fails to register with the powers that be as of value, there is the fall-back position of, or return to, personal capital — an existential justification for the work that redeems the work in the face of failure. Beckett's "Fail, fail again, fail better" is of this order. Works that are of no use to Capital will fail repeatedly in the attempt to find the necessary agency to go forward, while that forward motion will not depend entirely on external sources of benevolent capital. This is often where the agency of the work in progress kicks in — *as if* the work in and for itself carries with it both force and justification.

The term *before Capital* is not so much the test of the value of the work but a test of the merits of the work *for Capital* (for appropriation, expropriation, and assimilation). So-called failure before Capital is, therefore, the repeated step in the development of works in search of benevolent capital. The return to personal and symbolic capital is the return to the project as such, or to works for works.[6] The author returns to the *Muse,* with Muse the signature gesture of the event of the emergence (incarnation) of the work. As a fictive ontology for works, Muse signals the cosmological, immemorial figures inhabiting the work — the constellation of forces and factors (lights, intelligences, aeons) that brought the project or work into being. This vitalist gesture within works is backstory and history eclipsed.

---

6   See Bourdieu and/or Veblen on forms of symbolic capital. For example: Pierre Bourdieu, "The Forms of Capital," in *Handbook of Theory and Research for the Sociology of Education,* ed. John G. Richardson (New York: Greenwood Press, 1986), 241–58, first published as "Ökonomisches Kapital, kulturelles Kapital, soziales Kapital," in *Soziale Ungleichheiten,* ed. Reinhard Kreckel (Göttingen: Otto Schwartz, 1983), 183–98, and Veblen, "The Higher Learning as an Expression of the Pecuniary Culture," 363–400. See also Pierre Bourdieu, *Homo academicus,* trans. Peter Collier (Stanford: Stanford University Press, 1988). First published as *Homo academicus* (Paris: Éditions de Minuit, 1984).

Personal capital in search of the transpersonal inhabitation across works toward the life-work also represents not so much a banal investment of labor as the comprehensive configuration of what is irreducibly a confraternal order. Origins being half-unconscious, the conscious half is the artistic endeavor, whereas the unconscious half is the name of the Muse.

Return endlessly follows upon event, and return can be an inevitable aspect of the productive or generative élan of works that edge toward works for works. Event, Fall, Return — while apparently setting up eternal recurrence for works — is often an element of the field of the work that is incomprehensible to authors, experienced but non-negotiable in the accounting houses of capitalization for works. Capital vanishes at such moments — symbolic or otherwise — and personal capital is the zero degree that works pass through en route to extinction or re-play. Cultural systems betray a half-conscious knowledge of this ancient generative economy, while it is also quite evident that the guardians and gatekeepers of cultural systems rely on this vague knowledge to manipulate cultural production in the pursuit of privileges, fashions, and novelties.

What appears in this process of cyclical return from the search for benevolent capital is the delineation of the damaged ecosystems engaged — the forays into markets determining not the value of the work as work *for works* but the value of the work for capitalization across markets.[7] This pernicious reduction of

---

7   On this subject, see Terry Eagleton, "The Slow Death of the University," *Chronicle of Higher Education,* April 6, 2015, http://chronicle.com/article/ The-Slow-Death-of-the/228991/. "Education should indeed be responsive to the needs of society. But this is not the same as regarding yourself as a service station for neocapitalism. In fact, you would tackle society's needs a great deal more effectively were you to challenge this whole alienated model of learning. Medieval universities served the wider society superbly well, but they did so by producing pastors, lawyers, theologians, and administrative officials who helped to sustain church and state, not by frowning upon any form of intellectual activity that might fail to turn a quick buck" (ibid.). See also Erik Juergensmeyer, Anthony J. Nocella II, and Mark Seis, eds., *Neoliberalism and Academic Repression: The Fall of Academic Freedom in the Era of Trump* (Leiden: Brill, 2020), and *Social*

free intellectual inquiry to market ideology includes academic systems of exploitation that masquerade as platforms open to all (the ubiquitous open calls), claiming to privilege works versus reputations, though increasingly these platforms spell out in excruciating detail the rules of engagement (generally formulated in language and terms reducible to "return on investment" or "deliverables"). Generally, it is funding sources that dictate the terms that are subsequently handed down the academic food chain.

Justification of research merit proceeds in such instances as "product development" for institutions plugged directly into external industries of one kind or another. In the Arts and Humanities, the games of expropriation via residency, fellowship, or exhibition, while indirectly playing to the vanity of all concerned, are often openly or covertly constructed according to networks of privilege that service the professoriate — the openly careerist maneuvers of key players directly linked to escalating opportunities for key players. Works for works (forms of free inquiry without ideological bias) cancel this opportunistic gambit simply by existing as useless to what is nothing other than an institutionalized form of the production of cultural capital masquerading as benevolence offered — offered nominally on behalf of authors and works. If truly *open,* such calls are benevolent insofar as they are not also ideologically sustained or gamed (set up in advance to bring in fellow travellers for those who act as gatekeepers). The ecosystems involved may be judged by the language games perpetuated. These games include the use of linguistic agents of the order of Bourdieu et al., if the platform is sociologically biased, while any number of other linguistic agents may be brought into play to turn the operation toward cultural hacking or neo-avant-garde posturing. Return to zero for works *qua* free works is, then, the equivalent of return to resistance within the system, with the resultant electrical sys-

---

Anthropology 27, no. 52, "Politics of Precarity: Neoliberal Academia under Austerity Measures and Authoritarianism Threat," eds. Sabine Strasser, Georgeta Stoica, and David Loher (December 2019).

tem producing new doors left ajar or new windows through which to pitch the proverbial paper airplane. That the majority of these doors and windows are electronic doors and windows is the fundamental trait for exposing the class who partake of such vectorial systems that consistently and progressively act as protective borders for privilege, and as filters for "discovery" of works to be appropriated. It is not authors who are of interest to the vectorial class and their enablers in academia and elsewhere, but works and rent. And it is the accrual of works to the ledgers of the privileged that allows the game to move forward, with capture of works to systems the primary vehicle for the production of the matching precariat.

In most cases today truly free works are to be found outside of academia in both the accidental and the intentional wildernesses that form beyond the reach of Capital, in the most useless of endeavors (e.g., poetry and literature). The irony is that once these useless endeavors undergo a renaissance outside of academia and begin to attract attention, academia will attempt to re-incorporate what it has formerly driven from its hallowed halls.

IV. Ideology and Academic Networks

The extensive and insidious links between academia and various for-profit industries on the prowl for harvesting works from within academia for external capitalization is on display in the various internal and external offers for scholars to sign on to programs and events as guests. This includes the widening array of conferences, which may be judged or justified by their connections to industry or their distance from industry. Rarely do such opportunities offer the visiting scholar the freedom to do whatever they please. While this seems a foundational consideration for the Arts and Humanities, especially when understood as a super-discipline versus a discrete set of studies, the Arts *and* the Humanities historically offer two of the last places for something altogether off the map to be developed — e.g., works for works (orphaned or useless works). If it is increasingly a matter of pleasing one's masters in the age of the neoliberalization of the so-called knowledge commons, the proliferation of networks between the art world (which has been thoroughly neoliberalized) and academia (which is approaching complete capitulation to Capital) makes sense. Benevolent patronage may still exist within both worlds, but it will become increasingly difficult to locate until there is a widespread rebellion from within against the importation of market ideology to two worlds that once favored free inquiry.

Atop this layer of manufactured significance for programs and platforms is the proliferation of institutes and so-called cross-disciplinary activities led by scholars from within the fold of programs and disciplines that require external sources of meaningful activity to prop up the general lack of meaningful activity within academia other than the questionable production of platforms. These programs and platforms all substitute for research at the base, or for the absence of significance within disciplines that are internally exhausted. If PR-value reigns supreme within neoliberalized academia, useless works justified only by their abject and intentional uselessness will be either valorized as intellectual fashion statement or shunned as trivialities.

The ideological underpinnings of the discursive operations are generally spent generative causes that are also generally safe because they are spent causes — circularity of discursive appropriations being the chief sign of the re-cycling of motivation in absence of the Muse. Thus, personal capital is almost always imported into academia by way of the residencies, fellowships, and conferences utilized to compensate for the moral vacuum within universities beholden to the production of degrees, the securing of reputations, and the fostering of the horizontal networks of procurement, production, and dissemination of equity that substitute for the creation of works for works. These networks are eminently careerist in nature, as are most all bespoke or custom-designed institutes, and the personnel is vested insofar as their presence delivers vertically organized and capitalized cultural goods. The conference leads to the book-publishing enterprises of for-profit companies allied with academic networks that feed the increasingly digitalized production of value (e.g., the proliferation of online journals and e-books), whereas the institutes lead to external funding by industry or non-profit organizations toward the perpetuation of an ideological project (e.g., foundation grants for the mass digitalization of research, in whatever form that might take). The ideological underpinnings for such activities are in most cases crafted or themed for public consumption as progressive or liberal causes, while they are — quietly — neoliberal. The actual production of works then is incidental to the platform, and the platform is the primary means (primary venue) for leveraging works as intellectual property for regimes of privilege. "Author retains copyright" is a common refrain in most all instances of expropriation by academia of personal capital (e.g., author rights), appropriation from within or from without, while the author's presence as co-production assistant within the networks more closely resembles a case of work for hire than research as such. "Author retains copyright" is relative nonetheless to the useful life of the work within the network or system of appropriation, with digitalization of works dialogically locking down all works submitted to platforms (dialogically in this case meaning that the work in question is the property of the author only when it is no longer of any use to the platform).

Reputations rise and fall in a vast, interconnected system that requires incessant replenishment of spent intellectual goods. Works are assimilated and mined for value and forgotten or assimilated as fodder for the next-generation platform. Authors (and artists) are curated into oblivion and, if they are not assimilated to the machine as day laborers, they are replaced by the next generation of recruits trained to submit their wares in pursuit of holographic, stereophonic, or hyper-mediatized glory.

V. Inassimilable and Useless Works

Works for works are first of all inassimilable and useless to Capital. If they are also of no use to platforms, within the art world or within academia, they are paradoxically of maximum use for the development of alternatives. Shades of grey in this mathesis also suggest that some works might co-inhabit platforms or systems that are transitional states between parasitical and benevolent capital. Performance art and transmedia in the 2010s are examples of such experiments in longing (a collective desire to inhabit this grey zone), even if they were both more or less fully assimilated to the art-academic–industrial complex by the early 2020s. Yet all such works are essentially developed on the performative-formalist side (as lived works), and they may be re-naturalized downstream in markets or sent upstream toward extant spectral ecosystems, so-called weeping meadows, where no market is to be found. In the latter case, the role of the work as utterly useless is to wear the appropriate crown of thorns — as martyred work. It is here that a Christic development occurs for works of such an order that there is no sublunary place of taking-place present and the proverbial absence of a place for taking-place takes precedent. This place used to be called the avant-garde.

In the annals of literary and artistic history, for example, there are innumerable examples of such works. They generally return only as mockery of their former selves — tidily commodified for consumption by the art and literary worlds where they only half existed anyway. What is self-evident in the age of hyper-mediatic performance for both scholarship and the arts is that works that head upstream will generally vanish in the process — appearing here and then appearing there, ultra-temporally, but having no proper (i.e., home) address. The role of the author in such cases is transfigured by the orphaned works for works. Again, but for very different reasons than Barthes or Foucault theorized, the author does not exist.

The search for benevolent capital advances with the work, on cat's paws. The work *for works* inhabits multiple dimensions of socio-economic and socio-cultural intrigue simultaneously. It hovers here, and it dashes over there. It is cat's meow and cat's grin. Benevolent capital approaches insofar as the work is captivating, beguiling, or reminiscent of something Capital regrets having destroyed — wildness in a sense, but primordiality as cipher for freedom from exploitation and domestication. The next-level paradox is that Capital may need that beguiling something to redeem itself — not to save itself, which is hardly in the best interest of all, but to sacrifice itself to a cause other than itself. Mimicking the sacrifice of aeons as theorized in Gnosticism, and suggesting a War in Heaven, while also invoking Marxian teleology, concealed or vanquished prospects are revealed or reborn. Immemoriality and eschatology reveal themselves as, secretly, one thing.[8] Far from "immanentizing" the immemorial or the eschaton (a common complaint levelled against privileging that which formally transcends any direct relation with thought), both remain at a distance in works, effectively *crossing* works, and connoting the metric of the work. Alternatively, criticism of such a nuanced view of immemoriality and eschatology indicates an aversion to non-relational works, or to works that remain wilfully un-situated in utilitarian orders. All utility is internalized, and all relations are sublated.[9] Notably,

---

8   See Emmanuel Levinas, Jacques Derrida, Jean-Luc Marion — i.e., a sequence of scholars passing the flame from one to the next.

9   See Cacciari et al. on elective forms of nihilism — e.g., Massimo Cacciari, *Posthumous People: Vienna at the Turning Point,* trans. Rodger Friedman (Stanford: Stanford University Press, 1996). First published as *Dallo Steinhof: Prospettive viennesi del primo Novecento* (Milan: Adelphi, 1980). This elective nihilism is positioned in Cacciari's thought as a necessary condition, or existential transition, toward exiting actual nihilism. See also Emanuele Severino, *The Essence of Nihilism,* eds. Ines Testoni and Alessandro Carrera, trans. Giacomo Donis (London: Verso, 2016). First published as *Essenza del nichilismo: Saggi* (Brescia: Paideia, 1972). Regarding negative dialectics, in art and architecture, see Gail Day, *Dialectical Passions: Negation in Postwar Art Theory* (New York: Columbia University Press, 2010). Regarding Cacciari and Tafuri, see Gail Day, "Looking the Negative in the Face: Manfredo Tafuri and the Venice School of Architecture," 70–131, in ibid. For comments on the emergence of the society of the spectacle in relation to modern art and architecture, see T.J. Clark, "Origins of the Present Crisis," *New Left Review* 2, no. 2 (March–April 2000): 85–96. "Where once the nature of bourgeois rationality had been congealed into specific pieces or dreams of equipment — specific invasions of the body or the landscape by this or that network or instrument, monstrous or wonderful or most likely a mixture of both — now the new

nature was everywhere and nowhere, producing the very forms in which
it would be conceivable. There was no outside to the imaginary anymore;
or rather, no inside — no critical distance possible in the space between its
terms. 'Image', 'body', 'landscape', 'machine' — these (and other) key terms
of modernism's opposing language are robbed of their criticality by the
sheer rapidity of their circulation in the new image-circuits, and the ability
of those circuits to blur distinctions, to flatten and derealize, to turn every
idea or delight or horror into a fifteen-second vignette" (ibid., 88). Clark
is looking back, from 2000, over thirty or forty years and asking whether
the collapse of modernism included post-modernism — viz., whether post-
modernism is not actually the death-throes of modernism. Clark's "social
history" of art is on full display in this essay, as he masterfully demolishes
any real break between modernism and post-modernism, contra Jameson
and others, displaying nonetheless numerous anti-modernisms along the
way. The essay is, nominally, in response to Perry Anderson's *The Origins
of Postmodernity* (London: Verso, 1998), but with reference to Anderson's
earlier essay, "Origins of the Present Crisis," *New Left Review* 1, no. 23
(January–February 1964): 26–53. The fact that Clark is tackling Anderson in NLR is emblematic of arguments on the Left regarding art and its
politicization and/or abdication of a proper social role. Anderson became
editor of NLR in 1962, two years after its founding. Series One, extending
from 1960 to 1999 (with Anderson editor until 1983), ended with NLR 238.
A new series began in early 2000, with Anderson's return as editor. Series
Two opened with an editorial by Anderson, stating: "The only starting
point for a realistic left today is a lucid registration of historical defeat." See
Stefan Collini, "A Life in Politics: *New Left Review* at 50," *The Guardian*,
February 13, 2010, https://www.theguardian.com/books/2010/feb/13/new-
left-review-stefan-collini. "The message may have been bleak, but the tone
was resolute: the guiding principle for the review should be 'the refusal of
any accommodation with the ruling system, as of any understatement of
its power'" (ibid). Clark is defending both the Situationist International
and a role for art that is not reducible to mere socio-political agency,
against the high-handedness of the orthodox New Left. Verso — publisher
of Anderson's *The Origins of Postmodernity*, to which Clark is respond-
ing — is, notably, an off-shoot of NLR. Clark, former member of the Situationist International (SI), also refuses to situate the arrival of the society
of the spectacle historically, preferring to cite its incipient spectral qualities
within capitalist orders. "The spectacle was a logic and an instrumentation
inherent in the commodity economy, and in certain of its social accompa-
niments, from the very beginning. No doubt that logic became clearer as
the instrumentation became more efficient and widespread — why else the
peculiar mixture of lucidity and desperation to Debord's very tone? But
the logic had always been relatively clear, and the instrumentation notable — in a sense, pervasive. Why else *The Society of the Spectacle*'s epigraph
from Feuerbach? What else did its author think Marx was pointing to in

such works for works open onto revelation and reverie (dream-states and anamnesis). Once again, "the law disappears...."

Can Capital step out of its own way? Can Capital facilitate its own redemption? Is the figure of benevolent capital a figment of the imagination or a figure-eight within the ravages of rampant, bloodthirsty contemporary capitalism? The mining of the commons by Capital, while a long-standing affair, grows more desperate today as untapped resources to assimilate to the circuit of capital diminish. Additionally, there is the odd mis-use of the public domain or the commons, by Capital, to effectively park resources while awaiting a means (usually technological and legal) to convert collective capital into private capital.[10]

The hypostatization is evident. There is no one thing named Capital. Capital is a mask worn by souls — many waiting for another cause other than the worship of Mammon. The theological precepts are basically a-theological. There is no religion involved. There is only the hoped-for respite from centuries of hard-bitten penury for works, which always infers "for authors"; and all authors are mere laborers, which permits the search for benevolent capital and the transfer of rights to works to benefit all. The most abstruse work of all is to work on behalf of all. Artist and author, demoted over time to wage slave, represents

---

his account of 'the fetishism of commodities'?" (Clark, "Origins of the Present Crisis," 90).

10 For a brief summary of the main types of commons addressed in critiques of contemporary capitalism, see Fuchs, "Introduction," 1–31, *tripleC* 18, no. 1 (2020), Special Issue: "Communicative Socialism/Digital Socialism": 14–15. Fuchs references the following books as exemplary: Costas Douzinas and Slavoj Žižek, eds., *The Idea of Communism* (London: Verso, 2010); Slavoj Žižek, ed., *The Idea of Communism 2* (London: Verso, 2013); Slavoj Žižek and Alex Taek-Gwang Lee, eds., *The Idea of Communism 3* (London: Verso, 2016); Tariq Ali, *The Idea of Communism* (London: Seagull, 2009); Alain Badiou, *The Communist Hypothesis*, trans. David Macey and Steve Corcoran (London: Verso, 2010), first published as *L'hypothèse communiste* (Paris: Nouvelles Éditions Lignes, 2009); Michael Hardt and Antonio Negri, *Commonwealth* (Cambridge: Belknap Press, 2009); and Jodi Dean, *The Communist Horizon* (London: Verso, 2012). For a history of the commons, see Guy Standing, *Plunder of the Commons: A Manifesto for Sharing Public Wealth* (London: Pelican, 2019).

Everyman. Shelley knew this, both before and *when* he drowned at sea off of Viareggio, Italy…. Did he know it *after* he drowned? The life-work is a vector of another order. Certainly, he left this impression.

Titian's Hour returns every evening, under the right atmospheric circumstances. The glow is spellbinding. Yet for many it is merely a postcard to mail home after a day trip elsewhere.

7

The Spilled Cup: Part I

The whole world is his tavern, / His wine-cup the heart of each atom, / Reason is drunken, angels drunken, soul drunken, / Air drunken, earth drunken, heaven drunken. // The sky, dizzy from the wine-fumes' aroma, / Is staggering to and fro; / The angels, sipping pure wine from goblets, / Pour down the dregs on the world; / From the scent of these dregs man rises to heaven. / Inebriated from the draught, the elements / Fall into water and fire. / Catching the reflection, the frail body becomes a soul, / And the frozen soul by its heat / Thaws and becomes living. / The creature world remains giddy, / For ever straying from house and home.[1]

— Saʿd Ud Din Mahmūd Shabistarī

---

1   Saʿd Ud Din Mahmūd Shabistarī, "The Wine of Rapture," in *The Secret Rose Garden,* trans. Florence Lederer (London: J. Murray, 1920), 56–57. In Sussan Deyhim's "The Spilled Cup," a song included on Bill Laswell, *Hashisheen: The End of Law* (Sub Rosa, 1999), CD, the lyrics are based on "The Wine of Rapture" from *Gulshan i Rāz* (*The Secret Rose Garden*). Deyhim's version reads: "The Universe: His wine cellar; / The atom's heart: His measuring cup. / Intellect is drunk, earth drunk, sky drunk / Heaven perplexed with Him, restlessly seeking, / Love in His heart, hoping at least / for a single whiff of the fragments / of that wine, that clear wine the angels drank / from that immaterial pot, a sip of the dregs, / the rest poured out upon the dust: / one sip, and the Elements whirl in drunken dance / falling now into water, now in blazing fire. / And from that smell of that spilled cup / man rises from the dust and soars to heaven." Deyhim

I. New Augustinianism

> We might ask ourselves is there any need for an intervention
> from above in order to move our intellect? Could we
> understand anything if its forms were not given to us?[2]
>
> — Massimo Cacciari

For Dante, caught as we are between two worlds or two empires,
secular rationalist authority is autonomous. It is its failure that
requires divine intervention; empire must then concede ground
and "venerate the *transcendence* of the divine Author. But who
is called to furnish the interpretation of the supreme Author?
[…] Who is the custodian of his ultimate Word?"[3]

Thus today, the empire of Capital seeks dominion over all
of life — commodifying all. Law provides the interpretive apparatus for appropriation and the divine Author is assimilated to
the ideology of the markets (no longer "markets" but "market,"
as globalization seeks unity and uniformity across borders and

---

(presumable the author for this version or transcription of the Sufi poem)
has interpolated or changed the middle passage from "The sky, dizzy from
the wine-fumes' aroma, / Is staggering to and fro; / The angels, sipping
pure wine from goblets, / Pour down the dregs on the world; / From the
scent of these dregs man rises to heaven" to "Heaven perplexed with Him,
restlessly seeking, / Love in His heart, hoping at least / for a single whiff of
the fragments / of that wine, that clear wine the angels drank / from that
immaterial pot, a sip of the dregs, / the rest poured out upon the dust: /
one sip, and the Elements whirl in drunken dance / falling now into water,
now in blazing fire. / And from that smell of that spilled cup / man rises
from the dust and soars to heaven." In this poem and Deyhim's song, as
in the Sufi tradition, the concept of Agent Intellect is glimpsed, an article
of much disputation in the Medieval period, foremost between the Aristotelean Thomas Aquinas and the Augustinian-Franciscan Bonaventure.
See Gavin Keeney, "Agent Intellect and Black Zones," *P2P Foundation,*
March 8, 2018, https://blog.p2pfoundation.net/agent-intellect-and-black-
zones/2018/03/08.

2   Massimo Cacciari, *The Withholding Power: An Essay on Political Theology,*
trans. Edi Pucci (London: Bloomsbury, 2018), 86–87. First published as *Il
potere che frena* (Milan: Adelphi Edizioni, 2014).

3   Ibid., 89.

across states). Transnational finance capitalism seeks transhistorical import — for itself.

Saint Augustine's pessimism for any just earthly power combined with Dante's tragic view of earthly powers gone awry (for Augustine earthly power is never just, whereas for Dante it might be) suggests that the true protocols of cognitive capitalism and the conversion of the knowledge commons to a new form of feudalism are to be found in relation to the conversion of both symbolic and spiritual capital (terms constituting proper reflection on origins or prior art) to spectral commodity.[4]

Authors have slowly, since the 1500s, lost rights through regimes of copyright increasingly favoring industry — the term *industry* defined as the book trade or immaterial platforms associated with forms of patrimony of a cultural order.[5] The last vestiges of classical patronage were also slowly wiped out due to the emergence of copyright and the reproduction of works. Per Walter Benjamin, aura or authenticity vanishes under the mechanical reproduction of works.[6] While moral rights remain

---

4 For a definition of cognitive capitalism, see Yann Moulier Boutang, *Cognitive Capitalism*, trans. Ed Emery (Cambridge: Polity, 2011). First published as *Le capitalisme cognitif: La nouvelle grande transformation* (Amsterdam: Éditions Amsterdam, 2007).

5 See Gavin Keeney, "A Brief Sketch of *Privilegio* in the Venetian Renaissance," *Intellectual Property Watch,* February 7, 2018, https://www.ip-watch.org/2018/02/07/brief-sketch-privilegio-venetian-renaissance/ and chapter 2 in this volume.

6 Walter Benjamin, "The Work of Art in the Age of Mechanical Reproduction," in *One-way Street and Other Writings,* trans. J.A. Underwood (London: Penguin, 2009). First published as "Das Kunstwerk im Zeitalter seiner technischen Reproduzierbarkeit," 1935. Benjamin opens his text with a citation from Valéry's essay, "La conquête de l'ubiquité" (1928), First published in *Pièces sur l'Art* (Paris: Éditions Gallimard, 1934). Valéry: "Our fine arts were developed, their types and uses were established, in times very different from the present, by men whose power of action upon things was insignificant in comparison with ours. But the amazing growth of our techniques, the adaptability and precision they have attained, the ideas and habits they are creating, make it a certainty that profound changes are impending in the ancient craft of the Beautiful. In all the arts there is a physical component which can no longer be considered or treated as it used to be, which cannot remain unaffected by our modern

legally present today, they have no real effect. They are now of a wholly non-utilitarian nature though they once shaded toward economic rights, crossing the landscape of exploitation of works for or against the author like a benevolent, yet ever-shortening shadow. If High Noon, the time of the "shortest shadow," is the equivalent of high materialism (or high determinism), its antithesis, Living Midnight (mysticism), calls again, to authors.[7] The role of the author as intermediary for the transmission of knowledge, effectively personalized and then corporatized, remains a phantom concept at High Noon — viz., guide, voice, angel neutralized, and the Word demoted.

Prior to *privilegio,* as bestowed on works as early as the late 1400s in Venice, works existed as such — as works for works. The right to copy a manuscript (before the Early Modern printed book arrived) was left to whomever or whatever library held the manuscript, "in escrow" or "on behalf of...." With *privilegio* moral rights to works were recognized, even if to be formally

---

knowledge and power. For the last twenty years neither matter nor space nor time has been what it was from time immemorial. We must expect great innovations to transform the entire technique of the arts, thereby affecting artistic invention itself and perhaps even bringing about an amazing change in our very notion of art." Paul Valéry, *The Collected Works of Paul Valéry,* Vol. 13: *Aesthetics,* trans. Ralph Mannheim (New York: Pantheon, 1964), 225.

7   Regarding the Nietzschean concept of Noontide as the time of the shortest shadow, see Alenka Zupančič, *The Shortest Shadow: Nietzsche's Philosophy of the Two* (Cambridge: MIT Press, 2003). Regarding Living Midnight, see Gavin Keeney, "Living Midnight (The Night of the World)," in *"Elsewhere": Essays in Art, Architecture, and Cultural Production, 2002–2011* (Newcastle upon Tyne: Cambridge Scholars Publishing, 2011), 175–82. "In the paradoxical state of things outside becoming things inside (representation itself), or in the mirroring of two infinities in subjectivity itself, what arrives is the spectral (imaginary) place/'night' where two blind spots become one — or, that blind spot in the apparitional-phenomenal world (projected *there,* arguably, by the subject), and that blind spot as subject, again, and arguably, unable to observe itself. In an outside becoming inside (and vice versa), what appears is 'night-sky,' an (un)earthly silence, and the thing conferred by both — a conscious, willing some-thing, always formulated as world on the outside, and always formulated as primordial (primeval) 'mind' (*nous*) on the inside" (ibid., 175–76).

granted privilege the work had to be produced or appear (be printed). The ontic basis is obvious, while the issue of rights remains spectral. Yet the author lost privilege as the book industry took flight and modern copyright would appear in the 1700s, in England, to protect economic rights to works.[8] The author as intermediary (for works for works) vanished with the onslaught of socio-cultural determinism, plus the establishment of the Modern and Romantic concepts of inspiration and genius as articles of faith for authors (arguably as compensation for their collective, historically determined demotion to socio-economic or socio-cultural servitude). The source for works was pushed further and further into the background (both historically and transhistorically) until it had been thrust so far back that it returned by loop (via zero degree) as a form of hyper-commodity under the omniscient gaze of at-first-incipient and then full-bore cognitive capitalism.[9]

The loop is the figure of primordiality; but it is also the gesture within gesturalism in art and humanistic endeavors that strive for unity across worlds versus perpetuation of the schisms associated with or embedded in temporal and *authorized* socio-cultural systems based in utilitarianism and exploitation. Patrimony and paternalism perpetuate these schisms as part and parcel of systems. Expropriation of "the given" and conversion

---

8   Statute of Anne, 1710. Thus did statutory law overwrite Common Law.

9   A variant of this "loop" may be seen in Heinrich von Kleist's *On the Marionette Theatre* (1810): "Now, my excellent friend, said Herr C., you are in possession of everything that is necessary to comprehend what I am saying. We can see the degree to which contemplation becomes darker and weaker in the organic world, so that the grace that is there emerges all the more shining and triumphant. Just as the intersection of two lines from the same side of a point after passing through the infinite suddenly finds itself again on the other side — or as the image from a concave mirror, after having gone off into the infinite, suddenly appears before us again — so grace returns after knowledge has gone through the world of the infinite, in that it appears to best advantage in that human bodily structure that has no consciousness at all — or has infinite consciousness — that is, in the mechanical puppet, or in the God." Heinrich von Kleist, "On the Marionette Theatre," trans. Thomas G. Neumiller, *The Drama Review: TDR* 16, no. 3, The "Puppet" Issue (September 1972): 26.

to forms of capital (symbolic, cultural, etc.) is the rule. License, patent, law, treaty, and rule always already intercede in this ancient economy, *for* or *on behalf of* Capital.

Saint Paul's well-known comments in Ephesians on Grace and works contains a third principle — i.e., Law.[10] Works in his formulation fall under the law, and such works are notably therefore embedded in injunction, rule, and proscription as determined by law. If the New Dispensation Paul announces is to overturn mere law (e.g., habit, dogma, ritual, proscription) then Grace must be both antecedent and futural — *at once* — to any law as such. The *at once* is the key. If antecedent, it falls to time-based authority and to figures of whatever law or authority are cited. If futural only, it fails to appear and becomes a classic millennialist quest, forever deferred (propping up the irreal at the expense of the real). Grace in such a formulation, as Paul suggests, negates all present formalizations by law on behalf of earthly power — or negates what constitutes a universalist rule for works.

Is Grace not also the secret force in generative agency for works — in the senses that works for works might sidestep the rule regarding works and access the Word? Cacciari's divine Author returning, but only in such works that refuse incorporation (first-, second-, or third-order incorporations, per Badiou) and, instead, re-present event — e.g., the event of Grace, the event of pure Word, and the encounter with pure Word converted then to record (textual form, image economy, or archival reserve across multiple forms of presentation and re-presentation).[11]

---

10 Ephesians 2:8–10.

11 Alain Badiou, *Being and Event,* trans. Oliver Feltham (London: Continuum, 2005). Regarding first-order incorporations and the artwork, see Gavin Keeney, "The Art World," in *Art as "Night": An Art-theological Treatise* (Newcastle upon Tyne: Cambridge Scholars Publishing, 2010), 155–61. "Art as 'Night' is the re-appearance of the immemorial (the future anterior as Absolute Knowing in itself). Its poverty is its wealth, and vice versa. It (art as such) outfoxes and outmaneuvers all first- and second-level incorporations; it requires no history per se, and it eliminates by the fact of its embodiment via 'x' (Incarnation, Crucifixion, and Resurrection) its own biography. The artist is paid off for their labors with money, obscurity,

This theology of effects and affects inhabits works; it does not need to be added to works. How can generative agency then remain unproscribed and *free*? The loop denoted above (appropriated and converted to the apparatuses of appropriation by Capital) is the key to the mystery and enigma of works for works that constitute — contra Paul's situational judgment — evasion of the law and the rule dictating terms to authors. The theological problem with Paul's words in Ephesians has always been the context in which they are stated (or inserted). To universalize them requires throwing out reference to Jewish law — something that might easily be accomplished, ridding in the process the long history of these remarks being associated with incipient or supposed antisemitism.[12] This then signals a Law of Art that is diametrically disposed to counter (as historically grounded *concordia oppositorum*) all forms of vitalism. Under this Law of

immortality, and/or derision. In pleroma there is no longer any biography of Spirit. History and art history are finished, per se" (ibid., 160).

12 Both Alain Badiou and Slavoj Žižek have attempted this universalization of Saint Paul's writings, effectively ignoring any historical elements in the process. See Alain Badiou, *Saint Paul: The Foundation of Universalism*, trans. Ray Brassier (Stanford: Stanford University Press, 2003); Slavoj Žižek, *The Puppet and the Dwarf: The Perverse Core of Christianity* (Cambridge: MIT Press, 2003); and Slavoj Žižek, *The Universal Exception* (London: Continuum, 2005). For brief comments on Badiou and Žižek's "synchronized turn into the so-called 'theological turn,'" see Gavin Keeney, "Thought Itself," in *"Else-where,"* 59. The theological turn in French phenomenology occurred primarily across the 1990s, extending into the early 2000s. See Dominique Janicaud et al., *Phenomenology and the "Theological Turn": The French Debate* (New York: Fordham University Press, 2000). Badiou and Žižek came rather late to the game. Giorgio Agamben's "Homo sacer" project also, more or less, has its origins in the theological turn. In terms of an element of Kantian aesthetics that resembles what is proposed here as an excess in cultural production that opens onto immemoriality (and what in Kant's *Critique of Judgment* is to be found in the concept of the Sublime), see Jean-Luc Marion, *Being Given: Toward a Phenomenology of Givenness,* trans. Jeffrey L. Kosky (Stanford: Stanford University Press, 2002). First published as *Étant donné: Essai d'une phénoménologie de la donation* (Paris: Presses Universitaires de France, 1997). See also Jean-Luc Marion, *The Crossing of the Visible,* trans. James K.A. Smith (Stanford: Stanford University Press, 2004). First published as *La croisée du visible* (Paris: Éditions de la Différence, 1991).

Art, the primary question becomes: What constitutes works for works?

There does not seem to be much more than this to know. Prometheus has withdrawn — or has once again been crucified on his rock, and Epimetheus is at large and in our world opening ever newer Pandora's boxes.[13]

Why does hope remain within Pandora's box (jar) after she closes it? Hope was one of the two gifts Prometheus gave to mankind, against the diktat of Zeus. The other was fire. Yet Aeschylus, in *Prometheus Bound,* quotes Prometheus as saying he gave to man "blind hopes."[14]

---

13 Cacciari, *The Withholding Power,* 117.

14 Perhaps this is the origin of Blake's statement, "If the doors of perception were cleansed every thing would appear to man as it is, Infinite." William Blake, *The Marriage of Heaven and Hell* (1790). If the Promethean spirit includes hope ("blind" or otherwise), the classical theodicy sketched by Aeschylus in his trilogy, *Prometheia,* also includes a nod toward an archaic despotism that is matched in Blake's concept of the demiurge. Thus, it is entirely possible that Augustine's pessimism is a trait in his thought originating in what it has been claimed he *historically* overcame — i.e., Manichaeism. For the Romantic assimilation of the Promethean myth, see Percy Bysshe Shelley, *Prometheus Unbound* (1820). For Prometheus to be freed, in Shelley's account at least, Zeus (the demiurge) must be deposed and not replaced. Contrary to the classical *Prometheus Unbound,* Shelley was dodging the idea of reconciliation between the revolutionary and the despot: "I was averse from a catastrophe so feeble as that of reconciling the Champion with the Oppressor of mankind. The moral interest of the fable, which is so powerfully sustained by the sufferings and endurance of Prometheus, would be annihilated if we could conceive of him as unsaying his high language and quailing before his successful and perfidious adversary." Percy Bysshe Shelley, *Prometheus Unbound: A Lyrical Drama in Four Acts with Other Poems* (London: C. and J. Ollier, 1820), vii–viii.

II. Works for Works

> For want of a real object, by the power of my vague desires, I
> evoked a phantom which never quitted me more.[15]
>
> — Chateaubriand

The artist–author stands as witness to the event of the work. From there, in descending scales and according to the dictates of markets and platforms, degrees of accommodation set in, by markets and platforms and by artist–authors, with the loss of agency traceable through the descending scales of mere accommodation to authorized discourses. Assimilation of such works occurs incrementally, across markets and platforms, with authorized discourses effectively neutralizing the effects of works for works through tolerance, per Marcuse's diagnosis, yes, and per Veblen's reading of the role of the leisure class in the consumption of intellectual and artistic products.[16]

Could Marcuse and Veblen have been wrong though? Is it possible that the evolutionary assimilation is the only way forward and that such works, while revolutionary in spirit, can only take effect incrementally over time and across time? Over time and across time would re-introduce world-historical agency, or what has been generally dismissed in works for works by artist–authors in the modernist avant-garde tradition (the term *tradition* conferring retrospective agency to what was most often an attempt to neutralize historical agency in the very works later

---

15 François-René Vicomte de Chateaubriand, *Mémoires d'outre-tombe* (1849); cited in *Memoirs of Chateaubriand: From His Birth in 1768, Till His Return to France* (London: Henry Colburn, 1849), 133.

16 With reference to Herbert Marcuse, "Repressive Tolerance," 81–123, in Robert Paul Wolff, Barrington Moore, Jr., and Herbert Marcuse, *A Critique of Pure Tolerance* (Boston: Beacon Press, 1965), and Thorstein Veblen, *The Theory of the Leisure Class: An Economic Study in the Evolution of Institutions* (New York: Macmillan, 1899). See Gavin Keeney, "Anamnesis," in *Dossier Chris Marker: The Suffering Image* (Newcastle upon Tyne: Cambridge Scholars Publishing, 2012), 7–76, for a discussion of varieties of Marxism, including the late-modern, ultra-pessimistic variant known as "post-Marxism" (15–16).

assimilated to the historical record). The level at which generative agency departs from any form of vitalism whatsoever requires an analysis that privileges something nominally outside
of historical agency and often denoted transhistorical in art-historical and historical studies that are, by their own authorized
terms, reductive. Generative agency in works of art that privilege the event of works for works enters therefore into a vast
conundrum (almost a conspiracy) regarding authorial rights on
behalf of works, which, in turn, signals the necessity of deal-
ing with historical and transhistorical records that include artist–authors as witnesses and the attendant issue of what exactly
moral rights for authors implies. Antecedent to the Enlightenment declaration of moral rights, did moral rights exist for authors or for works? What type of works evade the historical and
deterministic field of rights as such? Indeed, which types *have*
evaded, *might* evade, and *will* evade this field? And what types
of vitalism or cultural determinism (Darwinian or otherwise)
capture works in a fold that is, reductively, a system of ascending
and descending scales?

In the interview "On the New Philosophers and a More General Problem," Deleuze specifically laments the surrendering
of philosophical thought to media. Here, writing and thinking are transformed into a commercial event, an exhibition,
a promotion. Deleuze insists that philosophy must instead be
occupied with the formation of problems and the creation
of concepts. It is the untimely of thought and the nonphi-
losophy of philosophy that will enable the creation of a truly
critical concept. But how do we overturn the presumed self-
erasure of critical concepts that stand outside the technosci-
entific regime of communication? Can a truly critical concept survive the indifferent new brutality of our post-truth
and post-fact world, driven as it is by automated thinking?
Doesn't this mistrust of technoscience ultimately prevent
philosophy from becoming a conceptual enaction of a world
to come? Why does philosophy continue to ignore thinking

machines that create alien concepts, acting as if [they] were beyond the capacity of machines to do?[17]

In this project of autonomy for disciplines, as Deleuze diagrams for philosophy and the Concept, a stalemate emerges between resistance and accommodation, one that also comes with a silver lining — mirroring more or less the way out proposed by Augustine. The compromise proposed by Dante, as noted above (and not necessarily all that divergent from Augustine's readings regarding accommodations with varieties of empire), also has a family resemblance to Pascal's famous nervousness within the folds of *Pensées* (1669) regarding the place the subject inhabits between the two infinities he identifies as extending outward in one direction and inward in another. Might works for works formally (via a version of autonomy for works versus for discourses) combine a type of "sumptuousness," as found in Chateaubriand, with the "nervous intensity of Pascal," precisely what Joseph Frank saw as the subtending chord for André Malraux's *The Voices of Silence*?[18]

---

17 Luciana Parisi, "Reprogramming Decisionism," *e-flux journal* 85, October 2017, http://www.e-flux.com/journal/85/155472/reprogramming-decisionism/.

18 "Nowhere else in modern art criticism can we find so magnificent a style (which combines the sumptuousness of Chateaubriand with the nervous intensity of Pascal) allied to so vast a knowledge of cultural, religious, and artistic history. A towering achievement." Joseph Frank, jacket blurb, André Malraux, *The Voices of Silence,* trans. Stuart Gilbert (Garden City: Doubleday, 1953). First published as *Les voix du silence* (Paris: Éditions Gallimard, 1951). Perhaps this is why we find Malraux in the opening credits for Godard's *Film socialisme* (2010). Under the intertitle "Textos" we find "W. Benjamin, J. Derrida, H. Arendt, J. Giraudoux, L. Aragon, H. Bergson et al.," while on "page two" of this now-classic technique (Brechtian sign boards resembling primitive PowerPoint slides) we find "F. Braudel, P. Ricoeur, A. Malraux, W. Goethe et al." Jean-Luc Godard, dir., *Film socialisme* (2010) (Kino Lorber, 2012), DVD. See Gavin Keeney, "The Film Essay," in *Knowledge, Spirit, Law: Book 1, Radical Scholarship* (Brooklyn: punctum books, 2015), 61–82, for Godard's version of sumptuousness combined with nervous intensity and the various justifications for it. Godard also draws on Malraux in *Histoire(s) du cinéma* (1988).

Works for works cannot connote autonomy as such for works as situated (held in thrall) within disciplines or discursive regimes of power. Autonomy, or the project of autonomy in a discourse or discipline, reverts naturalistically to formalism, and formalisms are always already incipient variants of vitalism. The circuit of self-signification closes in works that claim autonomy under the spell or sign of a discipline. Attempts by way of contemporary transdisciplinarity to break the spell and escape also almost always fail — the trans- or cross-disciplinary work caught nonetheless in the economies of representational values and orders negotiated, re-negotiated, or — as intended — erased, repressed, or transposed (not transfigured). It is self-evident (experientially) to authors that intentions to subvert conventions also often need to *meet and exceed* conventions while subverting authorized terms of engagement. This overarching determinism is the entropic force that also drives most assimilations of works to the circuit of Capital — eventually. Pascal's two infinities here are transposed to two versions of an outside — both leading back to incorporations via rote capture as commodity. The inside has assumed instead a false interiority (or contingency), under the spell of Capital, that mimics subjective states, and the question of what is *in* formalisms returns endlessly. What is *inside* this autonomous operation, as excess? It is the trace of what has vanished or been vanquished in the operation of assimilation. *It* is now an absence. As such, it is granted a halo by Capital — as exception.

Generative agency proceeds through an apparent series of absences and silences. The absences and silences are configured in formalist works as elisions, diremptions, estrangements, and erasures. These are the maneuvers that prepare a possible escape — the voids in such works suggestive of a space for something outside of or beyond the syntactical operations to appear inside. This return of the figure of the inside is the event that the author prepares and bears witness to. *The circuitous becomes fortuitous.*

Passing through this Barthesian degree zero and into the territory of the negative and the catasterism is a version of tarrying with the negative (*pace* Žižek and Hegel).[19] Adorno's negative dialectics and *minima moralia* are of this order as well.[20] This passage beyond zero, into negation upon negation, is also an apophatic path through determinisms and formalisms — a Dark Night of the Soul for authors and for works. At last, and as last word: *It* has *nothing to do or say* about autonomy or systems. The territory entered by way of the negative is paradoxically entirely positive — but as negative image of what passes as positive image (in positivist discourses, historical determinism, etc.).[21] Polarities shift, and aporias speak. Perhaps that is Mallarmé's point regarding the unsayable? In some ways it is image economies that reach this place or non-place first. Language per se seems to be the more obdurant of systems utilized by the law that must be overcome (the rule and the rules of patrimonial or paternal systems). Converting the law to images, or dynamic word-image economies, might then be a first-order means for bringing an operatic fold (works for works as life-work) closer to the originary economy of "no rights."

In the case of works for works the artist–author can rightly say, "I and the work are one." But the work does not belong to

---

19 Slavoj Žižek, *Tarrying with the Negative: Kant, Hegel, and the Critique of Ideology* (Durham: Duke University Press, 1993).

20 Theodor W. Adorno, *Negative Dialectics,* trans. E.B. Ashton (New York: Seabury Press, 1973). First published as *Negative Dialektik* (Frankfurt am Main: Suhrkamp, 1966). Theodor W. Adorno, *Minima Moralia: Reflections from Damaged Life,* trans. E.F.N. Jephcott (London: Verso, 1978). First published as *Minima Moralia: Reflexionen aus dem beschädigten Leben,* ed. Rolf Tiedemann (Frankfurt am Main: Suhrkamp, 1951).

21 See Thomas Ruff's strange play with this paradox in his photographic series and 2015 exhibition entitled "Nature morte." For a review of the August 6–September 26, 2015 exhibition of this work, see Gavin Keeney, "The Disembodied Gaze," in *Knowledge, Spirit, Law: Book 2, The Anti-capitalist Sublime* (Brooklyn: punctum books, 2017), 217–21. See also Hannah Freedberg, ed., *Thomas Ruff: Nature Morte* (London: Gagosian Gallery, 2015). Ruff uses found, "semi-antique" positives to create the missing negative (which would have been a glass plate) and then prints the newly created digital negative as negative image ("negative as positive," in technical-photographic terms). It is, in part, a linguistic game, but it also operates as a transgressive form of image economy. This all takes place in a somewhat charmed vortex of conflicting conceptual-formalist operations.

the author. Instead, the author belongs to the work. Everything is reversed or inverted regarding so-called author rights. "The law disappears…." Rights re-appear on the other side of the mirror, as rights for works — Breton's "other side of the mirror." All issues concerning rules and rights are subsumed in works for works under the sign of (hoped-for, never-presumed-upon) Grace. The author dis-owns him/herself. There is an extreme torsion, agonism, and process of renunciation and transfiguration, to be experienced on one side of the mirror, and on the other side, new-found freedoms.

Signals from 2014:

The University of Chicago Press recently released the third volume of its Trios series. *Excommunication* contains three extended essays written on the brink of the Snowden affair by three New York-based new media scholars — theory royalty who belong to the digital nineties generation: Alex Galloway, Eugene Thacker, and McKenzie Wark. The "three inquiries in media and mediation" open with the widely shared discontent that "new media" has become an empty signifier: "One of the things the trio of us share is a desire to cease adding 'new media' to existing things." As the nineties slogan says: new media are tired, not wired. Or, to put it in eighties theory jargon: new media have moved from the schizoid revolutionary pole to the paranoiac, reactionary pole. Fashion over, next hype? If so, how do we deal with the Media Question, knowing that it is over but hasn't gone away? To put it in the German context, what's media theory after Friedrich Kittler? This question has been with us for some time. It is not enough that the historical wing — media archaeology — is doing well. Can we speak of a next generation that grew up under postmodernism, matured in the post-Cold War era of digital networks, and is currently taking over? Taking over what? There is a lot to say for the thesis that the height of speculative media theory was in the 1980s. The rest has been implementation — a boring and predictable collision with the existing political economy of global capitalism. This leaves us with the question of the mandate and scope of today's media theory — if there is anything left. Are you ready to hand over the "new media" remains to the sociologists, museum curators, art historians, and other humanities officials? Can we perhaps stage a more imaginative "act of disappearance"? Are we ready to disguise ourselves amidst the new normality?[22]

---

22 Geert Lovnik, "Hermes on the Hudson: Notes on Media Theory after Snowden," *e-flux journal* 54, April 2014, https://www.e-flux.com/journal/54/59854/hermes-on-the-hudson-notes-on-media-theory-after-snowden/. "For the New York trio, the key question is: 'What is mediation?' To pose this question means to imagine the opposite: there is no communication without excommunication. What if we stop mediating? Instead of digging into the ongoing rise of the connected world, the authors favor studying the 'insufficiency of mediation,' and 'modes of mediation that refuse bi-directionality, that obviate determinacy, and that dissolve devices entirely.' Not everything that exists has to be represented and mediated" (ibid). And: "To what extent is this different from the traditional 'deconstruction' agenda, the 'glitch' aesthetics à la Rosa Menkman, or even the 'exploit' philosophy as formulated by Galloway and Thacker themselves? Already at that point the authors argued in favor of a 'counterprotocol,' an 'anti-web,' or, to put it in philosophical parlance, an 'exceptional topology.' If we exclude offline romanticism, how could we translate this analysis into a workable political program? It is one thing to imagine a specific aesthetic. There are multitudes of artists working in this direction. In the post-Snowden age, it is no longer sufficient to call for open-source alternatives that merely copy the corporate premises of the dominant platforms (the friends logic and so on). The social graph order itself has to be questioned. Can we bring together a collective intelligence that is capable of formulating the very principles of another communication order?" (ibid).

8

The Spilled Cup: Part II

Pessimism is not in being tired of evil but in being tired of good. Despair does not lie in being weary of suffering, but in being weary of joy. It is when for some reason or other good things in a society no longer work that the society begins to decline; when its food does not feed, when its cures do not cure, when its blessings refuse to bless.[1]

— G.K. Chesterton

I. Word-image Economies

Once more, once more / I am / your star. / Woe to the sailor with level / and compass / whose angle is false. / He will wreck on rocks / and hidden shoals. / Woe to you without love / or compassion / who angled me false. / You will wreck on rocks / and the rocks will laugh / at you / the way you did at me.[2]

— Velimir Khlebnikov

---

1   G.K. Chesterton, *The Everlasting Man* (Mineola: Dover, 2007), 149. First published in 1925 by Hodder and Stoughton, London. This often-cited passage illustrates what Žižek has expropriated from Chesterton's thought: i.e., that "orthodoxy" is quite often exceptionally radical versus conservative. For example, see *International Journal of Žižek Studies* 4, no. 4, "Žižek's Theology" (2010).

2   Velimir Khlebnikov, "Untitled Poem," in *The King of Time: Selected Writings of the Russian Futurian,* ed. Charlotte Douglas, trans. Paul Schmidt

With Schmitt, Freud, Lacan (Jung is exempt because he valoriz-
es versus corrupts or demonizes the mythic resources of immemoriality), and Heidegger, we enter uncharmed and charmed,
sinister and diabolical economies (libidinal and otherwise).
With Badiou and Žižek (Žižek and Hegel), we enter systems, to
extract "whatever" — e.g., event, sign, universal. All serve as encounters with a demiurge — Being displaced by "Being There,"
or by Event (plus Fall and Return). New word-image economies
therefore, to operate on the side of Grace, need to exit these
diabolical, proto-totalitarian "closed" systems, where Power is,
indeed (per Žižek), "obscene" and demiurge is an inflated sign
for "Being Thrown."[3] Cacciari's diagnosis in *The Withholding*

(Cambridge: Harvard University Press, 1990), 38. Is this Khlebnikov's
muse speaking to Khlebnikov? Is it Khlebnikov speaking to those who
have misunderstood his work? Or is it both, at once? There are echoes here
of Shakespeare's "Once more unto the breach …," in *Henry V,* intended or
not. In a conventional reading, it is the wounded artistic ego speaking to
their critics. Yet in the visionary universe of arts produced under the spell
of the Muse, there is no such ego as such. Artistic ego, work, and Muse are
one. And: "I am going out again today / Into life, into the marketplace, /
To lead a regiment of songs / Against the roar of rat and race." Ronald
Vroon, "The Poet and His Voices," in *Velimir Khlebnikov Collected Works
of Velimir Khlebnikov*, Vol. 3: *Selected Poems,* ed. Ronald Vroon, trans. Paul
Schmidt (Cambridge: Harvard University Press, 1997), 13. Vroon opens his
essay with the epigraph: "You still have not understood that my word / Is
a god howling in a cage" (ibid., 1). This is either megalomania on the part of
Khlebnikov or a nod toward the Muse. It cannot be both. The bard speaks
for the Muse, not for themself.

3 Two early texts by Emmanuel Levinas are worthy of close examination
   in this regard. They are: *De l'évasion* (1935) and "La réalité et son ombre"
   (1948). *De l'évasion* was re-published as *De l'évasion* (Montpellier: Fata
   Morgana, 1982), with notes by Jacques Rolland, and in English, *On Escape:
   De l'évasion*, trans. Bettina Bergo (Stanford: Stanford University Press,
   2003). The Stanford edition is based on the 1982 edition and includes
   Rolland's "notes," which constitute perhaps half of the book. "La réalité
   et son ombre" was first published in Jean-Paul Sartre's journal, *Les temps
   modernes* 38 (November 1948). Regarding *De l'évasion,* as response to
   Heidegger, see Gavin Keeney, "What Is Fate?" in *Art as "Night": An
   Art-theological Treatise* (Newcastle upon Tyne: Cambridge Scholars
   Publishing, 2010), 39–40. Levinas's meditation on transpersonal relations
   constructs a version of an extreme outside which is only further outside

Power is extreme (as it proceeds in part from Schmitt, head jurist of Nazism). The law, in such instances, is a fabrication — a complex fetish justifying dehumanization, imprisonment, and extermination of the Other. The superego in Freud and Lacan is ultimately also a fabrication of processes of subjectivization (that sickening internalization of rules diagnosed by both Kierkegaard and Nietzsche). In all cases, this situational anomie is used to offset the general or global anomie of the End Times. The katechon is, in such a scenario, the institutions of law, plus all the anomalies or brutalities associated with the historical subversions of the rule of law by incipient forms of imperialism, fascism, and/or totalitarianism. Yet the new demiurge of late modernity is Capital — plus its jurists, the vectorial class and its enablers.[4] And if political theology is the place where the

---

normative intersubjective time-space due to its being an attempt to escape Heidegger's definitions of Being. It is, in fact, "an ultra-sophisticated maneuver that returns in itself to 'what is,' in that this outside of the outside is the premiation of the austere 'what is' (pure coordinates) that sponsors 'what is' (the outside of the outside that eliminates the last residue of onto-theology)" (ibid., 39). For "La réalité et son ombre," see "Reality and Its Shadow," in Emmanuel Levinas, *The Levinas Reader,* ed. Séan Hand, trans. Alfonso Lingis (Oxford: Blackwell, 1989), 129–43. For the significance of "La réalité et son ombre" and Levinas's objections to the 1940s penchant to place visuality above discursivity, see Gavin Keeney, "Anamnesis," in *Dossier Chris Marker: The Suffering Image* (Newcastle upon Tyne: Cambridge Scholars Publishing, 2012), 57–60, n15.

4   This comes to acute expression, under the auspices of a discussion of the corrosive effects of the worship of technology, for Morris Berman: "Modern societies, said [Max] Weber, are governed by bureaucracy; the dominant ethos is one of 'rationalization,' whereby everything is mechanized, administered according to the dictates of scientific reason [i.e., determinism and utility]. Weber famously compared this situation to that of an 'iron cage': there was no way the citizens of these societies could break free from their constraints. Premodern societies, on the other hand, were permeated by animism, by a belief in magic and spirits, and governance came not through bureaucracy but through the charisma of gifted leaders. The decline of magic that accompanied the transition to modernity Weber called *die Entzauberung der Welt* — the disenchantment of the world." Morris Berman, *Why America Failed: The Roots of Imperial Decline* (Hoboken: John Wiley and Sons, 2012), 88. Weber borrowed the term from Schiller. For Romanticism, however, the dawn of disenchant-

greatest ambushes take place, as part of the superstructure of the Arts and Humanities, political theology and politico-cultural economy must be examined as, foremost, a force-field under contestation in the age of cognitive capitalism.

Exiting or avoiding operative criticism becomes one path forward, though that path may also include contesting, at first, the very premises of operative criticism.[5] For today, in the Arts and Humanities, the villains of Capital (the jurists of academia, the art world, and platform cultures in general) dictate the terms of engagement for artist–scholars, the entire operation excessively reductive and/or deterministic, especially in terms of the

---

ment also often presages a form of terrifying "liberty" from custom and illusion. Berman also notes, en passant, how the worship of progress, from the Enlightenment forward, is "ultimately Christian eschatology in modern dress" (ibid., 81). Berman cites Carl L. Becker, *The Heavenly City of the Eighteenth-century Philosophers* (New Haven: Yale University Press, 1932) and John Gray, *Black Mass* (New York: Farrar, Straus and Giroux, 2007). Berman also deploys the dialectic of *Gemeinschaft/Gesellschaft* to structure his arguments for a return to the past to recover "lost causes" associated with traditional communitarian values. See pages 88, 112, 133, and 135. He defines this dyadic and/or didactic analytic as weighing the *lived* virtues (not *intended* virtues) of a dynamic, capitalist society [*Gesellschaft*] against those of a traditional, neo-feudal one [*Gemeinschaft*]" (ibid., 133). These terms originate in Ferdinand Tönnies, *Gemeinschaft und Gesellschaft: Abhandlung des Communismus und des Socialismus als empirischer Culturformen Attribution von Ferdinand Tönnies* (Leipzig: Fues, 1887). Berman attaches both terms to his critique of American political economy, slightly distorting both. A better use for these terms is to denote them ~~Gemeinschaft/Gesellschaft~~ — i.e., discarding them altogether. For the appropriation of Tönnies by Heidegger and others, see Miguel de Beistegui, "Bordering on Politics," 8–31, in Miguel de Beistegui, *Heidegger and the Political: Dystopias* (London: Routledge, 1998), 20. See also Eugene McCarraher, *The Enchantments of Mammon: How Capitalism Became the Religion of Modernity* (Cambridge: Harvard University Press, 2019).

5   See Susan Carty Piedmont, "Operative Criticism," *Journal of Architectural Education* 40, no. 1 (Fall 1986): 8–13. "For the avant garde, intent and declaration become the object and in so doing reveal the role of the adversarial relationship of design by invention to existing context: progress is not necessarily found in the substance or the methodology, but in the dialectic process of contestation" (ibid., 12).

neoliberal machinations of the managerial university, but also via the neo-spectacular biases of the art world.[6]

Thus, the situational anomie noted above is systemic, crossing all disciplines and all discourses, as sinister shadow. The very idea of works that might escape this shadow plays directly into the entire field of politico-cultural economy. It is not just the discursive regimes of power, in concourse with critiques of the same, that condition this field. In fact, per Debord and the Situationists, it is more than self-evident that it is the visual regimes of spectacle that condition the field for most subjects, insofar as *most* citizen-subjects of Weber's "iron cage" do not read philosophy or criticism.

The escape route therefore engages both regimes in the Arts and Humanities (academia and the art world), but comes to fullest expression across regimes — across platforms and across media. Heedlessly testing, bluffing, and provocatively working its way through the existing opportunities for the production and dissemination of works, works for works as anti-capitalist adventure (form-of-life for life-works) wanders downstream to go upstream — and into markets to escape markets.

"Works for works" must also escape the trap of autonomy as defined within disciplines and within works (*pace* Tafuri) and depart company with arguments or justifications that are ultimately or penultimately reductive.

This then entails an apparent engagement with so-called thick and thin representational means to normative ends (historically determined or otherwise). As new avant-garde gestalt, new word-image economies will, indeed, include some measure of self-reflexion (self-referentiality), but only

---

6   These networks would seem to resemble what Jaron Lanier called "antigoras." "An Antigora is a privately owned digital meeting arena made rich by unpaid or marginally paid labor provided by people who crowd its periphery." Jaron Lanier, "The Gory Antigora: Illusions of Capitalism and Computers," *Cato Unbound,* January 8, 2006, https://www.cato-unbound. org/2006/01/08/jaron-lanier/gory-antigora-illusions-capitalism-computers.

as one aspect of the "voice" of "works for works". Both the object and the content (or the methodology) are temporal and this-worldly, while the "voice" is other-worldly — operating not as negative critique but as positive or anagogical escape route from both rules and Law.

The self-imposed or self-reflexive "dogma" is therefore positioned on the performative side, to distinguish works from established or authorized discourses. That dogma is always already provisional. The various methodologies employed across platforms — in production, post-production, and in dissemination of works — are thus also always already provisional (as part of the dogma), and the intent of finding new word-image economies, through both collective and individual effort (e.g., via Ivory Tower and Lonely Tower), is productive of an utterly untimely and dynamic engagement with rules and Law. Instead of a cursory, high-handed and/or dismissive departing of company with deterministic forms of "cultural patrimony", subtle or overt, "works for works" arise out of a spirited and enchanted foray by artist–scholar into contestation with rules and Law. Yet the results, as gestalt (or as form-of-life for works, *pace* Agamben's "ideational Franciscanism"), are to be re-performed and thus iterative toward leaving rules and Law behind for "else-where" — i.e., "lessons are learned from lessons learned", collectively and individually, irreducibly across "works for works" as life-works […].[7]

This agenda for works for works would, under some circumstances, resemble recent attempts in subaltern studies to escape so-called abyssal thinking.[8] Yet the privileging of entanglement

---

7   "Summary: 'Thick and Thin,'" from "QS: Lessons for Artist–Scholars" (001 Archive, 2018). Unpublished manuscript associated with the Out of India Collective.

8   "Modern knowledge and modern law represent the most accomplished manifestations of abyssal thinking. They account for the two major global lines of modern times, which, though being different and operating differently, are mutually dependent. Each one creates a sub-system of visible and invisible distinctions in such a way that the invisible ones become the

and its analogues (as circulating in the various worlds of digital media) effectively throws the baby out with the bath water. Horizontal and syntagmatic orders will consistently fail to challenge Power, which is always arrayed or positioned along the paradigmatic axis of politico-cultural production (and its ideological formulation as hegemony). The failing West's fascination with indigenous cultures and the suppressed regimes of magical thinking supposedly hiding out there represent a struggle to arrive at a locus in thought that is not premised on rationality. Instrumental reason is running out of frontiers to conquer and subjugate. Yet the failing West might look inward versus to its benighted former colonies for the source of that inimitable something else it seeks. The irony here is that abyssal thinking, while no doubt a correct analysis of politico-cultural imperialism and the subjugation of the Other, is a construct of subaltern studies (no matter the pedigree of its critical apparatuses, Marxist, neo-Marxist, post-Marxist or otherwise), and we now witness attempts to escape the construct by those very academics who have constructed and/or subscribed to it. Yet all the while abyssal thought is turned upside-down and backwards

---

foundation of the visible ones. In the field of knowledge, abyssal thinking consists in granting to modern science the monopoly of the universal distinction between true and false, to the detriment of two alternative bodies of knowledge: philosophy and theology. The exclusionary character of this monopoly is at the core of the modern epistemological disputes between scientific and nonscientific forms of truth. Since the universal validity of a scientific truth is admittedly always very relative, given the fact that it can only be ascertained in relation to certain kinds of objects under certain circumstances and established by certain methods, how does it relate to other possible truths which may even claim a higher status but which cannot be established according to scientific methods, such as reason as philosophical truth or faith as religious truth?" Boaventura de Sousa Santos, "Beyond Abyssal Thinking: From Global Lines to Ecologies of Knowledges," *Eurozine,* June 29, 2007, https://www.eurozine.com/beyond-abyssal-thinking/. For a symposium constructed upon the premise of escaping "abyssal thinking" (but perhaps caught nonetheless in the rhetorical trap of the language games of subaltern studies), see "Knowledge Entanglements," KfW Stiftung and DAAD Artists-in-Berlin Program, 2018, http://www.berliner-kuenstlerprogramm.de/en/veranstalt_detail.php?id=2061.

to privilege jumping into the abyss — e.g., crossing the dividing line and abandoning rationality in favor of seeking varieties of Deleuzian pure immanence. The games are legion, and the outcome almost always provisional until the next intellectual fashion statement appears to displace the outmoded. This cycle speeds toward exhaustion, often circling back to revamp spent agendas, as if something might have been missed along the way. It is not so much a case of recovering lost causes (as with Benjamin et al.), but instead a vicious circle given to intellectual inquiry that refuses to fully exit regimes of citation, appropriation, expropriation and ameliorization via the periodic production of the proverbial new black (the not-self-ironic pursuit of anything new for the sake of anything new).

Today we see well-meaning attempts by universities (e.g., Harvard and Aalto) to throw the sublime arc of the arts across all disciplines in the university in pursuit of a quickening of the pulse within otherwise empirically driven disciplines. It is wholly possible that the result will merely be additional mediatic spectacle for programs by which to add to the PR cache of programs and schools. For the agenda to have any real and/or significant impact it would have to actually alter the pedagogical constructs of the university, to effectively erase the prevailing biases of neoliberalism wherever they may have taken up residence within the Ivory Tower. The more likely outcome is a tidal wave of new performative studies, from Master's to PhD, conducted in service to the platform cultures currently acting as bespoke chapters in the conquest by Capital of the knowledge commons.[9]

---

9   "Traditional stock markets, or even flea markets, are a little like Antigoras, in that they are also private meeting places for business. One obvious difference resulting from the digital quality of the Antigora is a far stronger network effect; Antigoras enjoy natural monopoly status more often than physical marketplaces because it would be almost impossible for locked-in participants to choose new Antigoras." Lanier, "The Gory Antigora."

II. Villainy and Its Other

Thus does political theology crash into politico-cultural economy. One might expect the outcome, in terms of impact and
output, to resemble Jean-Luc Godard's car-crash of a film, *Week-
end* (1967). The history of the avant-garde is, after all, the history
of the production of new word-image economies that generally
resemble a car-crash, if not a train-wreck. Yet there are others
that exit the thematic of excitable mash-up. It might even be
said that Godard exited his own penchant for the filmic mash-
up with his late works (from roughly the 2001 masterpiece *Éloge
de l'amour* forward), or at least some of his late works. His film
essays post-2001 still drift toward the incomprehensible and
gloriously synoptic or selective assemblage he perfected in the
agit-prop works that punctuate his life-work. *The Image Book* of
2018 is such an example. What redeems many of these excessively montaged works (montaged by way of appropriated word and
image) is that they are positioned according to a word-image
economy they either seek to critique or create. *The Image Book,*
while almost a work intentionally created as provocation for
Cannes, in the spirit of *De l'origine du XXIᵉ siècle* (2000), which
was commissioned by the Cannes Film Festival, is notably to be
"supplemented" with a traveling exhibition.[10]

It is perhaps too easy to fixate upon modernist avant-gardes
when seeking examples of word-image economies that served
the purposes of escaping dominant narratives or imposing
ideologies that served power of one form or another. For if
the villains are poised or arrayed along the paradigmatic axis
(*pace* Ernesto Laclau) of politico-cultural or politico-econom-

---

10 See Alex Greenberger, "Jean-Luc Godard to Stage Exhibition Version of
His Latest Film, 'The Image Book,'" *Artnews,* May 11, 2018, http://www.
artnews.com/2018/05/11/jean-luc-godard-stage-exhibition-version-latest-
film-image-book/. As of late 2019, early 2020, this intended exhibition
appears to have turned into an installation at the Fondazione Prada,
Milan. "Jean-Luc Godard: Le Studio d'Orphée," *Prada Group,* December
2019, https://www.pradagroup.com/en/news-media/news-section/jean-
luc-godard-le-studio-orphee.html.

ic production, in the mysterious workings of works for works something slips past the sentries, almost ghost-like. Or, works for works maneuver around and/or outmaneuver authority by means that are paradoxically fully lodged in the paradigmatic while ascending and surpassing the paradigmatic. Kenneth Rexroth's statements about the inassimilable purposes or aspects of 1960s avant-garde poetry utilize the songs in Shakespeare's plays as an example of this mysterious something that slips past the sentry posts of disciplinary and political power structures. Shakespeare's *Cymbeline* is the perfect example.[11] Yet, by and large, the greater corpus of works by Shakespeare also slipped past the sentries of Elizabethan England. In some ways Shakespeare split himself in two to accomplish this feat. The plays work on two levels — as theater and as moral agenda. This splitting was also the case with Ruskin and Tennyson, in Victorian England. And it is possible to say that it was also the case with Veronese in the Venetian Renaissance. Indeed, Veronese's works are one source for Ruskin's famous unconversion to English pietism. Yet the splitting occurs by way of the work, and the work's inherent power or force is inescapable — for artists and for spectators.

Villainy famously creates villains of the Other to cover up true villainy. Yet there are extraordinarily subversive works that pass by the censors (literal or de facto censors) due to the nature of their qualities, not content. Form and content mean nothing in such instances. The structuralist analytic collapses. While the historical parade of modernist avant-gardes (one after another)

---

11 "The whole problem is to find works of art which remain permanently unassimilable and permanently corruptive. This means that they don't really differ very much from anybody else's work of art. The songs of Shakespeare are permanently indigestible and permanently subversive." David Meltzer, "Interview with Kenneth Rexroth," *Bureau of Public Secrets,* n.d., http://www.bopsecrets.org/rexroth/meltzer.htm. "This interview was conducted in summer 1969 at Rexroth's home in Santa Barbara, California. It was originally included in [David Meltzer, ed., *The San Francisco Poets* (New York: Ballantine, 1971)]. An expanded edition, *San Francisco Beat: Talking with the Poets* (City Lights, 2001), includes interviews with several more poets along with a few additional comments by Meltzer" (ibid.).

suggests that modernism and anti-modernism are, after all, one thing, and that modernism is half predicated on a perpetual destruction of the past (even the immediate past, as in the cases of a preceding avant-garde upturned and emptied out by the one immediately following it), there is a secret, not silver lining. This secret lining is to turn critique on its head and produce the proverbial " { } " of an utter break with conventions.

The oscillations across the spectrum of disciplines in the Arts and Humanities, in terms of the appearance and the disappearance of new avant-gardes, is structurally impossible to properly document. This is the reason for the reductive narratives of Art History; and this is the reason for the curiously abject cultural histories denoting life- and death-cycles in the various disciplines that come under the rule of the super-discipline of the Arts and Humanities. To the artist–scholar they make no sense, though they may be examined for traces of the mysterious anagogical spirit — " { } " — that animates works that escape these cycles and become immortal. The Western canon is essentially premised on such winged victories, while within most such works there is hidden, despite the canonization process generally being considered by critics a form of absurdist paternalism, the inassimilable and the subversive. Certainly, Melville or Flaubert exemplify authors whose works have flown past the sentries. If it takes centuries sometimes for the works to be acknowledged as masterpieces, that hardly matters. The point is that they contain a secret map of a secret exit route that is — per Thomas Mann — to be found in "homeopathic dilution." The songs of *Cymbeline* are other-worldly. Melville's novelistic satire conceals an entire reading of the onrushing failure of American exceptionalism — indeed, the absurdity of American exceptionalism. The secret map is a moral map, which defines the anagogical process.[12] It was present in Renaissance humanism, but

12 This was certainly the case with both Dada and Situationism, two of the most enduring of the anti-modernist insurrections. The term *enduring* means, in the art-historical context, the re-appearance of both scholarly interest in Dada and Situationism and in the periodic outbreak of neo-Dadaisms and neo-Situationisms, the latter outbreaks generally perpetu-

it took many forms. With Veronese it took the form of painting as tableau vivant. By the time of Caravaggio, Renaissance illuminism had failed and the mysteries of chiaroscuro supplanted illuminism.

Yeats's gyres are stretched today to the extremities. The time of working within despotisms is over. Wholesale departure is in order. Gracián to Calderon to Shakespeare and back is instructive (the "measure of things"). The possibility in the age of cognitive capitalism to alter the terms of engagement are increasingly marginal — with co-optation the usual result. The machinery that Thoreau saw encroaching on life has surpassed even his estimation at the decimation of life. The law has to be overturned. Overturning apple carts is not enough. New word-image economies can only emerge outside of all forms of law, as form-of-life — beyond the claws and tentacles of Capital. The university and the art world could be spared this assessment — but how? Via new walled gardens? Via the new monasticism?[13]

The proverbial clown cars of power take two principal forms: the truly dangerous (and thus ultra-obscene), and the merely symptomatic or posturing type (and merely annoying). The antics of power spread over ever-diminishing systems of return and effective or ineffective repression.

Where are those that are merely annoying pantomimes to be found? One such field of idiosyncratic and absurdist posturing is, for the most part, neoliberal academia. From Chancellor to

---

ated by artist–scholars. It was less true of Surrealism, though we see the presence of the moral map (sometimes distorted as absurdist libidinal economy of excess), in part, in the dissident Surrealists — i.e., Bachelard, Bataille, Serres, Leiris, and Caillois.

13 Life migrates for most artist–scholars from pen and paper to smartphone to laptop — to and fro — toward what? Correcting auto-correct becomes tedious and sows discord, frustration, and "ameliorative" bemusement (bemusement to improve benighted tolerance). Google, Gooogle, and Goooogle atones for its sins by building a spaceship — a life raft for itself... Hawthorne's Mr. Smooth-It-Away paces the spaceship/life raft... Adorno's "minima moralia" passes over into sub-zero territory. This pessimistic optimism was characterized by G.K. Chesterton as pessimism of the intellect, optimism of the heart.

Provost the rule and the law is a fabricated network of imposed standards via external industry—i.e., outside interests searching for purchase (Archimedean and financial leverage) inside of academia. The twisted performative value of neoliberal academia is two-fold—imposed rules to subjugate faculty and PR campaigns that are hyper-self-congratulatory (e.g., Web-based assaults on prospective clients, including students, and alumni). The absurdist quality kicks in with the excessive posturing and the self-congratulatory hype to turn heads.[14] Can power at both

---

14 In a review of the fiftieth anniversary of the *New Left Review,* in 2010, Cambridge academic and literary critic Stefan Collini makes a few curious remarks, en passant, about academia. He is, in effect, extolling the virtues of the NLR as semi-privileged bastion of critical inquiry against a backdrop of neoliberal capitalist conquest of academia. Yet he is also taking issue with some of the anniversary issue's ideological postures, foremost in the editorial by Susan Watkins: "When I'm told, for example, that 'the thought-world of the west' is increasingly determined by 'Atlantic-centred structures of wealth and power', *dragging academic disciplines in tow,* I find myself feeling that the search for pattern and causation is starting to lose sight of something no less important—the uneven, awkward diversity that is apparent when viewed from a little closer. All intellectual inquiry is a see-sawing between *abstraction and particularity,* and NLR's inheritance can still make it seem more indulgent of the former than the latter. Interestingly, the language of 'determinants' and 'system' falls away when it comes to self-description. 'NLR stands outside this world,' Watkins writes, 'defines its own agenda.' Excellent, but might not some other elements in 'the thought-world of the west' be doing the same, in their own way? Still, the audacity is admirable: I like the thought that a specially unillusioned, independent, global perspective on what's happening is to be had from a side street in Soho." Stefan Collini, "A Life in Politics: *New Left Review* at 50," *The Guardian,* February 13, 2010, https://www.theguardian.com/books/2010/feb/13/new-left-review-stefan-collini, italics added. Watkins opens the issue with an essay intoning the now well-rehearsed Gramscian "pessimism of the intellect, optimism of the will." See Antonio Gramsci, "Address to the Anarchists," 185–89, in Antonio Gramsci, *Selections from Political Writings,* Vol. 1: *1910–1920,* ed. Quintin Hoare, trans. John Mathews (London: Lawrence and Wishart, 1977). First published as "Discorso agli anarchici," *L'Ordine Nuovo* 1, no. 43 (April 3–10, 1920). "That neoliberalism's crisis should be so eerily non-agonistic, in contrast to the bitter battles over its installation, is a sobering measure of its triumph." Susan Watkins, "Shifting Sands," *New Left Review* 2, no. 61 (January–February 2010): 20. Collini dutifully closes his review with a last nod toward

levels be turned to other, more ethical and perhaps self-effacing purposes? At the level of government Capital is fully entrenched for the long run. At the level of sub-cultural, socio-economic activity the screws are not yet so tightly fastened — things could be pried free. Saving the knowledge commons may be possible, albeit in the long run, through inserting the equivalent of monkey wrenches into the works, or by the charmed auspices of new word-image economies.

How the clown car of neoliberal academia may be derailed includes convincing faculties to challenge the circuit of false power that runs from Chancellor to Provost.[15] That circuit,

---

that side street in Soho (i.e., 6 Meard Street): "When so much of even the so-called 'serious' media is given over to celebrity-fuelled ephemera and the recycling of press releases and in-house gossip; and when the academic world is struggling to mitigate the worst effects of *funding-driven over-production and careerist modishness*; and when national and international politics seem to consist of bowing to the imperatives of 'the market' while avoiding public relations gaffes; then we need more than ever a 'forum' like NLR. It is up to date without being merely journalistic; it is scholarly but unscarred by citation-compulsion; and it is analytical about the long-term forces at work in politics rather than obsessed by the spume of the latest wavelet of manoeuvring and posturing." Collini, "A Life in Politics," italics added. See also Alex Callinicos, "The Radical Left and the Crisis — A Tale of Two Journals," *Europe Solidaire Sans Frontières,* March 14, 2010, http://europe-solidaire.org/spip.php?article26129#nb4. Collini is the author of *What Are Universities For?* (London: Penguin, 2012) and *Speaking of Universities* (London: Verso, 2017).

15 This false circuit of power, aimed at disenfranchising faculty and students, is based on authoritarianism combined with opportunism. "What role might education and critical pedagogy have in a society in which the social has been individualized, emotional life collapses into the therapeutic, and education is relegated to either a private affair or to a kind of algorithmic mode of regulation in which everything is reduced to a desired measure-able outcome. How might education function to reclaim a notion of the democratic imagination and the importance of the social under a system that celebrates and normalizes the assumption that individuals are 'greedy, self-interested animals [and that] we must reward greedy, self-interested behaviour to create a rational and efficient economic system?' There is more at work here than a pedagogy of repression, there is an ideology of barbarism, one that flirts dangerously with irrationality and removes itself from any vestige of solidarity, compassion, and care for the other or the planet." Henry Giroux, "Culture of Cruelty: The Age of Neoliberal

which is simply serving market ideology, may be short circuited by shifting the terms of marketability. Rather than perpetuating the re-cycling of spent discourses (and this includes the technological hubris associated with ever-new versions of everything), faculties could break the model of citational scholarship and false innovation currently supported in the Arts and Humanities by metrics-based research standards, by the incorporation of a new avant-garde gestalt across disciplines. If of sufficient appeal and merit, markets would follow, fashion neutralized while paradoxically — or strangely — valorized.

III. Memo to Self

Thus, shorthand for artist–scholars: Eternity within Trinity... "How long is forever? Eternity and a day...." *It* contains every move you ever thought of, or might think of, and the counter-move. *It* neutralizes irony and dialectics — positive and negative. Tarkovsky's last scenes in *Solaris* and *Sacrifice*. Žižek, in *Angelaki,* takes Tarkovsky to task — reducing Solaris to the Lacanian psychoanalytical something that is nothing, calling it "The Thing from Inner Space."[16] Kris returns "home" from Solaris to the Father, by way of Solaris's mesmeric sea. In *Sacrifice* the economy (force-field) of post-apocalyptic broken promises and premises is burned to the ground. In *Nostalghia* the alienated scholar returns "home" via a spectral ruined cathedral. Thus, Tarkovsky's last three films: cosmologies of Grace....

Authoritarianism," *CounterPunch*, October 23, 2015, http://www.counterpunch.org/2015/10/23/culture-of-cruelty-the-age-of-neoliberal-authoritarianism/; with reference to Robert Jensen, *Arguing for Our Lives: A User's Guide to Constructive Dialog* (San Francisco: City Lights Books, 2013), 95. Giroux provides three main points of reference for a critique of neoliberal capitalist ideology: Stuart Hall, "The Neo-Liberal Revolution," *Cultural Studies* 25, no. 6 (November 2011): 705–28; David Harvey, *A Brief History of Neoliberalism* (Oxford: Oxford University Press, 2005); and Henry A. Giroux, *Against the Terror of Neoliberalism* (Boulder: Paradigm Publishers, 2008).

16 Slavoj Žižek, "The Thing from Inner Space," *Angelaki* 4, no. 3 (1999): 221–31.

The economy of Eternity is Grace Itself. All elements (instances and instantiations) exist as One — Force and Field. "The Law disappears…." "Water into wine…." IRWIN appropriated the mostly silent iconography of Triglav, the three peaks in northern Slovenia, for ironic purposes — three heads atop three peaks. Žižek, Dolar, and Zupančič did the same — the irony also self-ironically self-referential; mock triumvirate of Slovene Arts and Letters. Yet the trinitarian gestures of this economic gestalt are nonetheless one with the One.

9

The Icons of IRWIN

0. Nota Bene

This essay (intentionally enigmatic and elliptical) is not about NSK (the New Slovenian Art collective), IRWIN (part of NSK), Ivo Svetina (the playwright of *In the Name of the Mother*), or the Slovenian National Theatre (where Svetina's play was staged). It is, instead, about the agency of the works described (the icons), the ongoing or unfinished performative intervention via "séance," and the interplay of anonymous and often absurdist forces only activated by art and theater. Based on an actual performance project conducted in 2019, in Ljubljana, Slovenia, it is nonetheless written as a type of fabulation (i.e., a fantastic tale constructed after-the-fact and from memory) to purposefully put a distance between the event and its recollection and to invoke future sessions of a similar spirit and non-place. The time-senses invoked in the essay (as report) — i.e., before, during, and after the preliminary first two sessions — are also indicative of the affective regime of such a research methodology, where the aleatory, iterative, and generative aspects of the project run up against the self-imposed necessities of producing tangible records in order to archive the event for future re-play.

I. Questions and Answers

When a wall covered with icons produced by the Slovene art col-lective IRWIN appeared as the imposing backdrop for Ivo Sveti-na's play *In the Name of the Mother* (Slovenian National Theatre, 2018–19) something shifted, dramatically, in their ongoing serial presentation and production since the 1980s.[1] Always offered in relation to something else, in the case of Svetina's play the wall of icons interspersed with hunting trophies (taxidermy speci-mens of wildlife) became another world observing the world of the play, a play that spanned one hundred years in the life of one family. As backdrop for the entirety of the play, the minimal set at stage-level changed repeatedly while the backdrop remained the same, shifting only in mood and tenor with lighting effects.

Here is the last thing they witness:

> When the century is at its end and the Slovenians get their independent state, history spins around in a single August afternoon as if on a carousel; the living and the dead are dancing their casual Sunday chat. Among them, we spot a reader of *Anna Karenina*, leaving for a trip to the other side of the world, where her fears — born perhaps in a concentra-tion camp — will come alive again. Thus, on Christmas Eve, she throws herself into a dark river as cold as marble…[2]

In this sense the icons revealed themselves, finally, as witness-es — albeit silent witnesses that had often been installed in gal-leries in the same manner — i.e., as field effect.[3] Yet witnesses to

---

1   See the playwright's summary of *In the Name of the Mother,* Ivo Svetina, "Ivo Svetina: In the Name of the Mother," *Slovenian National Theatre,* n.d., https://www.drama.si/en/event/in-the-name-of-the-mother/.

2   Ibid.

3   These well-known works of retro-avant-garde art are part of the larger corpus of IRWIN works but register something historical and a-historical, at once. It is the a-historical merit of the works that the Question and An-swer sessions sought to access. Notably, in 2019, and at the time of the two

what? Operating as field effect, the icons of IRWIN immediately beg the asking of questions — i.e., questions posed first of all to the icons, and then questions asked by the icons to the five members of IRWIN. In other words, a conversation or séance. In order to achieve this end, and without the outright inventing of the answers, it is necessary to propose questions that the icons might actually answer, plus a methodology, while creating the time-sense that they might also answer *from within*. The questions, fielded to the icons, in turn, might suggest the subsequent questions to IRWIN regarding the icons they have effectively created primarily through appropriation and assemblage. And what better way to find these questions to be asked of IRWIN by the icons than to turn the initial answers that the icons supply *into questions* for IRWIN, thereby setting up a loop that could, hypothetically, go on forever?

This somewhat picturesque mirroring strategy, a theatrical operation in its own right, far from being a case of catastrophic mise-en-abyme, nonetheless does entail and engage the famous "tain of the mirror" — the precise element of the mirror that produces the reflection, plus that famous circularity that mirrors are famous for, where the mirage in the mirror recedes into infinity only to return again. That critical reflective component of mirrors is the generative and operative element of the icon in and for itself. For the icon is not merely a reflective pane or a window; it has its effective material presence and connotes a form of temporality that is utterly prescient while nominally

---

sessions at the Academy of Visual Arts, an exhibition of Russian icons was on exhibit at the City Museum, Ljubljana. In a separate room, effectively closing the circuit of the exhibition, IRWIN installed their own icons along with a video homage to Hugo Ball. Additionally, the exhibition design for the Russian icons, as developed by IRWIN protagonist Miran Mohar, included a type of "wallpaper" or "radiation" (in the graphic art sense) alluding to various modernist associations with icons and iconicity. This somewhat indirect conflation of Orthodox icons and the icons of IRWIN, plus the referential datum of other works as "radiation," confirms and underscores the underlying topologically inflected relationship the icons of IRWIN have with both art history and, the more provocative position of avant-garde art, "no history."

elusive. It is only nominally elusive when it is conferred with preternatural or supernatural agency. In fact, the icon merely exists. It is what it is. But by merely existing, as tautology, it cancels a great deal of art-critical mischief. What it cancels includes representational theories of mimesis and hypostasis, both of no use in the reading or contemplation of icons.

It is not for nothing that iconography and iconology are two different art-historical worlds, of two orders of representational praxis, though they overlap. The former concerns the sign and metonym, while the latter concerns agency and topology. It is the latter that opens up the possibility of a conversation with the icons of IRWIN; for through the establishment of a properly distanced interview the icons may be able to speak, versus art criticism speaking for them. How this might be played out refers back, in a sense, to Svetina's play, *In the Name of the Mother,* in which they do not speak but observe. Yet their presence does speak; they are witnessing one hundred years of drama and occasional trauma. They are aeons in the sense that they are there also as figures for the very passage of time. As aeons, they are also indicative of the Gnostic fable of the sacrifice by and of aeons to create worlds — they are genitive *fabula*. That they may speak at all crosses and negates that primary deception that sacrifice imputes silence. Nominally otherworldly, they are exceptionally this-worldly.

This problematic is resolved through seriality. The questioned icons will question IRWIN. And IRWIN will ultimately set into play a conversation that engages the agency of the appropriations they have indulged over three-and-one-half decades, plus why they have endured this thirty-to-forty-year dance with the topological jouissance of iconicity itself.

II. The Séance

To stage this problematic or provocation, two sessions were held with a Hierophant and a Sibyl facilitating the fielding of questions and the collection and recording of answers.[4] In the first session, the Hierophant held a blank white card up to a projection of an icon intercepting the image, asking the question without speaking.[5] He then handed the card to the Sibyl who transcribed with pen and paper the answer from the blank white card. No words were spoken. Documents had been prepared in advance with a slideshow of imagery to establish the properties or metric for the performance. The written record kept by the Sibyl created the register in which the questions and answers could be re-synchronized. The visual field and the discursive field were only separated in the event of the séance to create a temporary tension between word and image. The internal constructive logic of the presentation defined the subjective conditions and the questions never needed to be spoken aloud. They were embedded in the topology of the event and mediated by the silent interaction of the Hierophant and Sibyl.

In Session Two, the fifteen answers of Session One were posed to IRWIN for new questions.[6] The Hierophant again held

4   These sessions occurred at the Academy of Visual Arts, Ljubljana, Slovenia, on the evenings of May 29 and May 30, 2019. Personnel: Gavin Keeney, The Hierophant; Lili Anamarija, Sibyl; Diego Capriolo, Technical Assistant.

5   In Session One, May 29, fifteen projected images of IRWIN icons were presented with four questions, with the four questions repeated across the fifteen images. Set and properties included: the projection; a painter's wooden easel holding eight long white blank cards; a red foot stool; a desk lamp; and a short aluminum step ladder. The cast was comprised of the Hierophant and the Sibyl. To secure an answer from each icon, a portion of the projection of each of the fifteen icons was intercepted by the Hierophant with one of the eight long white blank cards. The card was then handed to the Sibyl to record (intuit) the answer. The music for Session One was Brian Eno, "Spirits Drifting" (*Another Green World*, 1975).

6   In Session Two, May 30, the fifteen answers to four questions from Session One were offered to a projected image of the five artists comprising the IRWIN collective. Set and properties included: the projection; a painter's wooden easel holding eight long white blank cards; a red foot stool; a desk lamp; and a short aluminum step ladder. The cast was comprised of the Hierophant and the Sibyl. The projected image of IRWIN (*The Golden Smile*, 2003), repeated fifteen times, was interspersed with the fifteen answers provided in Session One. Word and image were now both present in the

a blank white card up to a projected image, this time a group portrait of IRWIN, known as *The Golden Smile,* silently posing each of fifteen answers given by the icons toward securing a new question. The fifteen answers from Session One were however interspersed in the projection with the fifteen images of IRWIN, with the four questions again being repeated across fifteen images. The card was again handed to the Sibyl to transcribe the new question provided by IRWIN to paper. In both sessions, the sixteenth place in the sequence (4 × 4) was constituted as *nil*. It has dropped out due to the nature of the sequence (i.e., the use of fifteen, not sixteen images) and serves as zero. Music was played in both sessions to cast an appropriate spell. There was no light other than from the projection and a lamp illuminating the place where the Sibyl sat on a red leather hassock.

The resulting matheme for these sessions is also a type of ideogram that contains, in condensed fashion, the occluded apparatus of the operative, iterative, and generative internal logic.

4 + 15; 4 + 4 + 4 + 3; 15 + 15; (16); 4 + 15 + 5 + 15

That this logic was also, effectively, aleatory, and includes zero within the sequence, suggests that any further sessions will need to be elaborations of this fundamental datum — a multiplication of effects as affects.

III. Four Questions for Icons (Asked Four Times)

1. What kind of capital are you?
2. Where are you from?
3. What do you see?
4. How can we help you?

---

visual register. The projection of IRWIN was intercepted by the Hierophant with one of the eight long white blank cards, singling out one of the five artists to provide a new question to the answer from Session One. The card was then handed to the Sibyl to record (intuit) the question. The music for Session Two was François Couturier, "Nostalghia" (*Nostalghia — Song for Tarkovsky,* 2006).

IV. "Sixteen" Answers for IRWIN to Four Questions

First series

1. What kind of capital are you?

   Omnipresent in time and space …

2. Where are you from?

   Depth and mist…

3. What do you see?

   Myself, my twin?

4. How can we help you?

   Observe and enjoy…

Second series

5. What kind of capital are you?

   Fleeting…

6. Where are you from?

   Pristine nature…

7. What do you see?

   Chaos in order…

8. How can we help you?

   Speak out, loud, agitate…

Third series

9. What kind of capital are you?

   Historical…

10. Where are you from?

    Mythology, fire…

11. What do you see?

    Very solid foundation…

12. How can we help you?

    Decompose (me)…

Fourth series

13. What kind of capital are you?

    Exploited…

14. Where are you from?

    Home…

15. What do you see?

    Pitch-black emptiness…

16. […]

V. "Sixteen" Questions from IRWIN (to "Sixteen" Answers)

1. Omnipresent in time and space…

   Where do you see our/your works? (Andrej)

2. Depth and mist…

   What inspires (you)? (Dušan)

3. Myself, my twin?

   Who do you see in your/our works? (Miran)

4. Observe and enjoy…

   How should the IRWIN works be perceived? (Borut)

5. Fleeting …

   What quality of inspiration do you enjoy most? (Roman)

6. Pristine nature …

   What can be found in the depths of your/our souls? (Miran)

7. Chaos in order …

   What do you enjoy finding in art/life? (Dušan)

8. Speak out, loud, agitate …

   What should artists and art lovers do? (Andrej)

9. Historical …

How do you see the time/circumstances when IRWIN was established? (Borut)

10. Mythology, fire …

Where does the inspiration and imagination originate/stem from? (Miran)

11. Very solid foundation …

What does a powerful artwork require and/or deserve? (Andrej)

12. Decompose (me) …

What do/should the qualities of art do to the author/you? (Roman)

13. Exploited …

How do you feel art [feels]? (Dušan)

14. Home …

Where is art heading? (Miran)

15. Pitch-black emptiness …

What do you opt for: brilliant omnipresent whiteness or pitch-black emptiness? (Andrej)

16. […]

VI. Field Effects

Asked in reference to specific icons in the collection "Kapital 2018" (the collection of icons featured in the theatrical event, *In the Name of the Mother*), the questions elicited answers that are both circular and unitary or specific. A tautological presentism becomes self-evident in spite of the circularity. The circularity is further played out in the fifteen new questions provided by IRWIN to the fifteen initial answers. In reconstructing the sessions, after the fact, in graphic format, there is a slippage in the relational and discursive system that supported the inquiry into how the icons operate as field, but also how each icon speaks of its presence as icon — i.e., what it might have to say if asked a question concerning its imperative agency. This slippage implies that one answer to one question might actually be an answer to an entirely different question — that the answers might be shuffled and applied randomly to any of the other four questions in the series. The entire operation, proceeding by chance, parts executed and parts that might be executed, resembles the Surrealist exquisite corpse.

Foremost, there is a verbal intensity to the inferred answers from the icons, while there is a more prosaic or conventional, less semantically rich form of expression in the new questions provided by IRWIN to the answers. There is human agency and there is inhuman agency — i.e., nominally conscious and unconscious effect in the answers, and in the new questions for answers. The initial fifteen ("sixteen") answers are infused with that peculiar time-sense that is often called the present-present, the principal formal operation of such a field of rhetoric echoing the visual field of the icons, which have, after all, been asked directly, by singular image, the question to which the answer almost refers. The *almost* is telling; for the agency of the operation has permitted the slippage in time-senses to occur and the echoes within the field to appear. This is a type of temporal montage of effect and affect that inhabits the conversation. The echoes are magnified or multiplied in the four-fold sequence of the questions asked and the answers given. To align the answers with the images of the icons that provided them, as reconstructed after the fact, sets in play another level of inference and formal or generative operativity, insofar as the minimal iconographic detail of the icon seems to suggest one origin for the answer given. For example, the answer "Pristine nature" is elicited by the question "Where are you from?" by the image of a stag in the icon questioned. Yet, the iconicity of the field effect supplants or overrides that correspondence of answer to image and further conditions the field effect of the "sixteen" new questions provided by IRWIN to the fifteen answers.

The peculiarity of this syntactical compression and expansion, through the cycle of the inquiry, is more than matched by the overriding sense of the field as counterpoint to icon as object. If icons are wholly present and not merely painted or constructed figures of speech and thought, they are also wholly registered in a field that supports the speculative agency they contain. IRWIN's multiplication of the presentism of the icon is not accidental. How IRWIN has appropriated this a-historical operativity to a large degree lies in how they have also played with the historical or art-historical appropriations of icons that have occurred in advance of their own appropriation.

IRWIN's use of the icon is ultimately derived from Malevich's use of the icon. The manner in which Malevich's *Black Square* (1915) was first exhibited is also at play. In the First Suprematist Exhibition of 1915, "0,10," the painting *Black Square* was mounted amidst an array of paintings, a crowded field of paintings, but occupying an upper corner of the room almost as a mirror might be mounted there to capture the full field of the room.[7] Famously, *Black Square* effectively or polemically erased all normative content for icons, and subsequently served as zero degree for a new approach to what is, irreducibly, a semiological approach to the production of images. The Suprematist moment did not last long, but it launched a wholly new inquiry

---

7 Also known as "The Last Futurist Exhibition of Paintings, 0,10 (zero-ten)." "Poslednaia futuristicheskaia vystavka kartin, *0,10 (nol'-desiat')*," December 19, 1915–January 17, 1916. See Christina Lodder, "In Search of 0,10 — The Last Futurist Exhibition of Painting," *Burlington Magazine* 158 (2016): 61–63. The painting was first known as The Quadrilateral (*Chetyreugol'nik*). See Irina Vakar, "New Information Concerning *The Black Square*," in *Celebrating Suprematism: New Approaches to the Art of Kazimir Malevich,* ed. Christina Lodder (Leiden: Brill, 2019), 11–28.

into the power of revolutionary representation. *Black Square* has also appeared in IRWIN's work (as has Malevich's *Black Cross*), and it is to that register that in many respects all of the icons by IRWIN return — before departing again. Yet what in the nature of the iconographical detail or content IRWIN has superadded to the register of the *Black Square* must also be read against a type of profanation that has occurred along with that appropriation? Imagery does re-appear after that zero degree has been reached. That imagery, however, is misleading as mere iconographic content. The appearance of a coffee cup, for example, might connote bourgeois complacency or bohemian abandon. It has that peculiar everyday or day-to-day quality that serves to re-naturalize so-called fine art. To bring the quotidian and perhaps abject into the field of the icon is one level of provocation that slides toward profanation. But there is another level of profanation that is more expansive and operates within the field effect of the icons as array; and that particular case of profanation, while appearing bizarre, actually restores an auratic presentism to the icons that is in no way actually a profanation. It is similar to the moral agenda beneath the chaos of the Cabaret Voltaire, and it is noteworthy that IRWIN also refers repeatedly to the Dada-ist insurrection, most commonly through references to Hugo Ball.

VII. Profanations by Field

It is the presence of the animals within the representational field of the exhibited icons that is the primary form of profanation. In the presentation of the icons of IRWIN, this dates back at least to 1991. The animals are totemic versus iconic. They are a gesture toward the generativity of the collective presence of the icons — both IRWIN's icons and Orthodox icons. They restore a "givenness" that has been somewhat estranged from icons historically and transhistorically, and they serve to re-institute that givenness a-historically. Historicity, too, has multiple time-senses. This givenness is also closely allied with what Jean-Luc Marion has conceived of as the elastic distance in the aesthetic, which in turn permits contemplation. The iconographic detail of the IRWIN icons draws on art-historical resources, primarily through visual appropriation, whereas the icons as field effect draw on the theological impress of that field without returning to the aesthetic or to sublimity as de-naturalized state. The presence of the figures of the animals is not unlike the ultimate purpose of Leo Steinberg's reading of sexualized images of the crucified Christ, in *The Sexuality of Christ in Renaissance Art and in Modern Oblivion* (1983).[8] Those images were far from scandalous insofar as they were charged with symbolic versus libidinal meaning. The libidinal economy of those images is what may also be found in the operative field of the presentation of icons by IRWIN when they escape singularity and combine forces with the totemic natural largess of the animal, or, more properly, *animality*. This combination of animality and iconicity, far from being heretical, has a long lineage in religious manuscript art — Paradise often shown as human figures with animal heads dining in a garden. The combination of icons, or their configuration, re-empowers the very nature of iconicity through icons. The age-less essence of the mythic comes full circle — into the here and now — through a topological jouissance that invokes the transpositionality of Eros and Thanatos. In the icons of IRWIN, the daemon of the classical world has somehow come into the artwork through a back door, providing an élan vital, which, it may be argued, was always present in the icon anyway in sublimated form.

The answers provided to questions by the icons, most of all through the linguistic resources of those answers, combined with the new questions to those answers provided by IRWIN, as combined "conversation," conveys the elasticity of the presentism of the icon. That elasticity opens onto the issues of generativity and givenness. The icons of IRWIN, intimately related to the larger agenda of the NSK State, a "state of mind" after all, cannot be divorced from that dynamic field that includes operativity and inoperativity, historicity and a-historicity, plus theology

---

8   Leo Steinberg, *The Sexuality of Christ in Renaissance Art and in Modern Oblivion* (New York: Pantheon Books, 1983).

and a-theology. They register *there,* and then they depart *there.* Oddly, they depart in two directions: they head back to origins, or toward their absolute givenness and their tautological condition (mute or otherwise); and, they head out into generativity and re-combination, as artefacts and as artworks (propositions or provocations) — as aeons, as it were. As artworks, they endure the multiple transformations of the artwork across markets — a probable cause for their being assembled under the title of "Kapital 2018," and a nonetheless proper test of their premise as collective emissaries from NSK across several decades.[9]

In departing in two directions, in the manner noted, the icons of IRWIN may be said to "split themselves in two." Heading in two directions at once causes such a split. The split occurs however in the liminality of the methodology of the works, not in the works per se. The works per se escape this splitting, which might also be best provisioned as test of markets, while also an inescapably seminal address to markets on behalf of an austere givenness and a tautological justification for works. These two directions may be termed: further inward, and, out into the world. *Further inward* is, however, where we find the sought-after conversation.

A-theological and theological expressivity is present in the presentism that comes and goes in the eye of the beholder, in Orthodox icons, and in the icons of IRWIN. The presentism is a form of Grace, for works. This re-launches long-term and long-distanced reflection, in the post-phenomenological and post-contemporary sense. It is that paradox that inhabits the icon both as singular object and as field effect. The icons of IRWIN re-establish this possible conversation with icons through the two-fold operative field of profanation and splitting — both apparent artistic tricks to get icons to speak. That IRWIN transfers that agency back to the works as works suggests that the icons of

---

9   See *NSK from Kapital to Capital: Neue Slowenische Kunst — An Event of the Final Decade of Yugoslavia,* eds. Zdenka Badovinac, Eda Čufer, and Anthony Gardner (Cambridge: MIT Press, 2015). Catalogue of an exhibition held at Moderna galerija, Ljubljana, Slovenia, May 11–August 16, 2015.

IRWIN might, indeed, have a conversation with IRWIN about that agency and about that field effect from which they operate, proceeding and receding. No doubt that conversation is already in the works anyway, through their very incarnational spirit across artistic and historical times. In many respects the conversation is, then, merely overheard.

VIII. The Silent Metric of the Conversation

The metric of the work is not vitalism. Instead, the metric is vitalism and its other — vitalism and not-vitalism. Vitalism is cancelled in the tautological state the work embodies as autonomous and apparently mute work. As exquisite corpse, the iterative and aleatory qualities of the performative sessions described above, to prompt a conversation through silence, connote what is at play through the conversation — i.e., intentionality and accident, plus Freudian slip and coincidence. The sequencing or metric of the sessions sets in motion a developmental model for the writing of the work of artistic scholarship. The reconstruction of the event, through graphic means and text, also confers upon the open work (which could go on for some time) the possibility of agency doubled. This doubling of agency includes the art-historical origins and the art-critical merit of the icons of IRWIN, however eclipsed or obscured by their own tautological states, as icons and as works of art, and the history of the event of the ongoing performance-based sessions. That history, constituted by the textual and graphic documentation, before and after the event of the sessions, the silent interactions of the Hierophant and the Sibyl, both quite convinced they are only facilitating a conversation, and the peculiar silent conversation across and between images, with words appearing out of thin air, all confer upon the event of the conversation (séance) an ever-increasing fold into which participant and observer may fall and/or disappear. This developing internal metric is premised upon the visual and visceral resources of the icons and the linguistic resources of the ongoing conversation. The slippage noted above, while nominally Freudian, suggests that unconscious and conscious forces within the works proper (both the borrowed works and the developing work) have, in some other-worldly manner, begun to form a type of economy or compact bridging two worlds, revealing in the process what the icons have otherwise kept secret, their so-called unsayability a ruse.

A third scenario, or scene, in this theatrical questioning of the icons and of IRWIN might then take the following form.

IX. A Hypothetical Session Three

The Theater

The five members of IRWIN enter the darkened theater carrying a bundle of black cloth. Perhaps martial music is playing.[10] They unfold the black cloth to create a black square on the floor of the theater.[11] Furniture is brought into the black square to establish the set. The black square becomes a theater within the theater. They take their positions as "distinguished panel" at the long table.

---

10 For example, the music by Luciano Berio that opens Chris Marker's *Le fond de l'air est rouge* (1977) (Icarus Films, 2008), DVD. "Musica notturna nelle strade di Madrid de Luciano Berio, d'après le quintette n° 60 de Boccherini, Orchestre national de Radio-France, direction Pietro Belugi." Christophe Chazalon, "Longs métrages de Chris Marker," *chrismarker.ch,* n.d., http://chrismarker.ch/longs-metrages-de-chris-marker-52.html. For the opening sequence (about four minutes), see https://www.youtube.com/watch?v=dO1E4GYjF1s.

11 This scenario is based on the 30-minute action by IRWIN and Michael Benson known as "Black Square on Red Square," June 6, 1992. The 30-minute action (staged between 2–3pm) consisted of spreading out a 22m × 22m square made of black fabric in the central part of Red Square in Moscow. "IRWIN and Michael Benson performed the artistic action in collaboration with N. Abalakova (Tot-Art), D. Ariupin, M. Breznik, S. Bugayev (Africa), Charles, E. Cufer, B. Edelman, F. Fleck, J. Harten, J. Kollerova, V. Kesic, I. Koulik, E. and V. Kurlandzev, G. Kurierova, I. Smirnova, K. Tschouvaschew, K. Turchina and D. Zivadinov." A short video of this event was acquired by the Tate in February 2020. *Black Square on the Red Square,* 1992, digital file, 3'15", edition of 5 (footage of Moscow TV and Kinteticon Pictures, edited by Igor Zupe). Gregor Podnar, Berlin, "Press Release," February 22, 2020.

IRWIN is seated stage left as a distinguished panel of "experts" on the icons of IRWIN. The set up resembles an academic conference or symposium. A looped projection of the fifteen icons from Session One provides visual support for the ongoing conversation. Live or recorded ambient music provides the necessary soundscape.

A new set of white cards has been prepared. Set One and Two now have the original four questions to the icons printed on them and the resulting fifteen answers from the icons. There are nineteen cards. They are numbered to permit a second level of mathematical calculation to be inferred, after the fact. A third set of cards has the fifteen new questions provided by IRWIN for the fifteen original answers provided by the icons. They are also numbered.

These three sets of cards will become the basis for the conversation between IRWIN and the icons, yet based on chance or random selection. IRWIN is blindfolded and cannot see the cards or the questions or answers. The exchange will be conducted by fanning each group of cards and asking one of the artists to select a card. This card will then be paired with the next selection conducted in the same manner. Various versions of the combination of cards might be developed based on the pairings — i.e., four questions and fifteen answers; fifteen answers and fifteen questions; etc.

The cards will be presented to IRWIN for blind recombination, in this manner, the premise being that the internal agency of the ongoing constructed event will precipitate appropriate correspondences or alignments between questions and answers and answers and questions.

Three Sets of Cards

1. The original four questions
2. The original fifteen answers
3. The fifteen new questions

The Setting

The reading of the cards takes place in a small theater with table and chairs and a looped projection. Live or recorded ambient music sets the mood.

The Hierophant and the Sibyl from Sessions One and Two are present, to facilitate the conversation. The Hierophant presents the cards to IRWIN and the Sibyl records the outcome. Because the cards are numbered, the Sibyl may record simply the numerical pairings. The subsequent linguistic values may then be recorded at any time — i.e., after the session, and toward extension of the textual record.

The entire exchange is conducted in a wordless or silent manner. Gestures and properties are permitted to speak.

The Record

The silent conversation is filmed and photographed. The new alignment of questions and answers, and answers and questions, is then taken into post-production for transcription and interpretation. The video and photography become the basis for Session Four — thematics and scenarios to be determined by the outcome of Session Three.

The Topology

A topology of three interrelated, not-mutually-exclusive possibilities for "The Icons of IRWIN" study emerges:

1. The scenarios are entirely invented and have no real value or relationship to the icons of IRWIN;
2. The scenarios engage with and interact with the generative value of the icons of IRWIN;
3. The scenarios are entirely internal to "The Icons of IRWIN" event and have value only in terms of that event.

X. Postscript

Only Session One and Session Two of "The Icons of IRWIN" project have been staged as of this writing. Session Three, as outlined above, is a hypothesis in pursuit of a timeframe and venue.

10

Preposterous Presentism

I.

At the end of the night,
The Girl and The Book.
And all that has
Been lost to time
Is washed away.

In the slow ebb and flow,
The Girl and The Book.
And what's to come
Has passed away—
Into pages and through words.

At the end of the book,
The Girl and The Book.
And all that has transpired
No longer lost but made
To weather passing days.

In the eye and the heart,
The Girl and The Book.
And she now over nine years

Placed amongst the pages —
Words, winds, and waves.

At the sea and the shore,
The Girl and The Book.
And both are washed
By wind and waves —
All pages flown away.

At the end of the day,
The Girl and The Book.
And as the night descends
Two become one again —
And words all disappear.

As the stars rise and fall,
The Girl and The Book.
And in these borrowed words
Worlds are made to sing
Through holy, ancient vigil.

II.

At the end of the night,
The Girl and The Book.
And all that has
Been lost to time
Slowly gives way.

In the pale ebb and flow,
The Girl and The Book.
And what's to come
Has sailed away —
Into pages and through words.

At the end of the book,
The Girl and The Book.

And all that has transpired
No longer lost but made
To weather passing days.

In the eye and the heart,
The Girl and The Book.
And she now three years thrice
Placed amongst the pages —
Words, winds, and waves.

At the sea and the shore,
The Girl and The Book.
And both are washed
By wind and waves —
All pages made anew.

At the end of the day,
The Girl and The Book.
And as the night descends
Two become one again —
Where silent words appear.

As the stars rise and pass,
The Girl and The Book.
And in these borrowed words
Worlds are made to sing —
Through slow, archaic vigil.

III.

At the end of the night,
The Girl and The Book.
And all that has
Been lost in time
Slowly returns.

In the pale ebb and flow,
The Girl and The Book.
And what's to come
Now sails away —
Into pages and through words.

At the end of the book,
The Girl and The Book.
And all that has transpired
No longer lost but made
To weather passing days.

In the eye and the heart,
The Girl and The Book.
And she now three years thrice
Placed amongst the pages —
Words, winds, and waves.

At the sea and the shore,
The Girl and The Book.
And both are swept
By wind and waves —
All pages made anew.

At the end of the day,
The Girl and The Book.
And as the night descends
Two become one again —
Soliloquy and silence.

As the stars rise and pass,
The Girl and The Book.
And with these trembling words
Worlds are made to sing —
The lost, archaic timbre.

11

Agent Intellect and Black Zones

The first image he told me about was of three children on a road in Iceland, in 1965. He said that for him it was the image of happiness and also that he had tried several times to link it to other images, but it never worked. He wrote me: one day I'll have to put it all alone at the beginning of a film with a long piece of black leader; if they don't see happiness in the picture, at least they'll see the black.[1]

— Chris Marker

I. Aristoteleanism

And this is the purpose of all of the sciences, that in all of them faith is strengthened, God is honored, character is formed, and consolations are derived consisting in the union of the spouse with her Beloved: a union that takes place through love, to the attainment of which the whole purpose of sacred Scripture, and consequently, every illumination descending from above, is directed — a union without which all knowledge is empty.[2]

— Saint Bonaventure

1   Chris Marker, *Sans soleil* (1982).
2   Conclusion to Bonaventure, *Reduction of the Arts to Theology* (*De reduc-tion artium ad theologiam*). See Bonaventure, *Saint Bonaventure's De reductione atrium ad theologiam: A Commentary*, ed. and trans. Emma

To bury spent disciplinary or discursive justifications for knowledge as property and reverse the commodification of the knowledge commons to exploitable and scalable "intellectual property," do we need another Verdun, which Capitalism would appear to be only so happy to supply?[3] Or is it possible to restore the immemorial coordinates of cultural production as formalized in "common law" by turning to the Holy Trinity of conceptual thought proper — that elegant, spare, and wintry tableau that haunts all forms of formative knowledge production? Through T.S. Eliot's bleak visions, operating in apparent reverse, we might reach across centuries to examine Bonaventure's reduction of the liberal arts to theology — theology, not religion, and theology as inter-subjective truth, not dogma. This communitarian spirit of intellectual austerities is the transitional state between grey areas (instrumental reason) and black zones (revelation or reverie). If it passes through subjective night, as Jacques Maritain suggests, via negative or apophatic theology, inclusive of negative dialectics, it does so in service to the impersonal agencies of that anterior sky in which stars and constellations (both old and new constellations of thought) appear or re-appear out of a proverbial no-where.[4] "La vita nuova," perhaps — but also a strange diminution in the analogical, for/

Thérèse Healy, 2nd edn. (Saint Bonaventure: Franciscan Institute, Saint Bonaventure University, 1955); cited in Armand A. Maurer, CSB, *Medieval Philosophy* (Toronto: Pontifical Institute of Mediaeval Studies, 1962), 139–40. See also Bonaventure, *The Works of Bonaventure*, trans. José de Vinck, 5 vols. (Paterson: Saint Anthony Guild Press, 1960–1970).

3 Regarding the historic intransigence on the part of Capital to relinquish or reduce its outsized share of global equity, see the conclusion to Thomas Piketty, *Capital in the Twenty-first Century*, trans. Arthur Goldhammer (Cambridge: Belknap Press, 2014), 571–77. First published as *Le capital au XXIe siècle* (Paris: Éditions du Seuil, 2013). "In the twentieth century, it took two world wars to wipe away the past and significantly reduce the return on capital, thereby creating the illusion that the fundamental structural contradiction of capitalism ($r > g$) had been overcome" (ibid., 572).

4 See Theodor W. Adorno, *Minima Moralia: Reflections from Damaged Life*, trans. E.F.N. Jephcott (London: Verso, 1974). "Anterior sky" is derived from a line in Stéphane Mallarmé's justly famous poem "Les fenêtres": "À renaître ... / Au ciel antérieur où fleurit la Beauté."

toward the anagogical. Therefore, the strange, wintry, and wonderful — or, Bonaventure's "union without which all knowledge is empty."

The problem of Agent Intellect, as controversy, has never quite gone away — with its origins in Aristotle's *De anima* and its subsequent elaborations and disputations reaching from the Islamic Aristotelians, Averroes and Avicenna, to St. Thomas Aquinas.[5] The issue of whether Agent Intellect is independent of human agency or transcendent to all intellectual activity suggests that this possible impersonal agency is the ultimate ghost in the machinery of thought. The universalizing tendencies of such a power (or source of power) are exceptionally elastic and, ultimately, indeterminate. If it belongs to mankind, as Avicenna thought, and not to individual subjects per se (not embedded within the intellectual capacities of souls), the penultimate question/issue becomes, What or *where* is such a power? Is this not the very origin of the idea of a knowledge commons? Assimilation to cultural patrimony is quite obviously not the same thing as the assimilation to the circuit of Capital. More critically, *How* is such a power to be accessed? According to Averroes: "The agent intellect is the last of the celestial Intelligences and moves the lunar sphere; the material intellect receives intelligible forms abstracted by the agent intellect. These intellects are not united to individual man by their substances, but only by their activity."[6] Thus, signatures or intelligences (lights) are what matter. Grey areas shade into black zones, and reverie is birthright, whereas instrumentalized reason or abject utilitarianism is a prison-house for Spirit.

Notably, Aquinas disputed the Aristotelian views of Averroes and Avicenna (Latin Averroism) and placed Agent Intellect firmly within the bounds of the human soul, differing with other Medieval theologians in the process, yet primarily in terms of

---

5   Avicenna, *Liber de anima, seu sextus de naturalibus,* ed. Simone van Riet (Louvain and Leiden: Peeters and E.J. Brill, 1972), I:5.

6   Tomáš Nejeschleba, "Thomas Aquinas and the Early Franciscan School on the Agent Intellect," *Verbum* 6, no. 1 (2004): 70.

the relation between Agent Intellect and Possible Intellect — the latter term connoting mere cognition. Anselm of Canterbury, for example, considered Agent Intellect co-equivalent to angelic intelligences. More importantly, however, is what occurs when one follows the argument backward to the early Franciscan School, prior to Aquinas, when, in effect, the major schoolmen said "Yes" to utterly contradictory statements concerning what exactly Agent Intellect was once it was operative within human cognition proper. The key figures here are Alexander of Hales and John of La Rochelle, the latter a teacher of Bonaventure. For example:

> In John of La Rochelle's view we can call the agent intellect both God and angel, and part of the soul with respect to different objects of cognition. God is the agent intellect for our knowledge of things higher than the soul, the angel is the agent intellect (in the sense of revelation or instruction) for our knowledge of things on the same level as the soul and, finally, the agent is a light innate in the soul for our knowledge of things that lie within the soul or below it.[7]

Thus, Bonaventure and many Franciscans to follow maintained a dual vigil for the transcendental and contingent conditions for knowledge, both personal and collective:

> The reason for the double-meaning of the agent intellect lies in the Franciscans' characteristic and well-known attitude towards theology and philosophy. They tried to reconcile principles of Aristotelian philosophy with the Augustinian fundament of theology. With respect to noetics this means that they had to unify the Aristotelian theory of abstraction and the doctrine of the agent intellect, which Aristotle had already compared to light, with the Augustinian theory of illumination and the division of the human intellect into two

---

7   Ibid., 76.

faces, the higher, which is illuminated from God, and the lower, which is not illuminated.[8]

Thus we have grey areas and black zones, and all of the attendant problems of locating the place and means whereby the Imaginary (Possible Intellect) may be disciplined and/or illumined. Thus, the condemned thesis 118 of 1277 proceeds as follows: "That the agent intellect is a separate substance higher than the possible intellect, and that with respect to the substance, potency and operation it is separated from the body, and that it is not a form of human body."[9] This is but one of 219 Averroistic-Thomist theses condemned at Paris after Aquinas's death in 1274.

Certainly, this dual vision of Agent Intellect (both in its disputatious aspects and in the Franciscan doubling or tripling of its agency proper) suggests that the true issue is not whether it subsists as impersonal agency in the natural world (as a cosmological principle, for example) but, instead, whether it inhabits human intellectual activity and the products of the same. For the ambivalence seems less about whether Agent Intellect is outside *of* (or transcendent *to*) all human subjective states, as its other, than whether human agency without Agent Intellect has any merit whatsoever; and, in terms of disciplinarity or the knowledge commons, the question would be as to whether the production of forms of knowledge transcends mere utility and/or supports degraded forms of experience of this larger economy that, on the one hand, *is* cosmological and, on the other hand, *is* transcendental.

In the latter case, all of the various problems of privileging a universal intelligence collide with worldly endeavors that may, indeed, be productive of virtual prison-houses. The latter state would seem to be the path of Capital today as it serves merely its own interests — not the interest of individuals and certainly

---

8   Ibid., 77.
9   Ibid., 78; with reference to Roland Hissette, ed., *Enquête sur les 219 articles condamnés à Paris le 7 Mars 1277* (Louvain and Paris: Publications Universitaires and Vander-Oyez, 1977), 193.

not the interest of the commons. In the first instance, language is always the First Instance for suspect motives and/or ideological sleights of hand; for, false claims to transcendental categories via Reason do, indeed, produce monsters. Such is the source of ideology — market ideology or otherwise. In the former case, when Agent Intellect is cosmological, the multiple disciplines of natural science and philosophy (or natural philosophy) take on exceptional importance to the critique of disciplines and forms of knowledge production that purportedly rely on this vision of universal, non-ideological intelligence. In both cases, there are as many problems as possible virtues, insofar as, since the divorce of theology and natural science, the orphaned middle ground has most often been moral philosophy and ethics. One very obvious analogue for the potential fusion of these discordant worldviews is to incorporate the intelligence embedded in natural systems directly and without mediation into human systems, which need not to be at odds with that larger universal economy (a semi-divine economy). Yet the inordinate nightmare of entropy follows upon every attempt to build synthetic systems that absorb and/or privilege natural systems alone, and the technocratic bias of contemporary culture betrays, repeatedly, any accord between competing visions, provoking the endless recourse to Apocalypse.

II. Franciscanism

> It was as though the real were cut in half by a door …. The door is the same one on both sides. The Earth, the visible, the tangible, time and space, are on this side; Heaven, the invisible, the eternal, the infinite, are on the other side. But everything is one, congruent, logical and true. The door which is Christ simultaneously rules here and the beyond with his love, crucified on this side, glorified on the other.[10]
>
> — Carlo Carretto

---

10 Carlo Carretto, *I, Francis: The Spirit of St. Francis of Assisi* (London: Collins, 1982), 128–29. First published as *Io, Francesco* (Assisi: Cittadella

This Medieval debate is interesting *today* if only because *then* the problem was the differing worldviews of the Augustinians and the Thomists — with the Augustinians and Franciscans privileging black zones, and the Thomists privileging grey areas. In terms of historical merit, the debate has lasted well into the first quarter of the twenty-first century primarily because there was no unitary, Medieval scholastic worldview (as there is no unitary Modern worldview), despite attempts to claim such — and the debates at the University of Paris Faculty of Arts in the thirteenth century concerned not so much the production of canon or dogma but the relationship of philosophy to theology (notwithstanding the various attempts by the authorities to shut down debate, plus warnings to theologians not to become philosophers). Indeed, it would seem that the chief argument between Bonaventure and Aquinas had to do with whether these two forms of knowledge (what we would today call disciplines) are different, and whether they *should* be different. Aquinas seems to have solidified the separation, perhaps unwittingly, while the Augustinians and the Franciscans were arguing for the preservation of philosophy (and metaphysics) *as* theology — and a proper study of whether this truly meant philosophy *as* subordinate to theology, or not, would resolve many of the petty arguments that persist in terms of what constitutes knowledge and what constitutes mere instrumental reason. Subsequent skirmishes generally further developed the schism, while around 1900 the argument returned in terms of the historiography of the Medieval world system and the various forms of high scholasticism that dealt with the issue of the created (eternal) world, best described as the focus of the sciences, and the uncreated (ideal) world, the realm of ideas and the source for knowledge per se, inclusive of all of the associated questions and non-answers attributed to not-knowledge, or revelation, always more or less left unaddressed due to the failure of

---

Editrice, 1980).

language to properly reflect what was, after all, subjective, inter-subjective, and onto-subjective, pre-conscious experience.[11]

If Bonaventure and the Franciscans could say "Yes" (or "All of the above") to whether Agent Intellect "subsides" within human cognition, outside of it (in angelic beings, in the cosmos, etc.), or with a transcendent (absent) God, it is more than apparent that they were attempting to preserve the sacred province of affective thought as such — or thought undivided (precluding the production of two contradictory, and historically antithetical realms). "Hence, according to [Étienne] Gilson, the philosophy of Aristotle compelled the thirteenth-century theologians to reexamine the proper relation of natural reason to Christian revelation; as a consequence, the great scholastic systems were born."[12] Nevertheless, Gilson's most controversial conclusions may be said to revolve around his quarantine of Bonaventure and his claims that the Franciscan harbored an irresolvable antipathy to Aristotelianism. According to Gilson, Bonaventure evaluated Aristotelian philosophy as "one who has understood it, seen through it, and passed beyond it."[13] By 1270 the verdict was in. Bonaventure refused Thomism and Aquinas committed himself to the elaboration of an autonomous philosophy, one according to Bonaventure that exposed him to inevitable error. That Aquinas would dramatically stop writing altogether on December 6, 1273 suggests that Bonaventure was, after all, right.

Several differences of opinion between Bonaventure and Aquinas in the controversy concerning Agent Intellect are instructive in terms of the critique underway here of knowledge production and the biases given most especially to singular disciplines that rely on so-called objective knowledge (or natural reason), converting everything in the process to spectral com-

---

11 Regarding the pre-conscious self, see Jacques Maritain, *Creative Intuition in Art and Poetry,* A.W. Mellon Lectures in the Fine Arts (Cleveland: Meridian Books, 1954).

12 John Francis Quinn, *The Historical Constitution of St. Bonaventure's Philosophy* (Toronto: Pontifical Institute of Mediaeval Studies, 1973), 23.

13 Ibid., 24; with reference to Étienne Gilson, *La philosophie de Saint Bonaventure* (Paris: J. Vrin, 1924).

modity. For, as it has been said, in times of crisis Augustine almost always makes a re-appearance.

Thus, the Augustinianism of Bonaventure (and the term *Augustinianism* was only coined during the controversies of the thirteenth century) is the key. According to Gilson, Bonaventure was safeguarding certain traditional, patristic principles against creeping Aristotelianism. The main issue was what might be called the cosmological worldview that almost always signals a medieval mindset. The Agent Intellect controversy was part and parcel of a larger set of disagreements that were only resolved by the separation of Philosophy and Theology. "By founding his doctrine on the self-consciousness of the soul, Bonaventure clung to the Augustinian tradition while grounding his Christian philosophy in the experience of his interior life."[14] The struggle between Bonaventure and Aquinas (and they were, after all, colleagues) was quite simply about what constitutes the highest form of knowing anything. While they both reverted to revelation, they also did so in different ways. "Bonaventure, Gilson stated, did not formulate his theology according to the norms of Aristotelean science. Following rather the Augustinian tradition, he recorded his personal experience of the Christian life without expressing it in an objective, or scientific, manner.... Bonaventure modelled his theology after the ideal of Augustinian wisdom; so he developed a theological wisdom which was inseparable from his own experience."[15]

Accordingly, Bonaventure's and Aquinas's worlds collide in the manner in which the outer, objective world and the inner, subjective world are dealt with. The role of intellect is central — Augustinians reserved knowledge (truth) for the internal tableau of direct illumination from the divine, not Aristotelian abstraction as such, nor an operation of the intellect. Here Pascal's two infinities come into view. Bonaventure resisted permitting illumination (revelation) to be a guarantor of natural

---

14 Gilson, *La philosophie de Saint Bonaventure,* paraphrased by Quinn, *The Historical Constitution of St. Bonaventure's Philosophy,* 25.

15 Quinn, *The Historical Constitution of St. Bonaventure's Philosophy,* 41.

reason (Aristotelian abstraction); and, again, it required a certain acceptance of paradoxes, or the rejection of attempting to rationalize or reconcile discordant principles that effectively underscored that knowledge is not unitary.[16] As a result, "to solve some problems in the natural order, [Bonaventure's] philosophy relied on a supernatural principle."[17] One exceptional example is the concept of the necessity of grace for all creatures to merely exist. In the case of animals, Bonaventure simply resorted to Augustine's doctrine of seminal principles. In the case of humans, Bonaventure kicked the entire question upstream, placing infallibility out of reach of contingent intellect. Far from hedging his bets, in the case of the status of human existence, Bonaventure simply jettisoned the need to rationalize what was, in effect, a transcendental category of experience (Being as such). But he again turned to Augustine for support, this time utilizing the well-known metaphor of the double mirror that permits divine illumination to reach contingent intellect, if the latter is turned in the direction of the divine. This judgment of cognition as black mirror, a type of internal Claude glass, is the very image of black zones (and revelation as path to knowledge). The path taken by Aquinas and Duns Scotus was the path not taken by Bonaventure. "Bonaventure withheld from the human intellect a power which would be sufficient for knowing truth with certitude."[18] According to Gilson, Bonaventure was safeguarding a particular worldview (an interior/anterior vista) "to protect a Christian understanding of creation, divine providence, illumination and moral guidance."[19]

The Neo-platonism is palpable, and an intermediary world of *semi*-divine ideas seems to be the key nonetheless. If both Bonaventure and Aquinas more or less grappled with Aristotle's natural philosophy in different ways, and if each retained that

---

16 Ibid., 39.

17 Ibid.

18 Gilson, *La philosophie de Saint Bonaventure,* paraphrased by Quinn, *The Historical Constitution of St. Bonaventure's Philosophy,* 40.

19 Gilson, *La philosophie de Saint Bonaventure,* paraphrased by Quinn, *The Historical Constitution of St. Bonaventure's Philosophy,* 41.

which Aristotle rejected (the Platonic theory of divine ideas), the matter then returns (and rests) in where and how ideas are accessed; the result is a battleground between immutable, universal truths and contingent knowledge (or the mere administration of things). It might be argued that the historically determined triumph of the administrative intellect sponsored the emergence of capitalism.[20]

It is possible, then, to see the entire scholastic operation sliding downhill and the mere description and administration (manipulation) of things and people becoming the entire point. The great scandals coming, of course, were named Giordano Bruno, Galileo, and Copernicus, plus Savonarola.[21] Furthermore, it is possible to detect in the shadows the instantiation of new models of power and control, with the ascendance of Thomism unnecessarily burdened with the incipient power struggles within the Church between secular and sacred concerns. Thomism could be seen in such a light as a threshold crossed historically, never to be re-crossed other than personally (or existentially) — a metaphysical Rubicon. Augustinianism (as the antithesis), in turn, shelters a certain generous latitude within thought that privileges immemorial reserves within subjectivity (almost always the enemy and victim of power). The return (and/or the suppression) of the singular subject is, in this way, a constant theme in the symphonic histories of knowledge production and

---

20 See, for example, Max Weber's arguments concerning "the disenchantment of the world" (*die Entzauberung der Welt*) via the privileging of instrumental reason. Max Weber, *Readings and Commentary on Modernity*, ed. Stephen Kalberg (Malden: Blackwell, 2005). See also contemporary and post-contemporary re-wilding strategies in cultural production, which platform and finance capitalism nonetheless attempts to tame and mine. These strategies are, arguably, the result of the cyclical appearance of proverbial ubiquity, or the ennui that appears when cultural production has exhausted one set of representational or critical conventions and seeks to re-engage what has effectively been neutralized through assimilation to academic or artistic discourse.

21 Regarding this period, see Fernand Hallyn, *The Poetic Structure of the World: Copernicus and Kepler*, trans. Donald M. Leslie (New York: Zone Books, 1990). First published as *La structure poétique du monde: Copernic, Kepler* (Paris: Éditions du Seuil, 1987).

humanist disciplines. And the singular subject or, in modern terms, "citizen," is the foundation of both polis and commons. It is for this reason that the approach of Capital, or for that matter any exploitative ideology, to the gates of subjectivity is utterly frightening.[22]

It is ideational Franciscanism that merits a closer look today for traces of an alternative. And it is the "right to have no rights" that merits utmost scrutiny — a coinage credited to Hugh of Digne concerning the early Franciscan refusal of property and an elective embrace of holy poverty.[23] This highly principled embrace of Christian virtue defined subsequent anarcho-Christian forms of self-government and is not entirely inconsistent with anarcho-socialist agendas. That a schism between the Conventuals and the Spirituals centered on ownership of property (as the Franciscan order began to receive major gifts from generous patrons) only further underscores the significance of the renunciation of worldly rights for higher rights — the latter generally reducible to the right to live where and as one wishes. The chief merit of this renunciation of rights is, notably, that in renouncing such rights the arrogation of those rights by anyone else is impossible.

An extended citation from *Einzige und sein Eigentum* (1844) by Max Stirner, bête noire of Karl Marx, is instructive:

> The time was politically so agitated that, as is said in the gospels, people thought they could not accuse the founder of Christianity more successfully than if they arraigned him for "political intrigue", and yet the same gospels report that he was precisely the one who took the least part in these political doings. But why was he not a revolutionary, not a dema-

---

22 See Malcolm Harris, *Kids These Days: Human Capital and the Making of Millennials* (New York: Little, Brown and Company, 2017).

23 Giorgio Agamben, *The Highest Poverty: Monastic Rules and Form-of-Life*, trans. Adam Kotsko (Stanford: Stanford University Press, 2013); with reference to Hugh of Digne, "De finibus paupertatis," *Archivum Franciscanum Historicum* 5 (1912): 277–90. First published as *Altissima povertà: Regole monastiche e forma di vita* (Vicenza: Neri Pozza, 2011).

gogue, as the Jews would gladly have seen him? Why was
he not a liberal? Because he expected no salvation from a
change of *conditions,* and this whole business was indifferent to him. He was not a revolutionary, like Caesar, but an
insurgent: not a state-overturner, but one who straightened
himself up. That was why it was for him only a matter of "Be
ye wise as serpents", which expresses the same sense as, in
the special case, that "Give to the emperor that which is the
emperor's"; for he was not carrying on any liberal or political
fight against the established authorities, but wanted to walk
his *own* way, untroubled about, and undisturbed by, these
authorities. Not less indifferent to him than the government
were its enemies, for neither understood what he wanted,
and he had only to keep them off from him with the wisdom
of the serpent. But, even though not a ringleader of popular
mutiny, not a demagogue or revolutionary, he (and every one
of the ancient Christians) was so much the more an *insurgent*
who lifted himself above everything that seemed so sublime
to the government and its opponents, and absolved himself
from everything that they remained bound to, and who at
the same time cut off the sources of life of the whole heathen
world, with which the established state must wither away as
a matter of course; precisely because he put from him the
upsetting of the established, he was its deadly enemy and real
annihilator; for he walled it in, confidently and recklessly
carrying up the building of *his* temple over it, without heed-
ing the pains of the immured.[24]

---

24 Max Stirner, *The Ego and Its Own,* ed. David Leopold, trans. Steven T.
Byington (Cambridge: Cambridge University Press, 1995), 280–81. First
published as *Der Einzige und sein Eigentum* (Leipzig: Otto Wigand, 1844).
For Stirner and Marx, see Jacques Derrida, *Specters of Marx: The State of
the Debt, the Work of Mourning, and the New International,* trans. Peggy
Kamuf (New York: Routledge, 1994). First published as *Spectres de Marx:
L'état de la dette, le travail du deuil et la nouvelle Internationale* (Paris: Édi-
tions Galilée, 1993).

III. Coda

In terms of prior art, or the contorted logic of the legal arguments for subsuming previously existing forms of knowledge,
Agent Intellect is the foundation for immemoriality, immemoriality is the foundation for the commons and common law, the
commons and common law are the foundation for statutory
law, and statutory law is the foundation for intellectual property rights (patents, licenses, and copyright).[25] Given the above
arguments, Franciscanism and "the right to have no rights" may
be seen as an early, yet pivotal attempt to protect immemoriality itself (in Platonic terms, the dynamic field known as anamnesis) and the attendant internal prospects for individuals and
free subjectivity. In terms of the rights of citizens and the commons, this same logic suggests that the subjective conditions
here denoted *black zones* are the foundational state for access to
the "Kingdom of God" (which is always within), however that
is defined and however that is experienced. Capital would appear, then, to have its sights set on controlling and monetizing
Pascal's and Kant's two infinities. Indeed, "God did not die, He
was transformed into money."[26] The great copyright robbery underway since around 2000 races ahead as technology permits

---

25 What, for example, might we find "inside of" the various VR patents cre-
    ated by Jaron Lanier in the 1980s, before he sold them to Sun Microsys-
    tems in 1999? See also Caroline A. Jones, "In Praise of Wetware," *Ethics,
    Computing and AI, MIT SHASS,* February 18, 2019, https://shass.mit.edu/
    news/news-2019-ethics-and-ai-praise-wetware-caroline-jones. "As we en-
    shrine computation as the core of smartness, we would be well advised to
    think of the complexity of our 'wet' cognition, which entails a much more
    distributed notion of intelligence that goes well beyond the sacred cranium
    and may not even be bounded by our own skin" (ibid). And: "Our adaptive
    and responsive wetware, and its dependence on a larger living ecosystem,
    is something I recommend we try to understand more fully before claim-
    ing that it is 'intelligence' we've produced in our machines, or modeled by
    computation alone" (ibid).

26 Giorgio Agamben and Peppe Savà, "'God Didn't Die, He was Transformed
    into Money': An Interview with Giorgio Agamben," *Libcom,* February
    10, 2014, https://libcom.org/library/god-didnt-die-he-was-transformed-
    money-interview-giorgio-agamben-peppe-sav%C3%A0.

regimes of surveillance for collecting tribute or imposing fines, while the surveillance state takes care of negating civil rights or the rights of citizens.[27] This dual campaign, by Capital and by State, represents a turning point for the very concept of the commons and civil society. The double threat for resistance or insurgency is the usual threat — Apocalypse (a new Verdun).

A version of this essay first appeared as Section I of Part I, Essay III, "Mnemonics: Elegant, Spare, Wintry," in Gavin Keeney, Not-I/Thou: The Other Subject of Art and Architecture *(Newcastle upon Tyne: Cambridge Scholars Publishing, 2014).*

---

27 "In the shadows of the 'copyright grab' that is currently taking place at the European and international political level, a massive confiscation of authors' rights, possibly much more destructive to society, is taking place. Media concentration, media convergence and the lure of multimedia product development have inspired media companies all over the world to redraft their standard publishing or production contracts in such a way as to effectively strip the authors of their pecuniary rights entirely." P. Bernt Hugenholtz, "The Great Copyright Robbery: Rights Allocation in a Digital Environment," *University of Amsterdam Institute for Information Law,* April 5, 2000, https://www.ivir.nl/publicaties/download/thegreatcopyright-robbery.pdf.

12

"The Law Disappears ..."

The law which is studied but no longer practiced is the gate to justice.[1]

— Walter Benjamin

I. Subjects and Works

Everywhere the walls separate the desperate poor from those who hope against hope to stay relatively rich. The walls cross every sphere, from crop cultivation to health care. [...] The choice of meaning in the world today is here between the two sides of the wall. The wall is also inside each one of us. Whatever our circumstances, we can choose within ourselves which side of the wall we are attuned to.[2]

— John Berger

For the law of copyright and the various regimes of command and control given to the exploitation of the knowledge commons

---

1   Walter Benjamin, "Franz Kafka: On the Tenth Anniversary of his Death," 794–818, in Walter Benjamin, *Walter Benjamin: Selected Writings,* Vol. 2, *1927–1934,* eds. Howard Eiland and Michael W. Jennings, trans. Edmund Jephcott and Kingsley Shorter (Cambridge: Belknap Press, 1999), 815.
2   John Berger, *Hold Everything Dear: Dispatches on Survival and Resistance* (New York: Knopf Doubleday, 2009), 94.

to *dis-appear,* the relationship of the author to the work would have to be completely re-defined. To transfer moral rights to works would require the author privileging the autonomy of the work over any and all forms of commodification, spectral or otherwise. This becomes, then, an existential rite for works and for authors versus a legal right. For a class of works to be defined by such a transfiguration of author rights, ontic and de-ontic rights would also have to become one with the work as work. The author, under such terms, becomes witness to the work as event and subsequently protects the work from conversion to mere commodity status. In the absence of the author, the work would have to effectively defend itself.

What are these works? What is this class of works? Have they ever existed? Do they exist now? Might they ever exist? And, if possible, under what terms and under what auspices do they exist?

Ultimately, it is the status of subjects and states for works that matter most; and, more than anything else, it is the tautological status of the singular work that constitutes works for works. This tautological status is effectively the subjective state of the work, and it is what confers a proto-theological agency upon works. In the economy of rights, and in the commercium of the knowledge commons, this protean theological status becomes a-theological and merely utilitarian. It is de-natured by the regimes of capitalist exploitation of works in force since the conflation of author and work. The issue of prior art may demolish some claims to authorship, but it is only *in reverse* — i.e., when prior art is traced backward versus forward, from commodity to antecedent, versus antecedent to commodity — that the principal gestural economy of works appears as given. This is the secret force in the generativity of works that cannot be explained through genius or through exception. The elective transfer of moral rights to works by authors is, as experiment, the recognition of prior art as incorporated incorporeal generativity. The apparent vector of vitalism in works is primarily a temporal ruse or chimera; for, the tautological status of works for works produces the opposite effect. "History" disappears with the disappearance of law; or, it is law that preserves history and vitalism as spectral economy for works. The knowledge commons, irreducibly, is a field of commodification that shifts everything within its circuit to one form or another of product (product as object, immaterial or material).[3] The antithesis is the anterior motive, shifting direction, and shifting perspective. The useless beauty of the tautological status of works mirrors subjective states otherwise acculturated and assimilated to systems. Those systems are co-terminous with law. For the law to disappear, the systems, the rules, and the forms of acculturation must be reversed and neutralized through the proper exception of works without address. As with all retro-avant-garde maneuvers, this reversal of fortunes is also — quietly — futural.

"But what is capital? What are its limits? What forms does it take? How has its composition changed over time?"[4] Thomas

---

3   Much like the term *human capital,* the very idea of a knowledge commons has a distinctly negative connotation when associated with the ideology of neoliberal capitalism. This is also the reason why the knowledge commons, as public commons, is often seen as a place for parking cultural production until it might be mined for value by Capital. Rent-seeking and its associated practice of socializing risk is how Capital exploits the knowledge commons. It offloads or disowns what is of no use while mining those public resources it might take back inside of the circuit of capital to exploit. The vectorial class, abandoning actual production, has mastered the art of commandeering the infrastructure of the cultural commons, in part through semantics, thereby profiting from not-for-profit cultural production and selling its wares back to the very institutions and individuals that have created the so-called content or by servicing the "transfer of knowledge." These technical and semantical mechanisms have penetrated both academia and the art world neutralizing any possible instance or conception of an exception other than as intellectual fashion statement. For a brief history of the concept of "rent," plus its pejorative or anti-democratic senses, see Thomas Piketty, *Capital in the Twenty-first Century,* trans. Arthur Goldhammer (Cambridge: Belknap Press, 2014), 422–24. "The entrepreneur inevitably tends to become a rentier, more and more dominant over those who own nothing but their labor. Once constituted, capital reproduces itself faster than output increases. The past devours the future" (ibid., 571). For how semantics influence behavior, see Alfred Korzybski et al.

4   Ibid., 46.

Piketty asks this series of questions early on in *Capital in the Twenty-first Century,* a monumental tome arriving in the critical year of 2014, when the 2008 global crash has taken its victims and the various punishments associated with the supposed recovery are self-evident. He then excludes so-called human capital (nominally reducible to labor) to focus primarily upon directly and legally tradable commodities. Thus, Piketty's critique of Capital focuses on inhuman forms, or, as he calls them, "nonhuman" forms of wealth. He does include intellectual property insofar as it is incorporated in one form or another in the balance sheets of private or public accounts. He is concerned with measuring wealth. Piketty calls intellectual property a form of "immaterial capital" (patents, trademarks, etc.) that nonetheless influences how wealth is measured. Generally, he means forms of licensable property.[5] Yet a curious gesture is made when he speaks of "intermediate forms of collective property owned by 'moral persons.'" These moral persons include foundations and churches with "specific aims."[6] Is this a *socialist* remainder? Oddly, he does not include public or private educational institutions in this group.[7] This passing nod toward what is left of civil

---

5   Ibid., 49.
6   Ibid., 47.
7   Universities do appear in Piketty's analysis of global inequality in the form of extraordinary returns earned on endowments and increasing inequality in access to education by way of extremely high tuition fees. See ibid., 447–52, 484–87. Piketty's comments and data mostly regard US universities, while they are also indicative of the neoliberalization of academia worldwide. Piketty is discussing what he calls "pure return on capital" and how investments are managed, but he is also discussing how educational institutions favor or hinder social mobility (ibid., 484–87). Piketty closes his remarks on universities with: "Defining the meaning of inequality and justifying the position of the winners is a matter of vital importance, and one can expect to see all sorts of misrepresentations of the facts in service of the cause" (ibid., 487). The reason this subtle dodge of the inequities perpetrated by neoliberal academia also contains a warning is due to Piketty's main agenda; the increasing tensions between accumulated wealth and properly egalitarian social mores — i.e., social justice. "The consequences for the long-term dynamics of the wealth distribution are potentially terrifying, especially when one adds that the return on capital

society is followed by the most curious remark of all regarding his definition of capital and the intentions of the entrepreneurial classes over time. He states:

What private individuals can and cannot own has evolved considerably over time and around the world, as the extreme case of slavery indicates. The same is true of property in the atmosphere, the sea, mountains, historical monuments, and knowledge. Certain private interests would like to own these things, and sometimes they justify this desire on grounds of *efficiency* rather than mere self-interest. But there is no guarantee that this desire coincides with the general interest. Capital is not an immutable concept: it reflects the state of development and prevailing social relations of each society.[8]

Effectively, what comes into view is Piketty's version of "the law of capital."[9] As empiricist, Piketty has to bracket certain categories of capital accumulation that he cannot yet quantify. His critique ends at the outer gates of physical properties given to capitalist exploitation. Yet he clearly knows that the law of capital has progressed further, and that its appropriational and expropriational targets or frontiers now include knowledge itself, plus subjective states given to knowledge, inclusive of the

---

varies directly with the size of the initial stake and that the divergence in the wealth distribution is occurring on a global scale" (ibid., 571).

8 Or, capital is socially constructed (ibid., 46–47; italics added).

9 See Adam Tooze, "How 'Big Law' Makes Big Money," *New York Review of Books,* February 13, 2020, https://www.nybooks.com/articles/2020/02/13/how-big-law-makes-big-money/, a review of Katharina Pistor, *The Code of Capital: How the Law Creates Wealth and Inequality* (Princeton: Princeton University Press, 2019). "The closest that Pistor comes in *The Code of Capital* to analyzing what might be called a site of production is in her interesting discussion of intellectual property. Once again, she gives us fascinating insights into the role of legal lobbyists in the construction of the global intellectual property rights regime. The Agreement on Trade-Related Aspects of Intellectual Property Rights (TRIPS) secures extraordinary protections for large Western firms in their dealings all over the world, on the pain of sanctions by the United States" (ibid.).

human condition, misidentified here and there as human capital (now co-equivalent to identity and labor, subjects and states).

Piketty's picturesque recourse to the term *common utility* — which he derives from the 1789 Declaration of the Rights of Man and of the Citizen — refers all of his arguments, ultimately, to the idea of the commons. It hides in his critique. Here, too, is the origin of the extra-legally determined or overdetermined work of art as exception and its ultimate address as common property. His embrace of political economy as a social science concerned with "political, normative, and moral purpose" is also picturesque.[10] Its reasonableness is epic. Beneath the analytic resides what needs proper elaboration; for, that spring, from which all things he analyzes flow, concerns first and foremost subjects and works — or, works and states.

In the "Conclusion" of *Capital in the Twenty-first Century,* where a type of post-rationalization of his empirical model and methodology takes place, and where he settles a few scores, Piketty takes a rather wide swipe at the "clash of communism and capitalism," between scholars, in the period 1917–1989, claiming it sterilized versus stimulated "research on capital and inequality by historians, economists, and even philosophers.[11] To illustrate, but burying it in the last footnote of the book, Piketty singles out Sartre, Althusser, and Badiou, whom, he claims, "give the impression that questions of capital and class inequality are of only moderate interest […] and serve mainly as a pretext for jousts of a different nature entirely."[12] The only clue to what he is speaking about (the "different nature") comes through an allusion to historian François Furet's late battles with Marxists and post-Marxists, and a not inelegant plea to "abandon simplistic and abstract notions of the economic infrastruc-

---

10 Piketty, *Capital in the Twenty-first Century,* 574. "It is illusory, I believe, to think that the scholar and the citizen live in separate moral universes, the former concerned with means and the latter with ends. Although comprehensible, this view ultimately strikes me as dangerous" (ibid.).

11 Ibid., 576.

12 Ibid., 655n2.

ture and political superstructure."[13] "Different nature" translates to "different order." One senses that he objects to the very abstractions given to meta-criticism and structuralist critique, and that his empirical bias blinds him to the value of abstract analysis of cultural production. This implied anima negates key elements of his critique of Capital insofar as it demotes a register within critique that has its own purposes, and which circles a necessary existential conditionality for a critique of the commodification of culture and the production or perpetuation of patrimonialism and inequality. The fact that he cannot enter into a proper analysis of immaterial capital also underscores the weaknesses of the empirical model he privileges but then modestly de-privileges in the "Conclusion." The masterful sweep of *Capital in the Twenty-first Century,* with its occasional plunges into literary-critical allusions or analogies (Austen, Balzac, etc.), suffers from its attendant suspicion of abstraction and no utility.

---

13 Ibid., 577. The swipe at Louis Althusser is most likely a swipe at structuralist Marxism. Regarding Althusser's alleged methodological shortcomings, and for a review of *Capital in the Twenty-first Century,* inclusive of Piketty's alleged methodological shortcomings, see Thomas Jessen Adams, "The Theater of Inequality," *Non-site,* August 12, 2014, https://nonsite. org/feature/the-theater-of-inequality. "Thomas Piketty's thousand-page economics bestseller reduces capital to mere wealth — leaving out its political impact on social and economic relationships throughout history." Frédéric Lordon, "Capitalism in the 21st Century Short on Capital: Why Piketty Isn't Marx," *Le monde diplomatique,* May 2015, http://mondediplo. com/2015/05/12piketty. "The worst is that Piketty's book has an explicit 'social philosophy': labour is deserving, but wealth generated through business enterprise is good — unless the rich merely sit on that wealth. The formula 'every fortune is partially justified yet potentially excessive' is not scary. The media, controlled by their shareholders, did not misjudge Piketty. In his desire for generalised peace — between capital and labour, the peace of the 99.9%, the peace of 'global governance' — Piketty, who mentions 'institutions', 'politics' and 'conflicts' only as a matter of form, delivers his vision: 'The bipolar confrontations of the period 1917–89 are now clearly behind us.' This does not sound like our moment in time, when a historic crisis of capitalism has returned the idea of ending it to the intellectual agenda" (ibid.). Piketty returns to attempt to answer these criticisms in his 1,104-page sequel, *Capitalism and Ideology,* trans. Arthur Goldhammer (Cambridge: Belknap Press, 2020). First published as *Capital et idéologie* (Paris: Éditions du Seuil, 2019).

Everything must still serve a purpose or illustrate an agenda, including literature. The exception of the Enlightenment returns with its utilitarian and instrumental bias. The commons is reducible to social utility. *Capital in the Twenty-first Century* also misses the menaces of algorithmic, finance capitalism, although it senses those ravages in the analysis of the 10% return on capital ($r > g$) for the 1% as opposed to an average 1.5% growth in GDP for everyone else. The investment strategies of the 1% are summarized by Piketty as a privilege based in the sums associated with the accumulation of capital at the highest reaches of the neoliberal rentier class. The subsummation of the cultural commons is, however, lost in the numerically established model that is dependent upon available data. The necessary data for an up-to-date forensic analysis is missing, as is historical nuance. The occasional picturesque return to common utility is, in fact, an abstract gesture toward concepts that Piketty otherwise feels compelled to elide or leave aside. The grand utility of his project duly suffers as a result. His remedy for inequality is also incremental and ineffective. The analysis falls victim, by default, to the law of capital. Piketty's disparagement of any criticism of socially constructed statistics demeans his own model.[14]

II. Works and States

> For the buttercups grew past numbering, in this spot which they had chosen for their games among the grass, standing singly, in couples, in whole companies, yellow as the yolk of eggs, and glowing with an added luster, I felt, because, being powerless to consummate with my palate the pleasure which the sight of them never failed to give, I would let it accumulate as my eyes ranged over their golden expanse, until it became

---

14 "Social scientists in other disciplines should not leave the study of economic facts to economists and must not flee in horror the minute a number rears its head, or content themselves with saying that every statistic is a social construct, which of course is true but insufficient." Piketty, *Capital in the Twenty-first Century*, 575.

potent enough to produce an effect of absolute, purposeless beauty; and so it had been from my earliest childhood, when from the tow-path I had stretched out my arms towards them before I could even properly spell their charming name — a name fit for the Prince in some fairy-tale — immigrants, perhaps, from Asia centuries ago, but naturalized now for ever in the village, satisfied with their modest horizon, rejoicing in the sunshine and the water's edge, faithful to their little glimpse of the railway-station, yet keeping nonetheless like some of our old paintings, in their plebeian simplicity, a poetic scintillation from the golden East.[15]

— Marcel Proust

In effect, everything is always already given. That, in its most expansive definition or sense, is the status of both prior art and the commons. It is the transformation across states and across processes of subjectivization that plays the key role in any analysis that will also indicate a possible way out of the increasingly predatory practices of neoliberal capitalist exploitation of things given, inclusive of subjects. The abstract and structuralist level of such an inquiry is a necessary rite, as is the existential limit incurred for such. But, ultimately, it does returns to things and to works. For things given not to be taken, they will effectively have to be taken off the table. "Render unto Caesar…."[16] We re-

---

15 Marcel Proust, *Remembrance of Things Past,* Vol. 1: *Swann's Way, Within a Budding Grove,* Pléiade edition, trans. C.K. Scott Moncrieff and Terence Kilmartin (New York: Vintage, 1982), 183. *Swann's Way* first published as *Du côté de chez Swann* (Paris: Éditions Grasset, 1913).

16 If the knowledge commons in its instantiation as platform culture is, in fact, an antigora, then exiting the law of that model requires wholly new works. "The phenomenon of Antigoras exemplifies the intimate and unprecedented relationship between capitalism and digital information. Because of the magic of Moore's Law and the network effect, the Invisible Hand has come to be understood not just as an ideal distributor, smarter than any possible communist central committee, but as a creative inventor outracing human wits." Jaron Lanier, "The Gory Antigora: Illusions of Capitalism and Computers," *Cato Unbound,* January 8, 2006, https://www.cato-unbound.org/2006/01/08/jaron-lanier/gory-antigora-illusions-capitalism-computers. Lanier concludes his essay with a remarkable assertion,

turn, then, to the Augustinian point of purchase — that the internal prospects of subjects and of works are off limits to the commercium of ideological or capitalist expropriation. We find again the necessary reverse praxis in works that separates them from mere commodity status and protects the subjective conditions of their appearance as works. The various states for works include "no works" — a preliminary position often taken prior to new works. Tactical withdrawal precedes re-engagement, yet at another level. The elective exit signals an elective return, but under wholly other auspices.

Works for works, if to embody a new exception to the variable and deterministic forms of de-natured exception that rule the knowledge commons, as constituted under the law of capital, will require a new instantiation of what has come to be called the futural within cultural production. "History" and "No History," forms of presentism, vitalism and its other, and the internal prospects of works as states will all have to be addressed through the iterative and existential processes of works for works. The primary concern of a focus on the futural will, then, require re-examination of and exit from spent premises for works that merely operate within the commercium of the neoliberalized knowledge commons — foremost the neoliberalized, digital knowledge commons. Inoperativity and operativity are the key terms in that transitional analytic, while operative inoperativity points to the internal time-sense for works denoted as futural.[17]

---

even if meant half-ironically: "Culture, including large-scale volunteer connection and boundless beautiful invention, has been somewhat forgotten because of the noisy arrival of capitalism on the Net in the last decade and a half or so. When it comes to digital systems, however, capitalism is not a complete system unto itself. Only culture is rich enough to fund the Antigora" (ibid.).

17 Regarding knowledge production on behalf of capital, or regarding attempts at conditioning or predicting future scenarios for capital, see Stefan Collini's comments on the history of *The Economist*. Within this review of a book on *The Economist*, a review which Collini establishes as a half-hearted defense of *The Economist*, the history of the journal (paper) is discussed across the history of modern capitalism. Collini calls *The Econo-*

If there is an attempt in scholarship to map ideological praxis across works, and to lodge new forms of socio-cultural criticism through such readings, the fact remains that the entire ecosystem is constructed with very little or no place for the exception proper to function other than in opposition to what it comments upon — i.e., the formerly constituted modernist work of avant-garde art or scholarship is increasingly co-opted or, as last resort, reduced to intellectual or artistic fashion statement.[18] Arguably, this ecosystem contains what is permitted.[19] The platforms and the institutional biases that obstruct any proper ex-

---

mist "Cosmopolitan for the capital-owning classes." In other words, it is a type of brain candy for the elite — foremost when it goes "global" after the "big bang" of the 1980s. "At some points in its history, it may have seemed like a cross between the *Spectator* and the *Banker,* at others an amalgam of *Time* and *Investors' Chronicle,* but it now has a unique position in the global media landscape that can be expressed as follows: if you want to know what's happening in the world, read the *New York Times.* If you want to know what's wrong with what's happening in the world, read the *Guardian.* If you want to know what's going to happen next in the world (unless tinpot leftists wreck everything), read *The Economist.* After all, omniscience extends to the future, too, the one period of time that investors are really interested in." Stefan Collini, "In Real Sound Stupidity the English Are Unrivalled," *London Review of Books* 42, no. 3 (February 6, 2020), https://www.lrb.co.uk/the-paper/v42/no3/stefan-collini/in-real-sound-stupidity-the-english-are-unrivalled; with reference to Alexander Zevin, *Liberalism at Large: The World According to the "Economist"* (London: Verso, 2019). Collini notes, in a semi-mock defense of *The Economist,* that Zevin is "on the editorial committee of *New Left Review*" (ibid.).

18 See Collini, "In Real Sound Stupidity the English Are Unrivalled," for a description of this process in terms of the ideological cut of journals and an attempt to use them to illustrate passages in intellectual history. "This can work well for relatively short-lived journals with strong editors and a clear identity, though even in those cases features that don't yield the right kind of evidence tend to be ignored. More recently, there have been sophisticated attempts to place a periodical in a network or economy of parallel and competing publications, exploring the dynamics of a field and the cultural logic governing the production of various kinds of media." These latter two terms — "dynamics of a field" and "cultural logic governing production" are essentially post-Marxist terms quietly connoting "Bourdieu" and "Jameson."

19 For example, see *Flash Art* 329 (February–March 2020), the "Post-copyright" issue.

ception are also those that survive only if they anticipate the future and shift with the prevailing winds, with prevailing winds typically defined as funding sources. Reading Capital today requires, as it has in the past, engaging with Capital's own attempts at conditioning all futural time-senses within cultural production, if only to preempt anything that threatens the law of capital. The avant-garde position of Capital is subsummation of any possible avant-garde position against Capital.[20]

What is this futural time-sense given to cultural production? If it operates within works as dark vitalism and its other, it is also indicative of a trajectory — e.g., it would seem to be eschatological and teleological, at once.[21] It has, as it were, two functions — or, a dual function that under certain circumstances functions as dialectical operational ambit (i.e., dueling functions) for works of a discursivity that conceives works as non-ideological intellectual force.[22] It is in the types of works that eschew or bracket the direct intellectual or ideational critique for other forms of criticality (e.g., visuality or visual agency, affect, atmosphere, etc.), that the time-senses are less dialectically composed and more integral to the operativity of the internal-

20 An example, as of early 2020, is the fury with which the discourse on inequality and economic justice has swept through bespoke and elite academic institutes — e.g., so-called institutes of advanced study — that focus on political economy while also doing nothing to alter the terms of engagement at the level of capitalist intervention in the very institutes or institutions involved.

21 Here we see spectral versions of Benjamin and Hegel in a type of pre-apocalyptic wrestling match with angels that are actually devils, or a dance with devils that are actually angels. This particular form of dance is what animates the works of Dostoevsky and Gogol, insofar as their dance with onrushing modernity and Russian history almost always invokes an a-historical mystical time-sense or quasi-dialectical strains given to historical time-senses.

22 It is important to distinguish between ideological and intellectual or ideational force. It is ideological force that Capital uses to pre-empt any and all possible *anti*-capitalist futures, while it is quite content to service the aspirations of *post*-capitalist fantasies, including Fully Automated Luxury Communism (FALC). See Aaron Bastani, *Fully Automated Luxury Communism: A Manifesto* (London: Verso, 2019).

ized inoperativity of works.[23] These terms are effectively the very terms given to, or dictated by, the knowledge commons as integrated discourse and/or integrated spectacle. The implied exit from that discourse, through works, cannot occur within any normative field of engagement with the very ideological forces (immanent or otherwise) that neutralize actually existing exception.

Current ecosystems for forms of apparent artistic scholarship are premised upon the values of the law of capital. Even open-access and alt-academic works are assimilated to this circuit.[24] Any futural time-senses for or embedded in such works,

---

23 See the so-called theatrical turn in the art world and culture industry.

24 See, for example, the proliferation of various proprietary open-access platforms that collect and offer works for text- and data-mining that have been published elsewhere in open-access fashion. See bepress, SSRN, ResearchGate, Academia.edu, Core, Project MUSE, etc. These include social-media platforms that operate as academic networking sites while nominally serving as pre-publication or post-publication sites for working and/or published papers. The appearance of the latter on these sites — i.e., published papers — is also an end run on paywalls, or instances where the author has taken the liberty of sharing their work with the permission of, or in defiance of, the for-profit publisher of the journal or book their work has appeared in. Both bepress (Berkeley Electronic Press) and Research-Gate are actually for-profit companies. Each has effectively masqueraded as a repository for academic works in the open-access ecosystem that is now undergoing neoliberal capitalist colonization. Core and Project MUSE are, in part, attempts to systematize and safeguard forms of scholarship that circulate beyond the authorized publications ecosystem that academia polices for institutional and careerist purposes. Both collect, re-digitize, and archive works that have appeared on other platforms. The neoliberal academic apparatus of bepress was subsequently acquired by Elsevier. "In a move entirely consistent with its strategy to pivot beyond content licensing to preprints, analytics, workflow, and decision-support, Elsevier is now a major if not the foremost single player in the institutional repository landscape. If successful, and there are some risks, this acquisition will position Elsevier as an increasingly dominant player in preprints, continuing its march to adopt and coopt open access." And: "Elsevier has invested substantially in tools to help universities comply with funder mandates, assess their research outputs, and showcase the expertise of their faculty members. The general category of systems has become known as current research information systems (CRIS)." Roger C. Schonfeld, "Elsevier acquires bepress," *Scholarly Kitchen,* August 2, 2017, https://scholarlykitchen.

whether critical, diacritical, pseudo-avant-garde, militantly an-archistic, or such, will be co-opted and neutralized within those systems. The austerities and nuances of such works, while serv-ing quite often as toxins for the systems that have been used, or that have co-opted such works, are the classic test cases for works.[25] Every instance has been tested. Every platform has been approached and often broached with intent for conciliation or enforced contretemps. These positions taken are well-known and well-rehearsed; yet they fail every time, unless they quietly alter the terms of engagement for such works. Whether that is possible, and whether it justifies the evolutionary predicament for free expression, is a matter of whether incrementalism is of any value in the face of totalitarian, expropriational Capital.

Again, it becomes elective — a matter for artist–scholars, not masters and slaves. The futural time-sense, while wholly imma-nent, becomes the necessary rite of passage to "no rights" and "no works" for/before Capital and the instantiation of a new dis-pensation for works beyond the law of capital.[26] If it is "Christic," or messianic, it is also a-theological and properly constituted

---

sspnet.org/2017/08/02/elsevier-acquires-bepress/. "Showcasing and insti-tutional promotion" are the two foremost "products" Elsevier sought in its acquisition of bepress, as it transitions from mere publisher to full-service platform for the management of academic IP.

25 See the admirable Lacanian and Žižekian attempt to define a possible cultural position for a late-modern avant-garde in Marc James Léger, *Don't Network: The Avant-garde after Networks* (Brooklyn: Minor Compositions/Autonomedia, 2018). Unfortunately, the Lacanian universe is demented, or irreducibly tragic, and a moebius strip without exit, whereas Žižek's Lacanian-inflected multiverse is a cover for his unrepentant Romantic ide-alism. See, for example, Slavoj Žižek, *Event: Philosophy in Transit* (London: Penguin, 2014).

26 This immanent power for works overwrites immanent power per se — or, imposes forms of power for works. It operates, foremost, on the paradig-matic axis of cultural production. Deleuze attempted a definition of this state for works in the essays collected for his last book, *Pure Immanence*. Gilles Deleuze, *Pure Immanence: Essays on a Life,* trans. Anne Boyman (New York: Zone Books, 2001). Deleuze constitutes this time-sense or state for works as a Nietzschean "will-to-art." The third and last essay, "Nietzsche," was first published in 1965. Regarding this essay, see Gavin Keeney, "Kant Nietzsche Undo Lacan," in *"Else-where": Essays in Art,*

upon the justification of the good and of the higher rights that supersede and/or subtend economic rights. The moral law of works for works cancels the law of capital. It does so through the auspices of the given (as prior art) and the conversion of the given into the real of the work. Works for works depart both political geography and political economy and all forms of critique of immanent power associated with such disciplinary boundaries — i.e., of or within such disciplines. Such critiques are, at best, rites of passage for works for works in terms of what such works seek to escape.[27]

Perhaps this model inhabits Chris Marker's *La jetée,* where visitors from the future offer up, to the post-apocalyptic Paris Marker has situated the story within, a power source that restarts civilization. This Markerian maneuver is outlandishly eschatologically teleological. The present is saved by the future — and vice versa. But that future would never have existed without that future visiting the present as future past. The cryptic power source is the internal metric and time-senses of *La jetée* — i.e., internalizing time-senses hypostatized as time-traveling.[28] Works for works, to adopt this properly Markerian

---

Architecture, and Cultural Production, 2002–2011 (Newcastle upon Tyne: Cambridge Scholars Publishing, 2011), 93–94.

27 Such critique is often, subtly or overtly, ideologically based. This also, arguably, demolishes all rhetoric regarding the "distribution of the aesthetic" and "relational aesthetics" in the arts and artistic scholarship. See Jacques Rancière, *The Politics of Aesthetics: The Distribution of the Sensible,* trans. with an introduction by Gabriel Rockhill (London: Continuum, 2004), first published as *Le partage du sensible: Esthétique et politique* (Paris: Fabrique: Diffusion Les Belles Lettres, 2000), and Nicolas Bourriaud, *Relational Aesthetics,* trans. Simon Pleasance and Fronza Woods with the participation of Mathieu Copeland (Dijon: Les Presses du Réel, 2002), first published as *Esthétique relationnelle* (Dijon: Les Presses du Réel, 1998).

28 *La jetée* (1962) only appears to be a sci-fi film. It is actually a strange outtake from *Le joli mai,* shot at the same time. It is, effectively, a version of Marker's answer to *cinéma vérité* — viz., *"ciné, ma vérité."* Chris Marker, dir., *La jetée* (1962)/*Sans soleil* (1982) (Criterion Collection, 2007), DVD. For Marker's very early associations with Surrealism and — then — Catholic personalism, pre- or post-WWII, well before and underlying his turn into cinema, see Gavin Keeney, *Dossier Chris Marker: The Suffering Image* (Newcastle upon Tyne: Cambridge Scholars Publishing, 2012). Marker

maneuver, will also indulge the consequential intellectual-conceptual whiplash of the operation to counter and cancel the perpetuation of the apocalypse within the field of cultural production — a perpetual apocalypse founded upon the twin horns of the dilemma. But such works will cancel by restoring. Such works will travel by homeopathic stasis in motion. Such works will inhabit a regime in thought that enters into dialogue with prior art as a substantial field overwriting Bourdieu's corruptible and corrupted "field of cultural production."[29] Works for works will indulge the late deconstructivist penchant for post-phenomenological excess through works — as passage or passageway. Works for works will crawl on cat's paws toward the futural that always already visits the present — i.e., a futural time-sense that also inhabits the past. Acts of recovery for things lost or left behind, plus acts of futural intensity through works, are the hallmark gestures of justice performed through works.[30] "The law disappears …." The tautological status or state of the work merely reflects its provenance, "from the future" — viz., beyond circular and incrementalist forms of the versioning of the real of the work of artistic scholarship.

The fuse of futural intensity for works for works is the time-sense of the internal metric of the work plus its tautological

---

was, more or less, a High Romantic Christian Marxist. His works are, thus, "Christic."

29 Pierre Bourdieu, *The Field of Cultural Production: Essays on Art and Literature,* ed. Randal Johnson (New York: Columbia University Press, 1993).

30 It would appear that, through a peculiar variety of parallax given to temporality (i.e., a temporal parallax), the futural is the time-sense that allows the past to be altered. In this sense, we may not be able to change the past from within the present, but we may be able to change the present and the past through the futural. In order for this to occur, the futural would have to be present — latent or active — in all time-senses. If theology privileges an *eternal presence* (not eternal present tense per se), it suggests that specific forms of expressivity transcend normative senses of temporality. It is, for example, both a canonical and existential error in Christian Eastern Orthodoxy to speak of Christ or The Passion in the past tense. Both are always already present. This is especially true in the case of Orthodox liturgy, which is exercised as a form of perpetual charism. See, for example, the fate of Maxim Grek in Russia.

state as Kantian "thing-in-itself." Things given constitute the foundation for any theory of the sublime and any theory of the exception. That fuse is the operational and situational status of the work in relation to the negations performed by a proper assimilation of works to the conceptual field of prior art, the true commons — i.e., to the nature of the exception defined by the auspices of that negation of proprietary rights. Moral rights transferred to works is part of that situational ambit en route to works for works. The nature or anti-nature of works for works is the intense internalization and neutralization of "History" and "No History," and the proper fielding of a new proprietary right for works against the dictates of markets and the dictates of systems of use or valorization as commodity. Yet this proper fielding of higher rights for works leaves all of that behind, insofar as all of that is the operative field of the law of capital.

Artistic scholarship and works for works constitute an aleatory and iterative re-combinatory embrace of the so-called canonical (prior art as "History" and "No History") and the existential (the lived rites of works for works). Such works re-encompass the quest of the Romantic epic, yet as life-work for works. They speak in the time-senses and verb tenses of the futural, here and now — i.e., through the often dizzying array of generic impulses inhabiting grammar and syntax.[31]

"I am leaving. But I have not left."

"I am here. But I have not arrived."

---

31 Ian Balfour, with reference to Wordsworth's semi-autobiographical *Prelude,* which was published posthumously. Ian Balfour, "In the Romantic Era and Beyond," lecture at Williams College, September 24, 2018. See Proust's attempt to deduce "moral thunder in buttercups," in *Swann's Way,* volume one of *Remembrance of Things Past (À la recherche du temps perdu).* This figure of speech references Proust's relationship to Ruskin, and Ruskin's relationship to English Romanticism. This grammar and syntax, not merely reducible to literary or linguistic content or style, includes visual grammar and syntax. It is, effectively, the so-called voice of works that speaks on behalf of works in/for themselves — even when they are silent.

The combined tenses and senses of these statements, bordering on tautology, confer a missing — or concluding — yet.[32] The canonical and the existential collide in works that infer the singular event of Art, Love, and Revolution.

---

32 In the senses and states of works for works, the "Markerian" slippage between word and image is also a type of radically immanent grammatology for word-image economies. This grammatology is nonetheless intimately or integrally tied to the ontic nature of works, insofar as it is part and parcel of how they speak. Thus, Marker's unique or oblique take on the genre of *cinéma verité* is also based in dissonance as dissident gesturalism for literary-cinematic works. His documentaries are also film-essays. This grammatology is, in many respects, coincidental to the early 1960s passage from structuralism to post-structuralism. For Marker's relationship to the film-essay, see Gavin Keeney, "Film Mysticism and 'The Haunted Wood,'" in *Knowledge, Spirit, Law: Book 2, The Anti-capitalist Sublime* (Brooklyn: punctum books, 2017), 83–104. For Godard's, see Gavin Keeney, "The Film-essay," in ibid., 61–82.

Topological Summary

The following questions, extracted from a failed Fulbright Scholar application (September 2020), were posed in and across Phase One: "Useless Beauty" (2019–2021) of the ongoing Works for Works (w4w) project. Drawing upon OOI-MTA[1] experiments in artistic scholarship across that two-year trajectory, the preliminary answers (as below), which may also appear to some as paralogisms, suggest what is at stake in Phase Two: "No Rights" (2022–).

1.1 Intellectual Property Rights (IPR) and Its Discontents

Given the contemporary transposition of immaterial labor to forms of spectral commodity, with a focus on monetizing the knowledge commons, what possible means of **restoring value to so-called useless works in the Arts and Humanities** might impact both academia and the art world, where, on the one hand, we have an increasingly intense metrics-driven culture conditioning and evaluating all research, and, on the

---

1 The Out of India Collective (OOI) was founded in Ahmedabad, India, in early 2017, at CEPT University, with theatrical-cinematic events staged in both Ahmedabad and Venice, Italy. The troupe is comprised of Gavin Keeney, Harsh Bhavsar, Ishita Jain, and Owen O'Carroll. MTA, the Metropolitan Transmedia Authority, was created in 2019 as a successor to OOI. The hybrid acronym connotes the presence of the OOI archive in MTA projects.

other hand, we have an advanced form of Guy Debord's integrated spectacle subsuming all artistic production, both a status for works that places author rights at risk of systematic conformity to the prevailing neo-utilitarian bias and/ or hegemony of new forms of patrimonialism and platform culture?

Preliminary answer: Through production and dissemination either beyond or across academic and art-world auspices, the works-for-works model introduces dissonance and exposes biases. In doing so, it also opens up other options that may then be further tested.

1.12 The Privatization and Digitization of the Knowledge Commons

With the mass digitization of cultural production advancing on two fronts, the for-profit and the not-for-profit, the author has been summarily caught in the crosshairs, reduced to working for careerist motives and/or servicing the aspirations of the vectoral class. What might permit the author to escape both forms of marginalization and co-optation and return to works that have no relation to either system of commodification of works?

Preliminary answer: Escape occurs through works, not in advance by negating options. Other options appear, some within the existing exigencies of systems as exception. This occurs most often when the system engaged is undergoing a shift and/ or deconstruction from within (versus from without).

1.13 Platform Cultures and Moral Rights of Authors

The advance of globalization of the knowledge commons is premised on making the knowledge commons "available" and "open" to all. What are the true motives for this agenda and what do capitalist and not-for-profit institutional prerogatives have in common? What is the **position of the artist–scholar** in the dialectical machinery of such a political economy? What is "artistic research," as opposed to artistic scholarship, and why is contemporary artistic research said to service platform economy and art-world spectacle?

Preliminary answer: The artist–scholar is foremost, under present conditions, a nomad and rebel. This takes the form of precarity — but with precarity also operating as voluntary exile.

1.14 Forms of Artistic Scholarship Present and Past

Setting aside the current penchant for practice-based artistic research, as espoused by art schools around the world, and leading to a peculiar "sameness" to works to be found in all such schools, plus a sameness that may be found in the art-industrial establishment worldwide (biennales, residencies, *kunsthallen,* etc.), **what types of artistic scholarship might be developed, or re-developed, toward freeing the artist–scholar from both careerist agendas, as enforced by academia and the art world, and commodification of works** toward mere survival in an increasingly oversaturated mediatized cultural commons?

Preliminary answer: The primary exit strategy is through a collectivist ethos (and telos) for works. "For works" also indicates that the collectivist ethos is based on the necessity of honoring the inborne agency of works, such that they also remain free of overt or banal attempts to leverage them by members of the collective as symbolic capital, thus serving to reinsert them into the very games exposed as given to corrupting and/ or co-opting works.

1.2 Transitional States for Works

If precarity is now the standard operating position for artists and scholars, and for artist–scholars, **what are the possible or extant transitional states** that will lead to works that do not fall prey to the twin exigencies of academic careerism and art-world opportunism?

Preliminary answer: The primary modus vivendi for artist-scholars is to enter into the existentialist paradoxes of non-proprietary works (often an alchemical "nigredo") and observe what occurs. Given contemporary biases that may be said to counter works-based agency from without (e.g., the application of PC agendas and/or ideological posturing), the transitional state for works of an entirely useless tenor ("useless" being utilized in tension with what is otherwise defined as "useful" by prevailing standards and neo-utilitarianism), the transit through the existentialist paradoxes will tend to engage variations on the theme of authorial privilege versus collectivist ethos (and telos).

1.21 Transmedia as Transitional State for Works

The emergence of time- and performance-based work as the new ultra-contemporary modality in which to pursue artistic research prompts numerous questions regarding the assimilation of performance, installation, and forms of postcinema to art-world spectacle. What are the **cross-platform, transdisciplinary editioning strategies** for such works that might also lead the artist and author to counter the hypertemporality of such works and the spectral commodification via "event" that serves to privilege such works?

Preliminary answer: Privileging works-based agency tends to produce works that may take any number of forms, although in terms of forms of artistic scholarship the prevailing modalities of academia and the art world may be utilized and/or custom-

ized to edition and disseminate "records" and "reports" on projects that otherwise remain within a circumscribed zone best described as "portfolio" or "archive."

1.22 Time- and Performance-based Works

If **time- and performance-based works** are the latest fashion statement in the art world and in art academies, are they forms of critical inquiry and how so? Is the present-day penchant for socio-cultural criticism in such works, or by way of such works, a subtle form of appropriation and neutralization of the artwork's autonomy and formal agency or is such content a valid transitional state toward a new avant-garde for post-capitalist artworks? Additionally, why has the art-critical and art-curatorial establishment declared the modernist concept of an avant-garde elitist and/or a fiction?

Preliminary answer: Time- and performance-based works are not guilty in and of themselves as serving intellectual and artistic fashions. How they are used is what determines whether they escape the overt and/or subtle mechanisms of control exerted by academia and the art world. Thus, time- and performance-based works may be a part of, but not the overriding concern of, new forms of avant-garde artistic scholarship. Moreover, the inherent or inborne radical agency of such works will negate any re-imposed socio-cultural "cut" or "bias" that might re-insinuate itself as new fashion statement. In observing and honoring the agency of the work, the artist–scholar will also refuse any accommodation with empty rhetorical gestures and/or posturing, except in the transitional states noted above, where such gesturalism may serve as vehicle for "report" or "record," whereas the inborne agency of the work remains offstage in the "portfolio" or "archive," to be re-played or re-mixed another time toward wholly new ends or no ends.

1.23 The Transfer of Moral Rights to Works

What possible means exist, or might exist, for the **transfer of moral rights of authors to works**? Does this require a wholly new form of the editioning and archiving of works?

Preliminary answer: The transfer of moral rights to works is carried out through the renunciation of authorial privilege. Renouncing rights includes preventing the theft or appropriation of such renounced rights by others. In this manner, the artist–scholar becomes a steward versus author of works.

1.24 Beyond the CC0 License and No Rights

How might the **final breach with IPR law** be made for works and through works in order to escape the last restriction — i.e., the fact that by IPR law moral rights may not be transferred and/or renounced, as is evident in the CC0 license? Additionally, why and to what end have moral rights been made subservient to statutory law and copyright?

Preliminary answer: Through the editioning and dissemination strategies of the works-for-works idiom, it is thereby the "idiomatic" in/for itself that provides the final breach. Multiform, hybrid, and occasional stealth modalities permit elements of works to reside in various places, with the predictable outcome(s) minimized and the unexpected outcome(s) maximized. Works will, under this model, generally choose their own path beyond IPR law through where they are welcome and where they are not.

1.3 Prior Art after IPR

What is the status of the concept of **Prior Art after IPR**? What possible future scenarios may be devised and/or theorized toward making Prior Art the basis for a futural class of works that have no relation to IPR? Is the Enlightenment-era concept of the "exceptional" status of the authored work not also the foundation for many of the fictions underlying IPR and the contested or strained relation between moral rights and economic rights? How can this idea of "exception" be re-purposed?

Preliminary answer: Prior Art becomes the landscape of possibilities that opens up after intellectual property rights and abject careerism are abandoned. Examples of such landscapes also illustrate the recursive nature of the exit strategy (leaving to return), inclusive of negotiating current or incipient ecosystems in academia and the art world while denoting aporias and forms of dissension through analyses and reports on subjects such as: Art + Law; Performative Research; and Rites of Works.

1.31 Works for Works

If "Works for Works" is to be defined as a class of works that has no relation to commodity status for works of artistic scholarship and no relation to IPR, have such works existed in the past, do they exist now, and how might they exist in the future? Does such a class of works re-constitute a past state for works or does it augur **a revolution in the very concept of works** and proprietary rights?

Preliminary answer: Works for Works, as an idiomatic quest for new forms of artistic scholarship with no relation to Capital and its edicts, "builds" across works (as life-work for works) a "catalogue," "portfolio," or "archive," which, in turn, specifies its own preferred means of expression (production and dissemination). This ecosystem is thus a proto-ecosystem for works that eventually come to reside in no one place and in no one time. Scriptorium and archive describe merely the surface of the extensivity of the model and its often-preposterous presentist time-sense.

1.32 The Artist—Scholar

What is the "fugitive" **status of the artist–scholar past, present, and yet to come?** Where, how, and when did the separation of artist and scholar occur, or is it a false dichotomy?

Preliminary answer: The artist–scholar, as steward for works versus author, effectively abandons time as normally conceived. In the agency of works produced as "useless," other times and other places emerge as expressive gestures and synchronistic time-senses. The works-for-works modality for artistic scholarship underscores what has always been at stake in the Arts and Humanities and which is increasingly imperiled by rote utilitarianism and the commodification of knowledge.

Notes on Language and Its Other

The following is a somewhat subjective, non-exemplary, impressionistic sample — with intentional gaps — of positions taken across roughly fifty years (1967–2017) regarding visual and discursive agency in the Arts, Humanities, and Social Sciences, culminating in the field of theoretical inquiry in Law denoted Jurisprudence. It begins with the emergence of post-structuralism in the 1960s as the defining style of the left critique of culture and then crosses the decades of the post-modernist inquest concerning what constitutes a proper evaluation of the linguistic and ideological stakes given to modernist cultural production, with the clash between Derrida and Agamben (c.2000) signaling an arrival at the gates of an instructive aporia (ban versus silence) that suggests either an impasse for left critique or a possible return of repressed transcendentals — oddly, a return to "Plato versus Aristotle," with Aristotle's definition of gramma as the bone of contention between Agamben and Derrida. The Western bias is obvious, as is the circling of what constitutes rationality or instrumental reason. Epigones of irrationality (past and present) come and go over the fifty-year period. While the "biopolitical" discourse (an academic cottage industry launched by Agamben's development of themes first broached by Foucault) centers upon the concept of the political "state of exception," this form of enforced exception, which reduces subjects to mere chattel and/or sacrificial victims, is then turned on its head and given a new existential primacy as "positive" or elective form-of-life. Agamben's Homo Sacer project (1995–2014) is the "site" of this crisis and transformation/transfiguration of fortunes for subjects. This project is effectively registered within the discipline of Political Theology, coinciding with aspects of post-phenomenology and a-theology in the 1990s. The late poststructuralist-influenced critique of law (and language as a form of law with theological and/or metaphysical underpinnings) suggests that language and law conceal the same primordial or immemorial resources privileged by repeated attempts to escape discursive systems, authorized or otherwise, through modernist, anti-modernist, and pre-modernist avant-garde visual and linguistic systems (Susan Sontag's point in her essay "The Aesthetics of Silence") — primarily by letting the "thing itself" speak for/on behalf of itself. Notably, the figure of "the event," traceable at least to Husserl's phenomenology, is present across the entire arc of this fifty-year critique of language and its other. Curiously, as of early 2020, the latest intellectual fashion statement in Jurisprudence is "*visual* jurisprudence."

N.B.: Books and texts referenced in this sampling of the emergence, ascendance, and decline of post-structuralist critique are not included in the Bibliography to this book.

I. The Game Opens...

As some people know now, there are ways of thinking that we don't yet know about. Nothing could be more important or precious than that knowledge, however unborn. The sense of urgency, the spiritual restlessness it engenders, cannot be appeased, and continues to fuel the radical art of this century. Through its advocacy of silence and reduction, art commits an act of violence upon itself, turning art into a species of automanipulation, of conjuring — trying to bring these new ways of thinking to birth.[1]

— Susan Sontag

Regarding "nihilisms" (versus "nihilism"), see Susan Sontag's remarks on silence as a form of "via negativa" in late-modern contemporary art in "The Aesthetics of Silence," in *Styles of Radical Will* (New York: Farrar, Straus and Giroux, 1969), 3–34. First published in *Aspen* 5–6 (Fall–Winter 1967). For Sontag the elective nihilism found in conceptual art in the late 1960s — an apophatic tradition found in philosophy and religion as much as in the arts, intimately related to negative dialectics, and a perennial element of art insofar as art is an inquest conducted on forms of consciousness for artists and for works — is not reducible to mere escape from the commercium of the art world.

Regarding negative dialectics, see Theodor W. Adorno, *Negative Dialectics,* trans. E.B. Ashton (New York: Seabury Press, 1973). First published as *Negative Dialektik* (Frankfurt am Main: Suhrkamp, 1966). See also Theodor W. Adorno, *Minima Moralia: Reflections from Damaged Life,* trans. E.F.N. Jephcott (London: Verso, 1978). First published as *Minima Moralia: Reflexionen aus dem beschädigten Leben,* ed. Rolf Tiedemann (Frankfurt am Main: Suhrkamp, 1951).

Regarding "the birth of the death of the author," see Roland Barthes, "The Death of the Author," trans. Richard Howard, *Aspen* 5–6 (Fall–Winter 1967).

Regarding Barthes and *Aspen* 5–6, see John Logie, "1967: The Birth of 'The Death of the Author,'" *College English* 75, no. 5 (May 2013): 493–512. Barthes's *Writing Degree Zero* appeared in 1967 as well. Roland Barthes, *Writing Degree Zero,* trans. Annette Lavers and Colin Smith (London: Jonathan Cape, 1967).

---

1   Susan Sontag, "The Aesthetics of Silence," in *Styles of Radical Will* (New York: Farrar, Straus and Giroux, 1969), 18.

First published as *Le degré zéro de l'écriture* (Paris: Éditions du Seuil, 1953). For the "minimalist presentation" of Barthes's "The Death of the Author," *Aspen* 5–6 (Fall-Winter 1967), see http://www.ubu.com/aspen/aspen5and6/threeEssays.html#barthes.

As first published in *Aspen* 5–6, along with Barthes's "The Death of the Author," Sontag's "The Aesthetics of Silence" concerns the emergence of a form of conceptual artistic inquiry (not necessarily reducible to minimalism) that brackets or troubles discursive "noise," questioning the "modernist" privileging of content and authorial intent over form and sense. Barthes's essay, in this context, reinforces the post-structuralist focus on the autonomy of the work, yet on behalf of the literary work of art.

The editor of *Aspen* 5–6, art critic and artist Brian O'Doherty, is generally credited with establishing the critique of the "white cube" (in *Artforum,* 1976) — i.e., the modernist art gallery as de facto commercium, generally guilty of de-naturing art. "At the time he edited *Aspen* 5–6, O'Doherty was trying to develop a poststructural artistic language using installation, drawing and performance." Lucy Cotter, "Between the White Cube and the White Dom Brian O'Doherty's *Aspen* 5 16, an Early Exposition" in *Artistic Research Expositions: Publishing Art in Academia,* eds. Michael Schwab and Henk Borgdorff (Leiden: Leiden University Press, 2014), 221.

Aspen (published intermittently by Roaring Fork Press between 1965 and 1971) was effectively an "artists' multiple," or gallery/museum unto itself. See also Brian O'Doherty, *Inside the White Cube: The Ideology of the Gallery Space* (San Francisco: Lapis Press, 1986).

Aspen 5–6 (Fall–Winter 1967), "The Minimalism Issue," adapted for the web by Andrew Stafford, *UbuWeb,* n.d., http://www.ubu.com/aspen/aspen5and6/index.html.

"Twenty-eight numbered items, including advertisements folder. Edited and designed by Brian O'Doherty, art direction by David Dalton and Lynn Letterman. Published Fall-Winter 1967 by Roaring Fork Press, NYC." (Ibid.)

This late-1960s "avant-garde" journal was published by Phyllis Glick (née Phyllis Johnson), a former journalist and editor of *Women's Wear Daily* and *Advertising Age.* See Giulia Mutti, "Aspen Magazine: A Surprise Box of Delights," *AnOther Magazine,* March 31, 2015, https://www.anothermag.com/art-photography/7220/aspen-magazine-a-surprise-box-of-delights. It was conceived in Aspen, Colorado, in 1964, "one of the few places in America where you can lead a well-rounded, eclectic life of visual, physical and mental splendor," where Glick, skiing and working as a photographer, happened upon the Aspen International Design Conference. See "Letter from Phyllis Johnson," in *Aspen* 1 (1965), http://www.ubu.com/aspen/aspen1/letter.html.

Anna Gallagher-Ross, "Magazine as Storehouse: Merce Cunningham and *Aspen* 5+6 (1967)," *Sitelines,* Walker Art Center, July 20, 2016, https://walkerart.org/magazine/on-merce-cunningham-and-aspen-56-1967.

See Gwen Allen, "The Magazine as a Medium: *Aspen* 1965–1971," in *Artists' Magazines: An Alternative Space for Art* (Cambridge: MIT Press, 2011), 43–67.

"The initiative of former *Women's Wear Daily* and *Advertising Age* editor Phyllis Johnson, *Aspen* began as a lifestyle magazine about the Colorado ski resort after which it was named." "The Magazine That Wasn't," *Eye Magazine,* October 10, 2012, http://www.eyemagazine.com/blog/post/the-magazine-that-wasnt. Review of the exhibition, "Aspen Magazine: 1965–1971," September 11, 2012–March 3, 2013, at Whitechapel Gallery, London.

Prior art: "The text is a tissue of citations, resulting from the thousand sources of culture." Roland Barthes, "The Death of the

Author"; cited in Logie, "1967: The Birth of 'The Death of the Author.'" Logie argues that Barthes's essay must be considered a "site-specific" artwork versus the "literary essay" it became upon re-publication.

The "literary version": Roland Barthes, "La mort de l'auteur," *Manteia* 5 (1968): 12–17. Re-published in Roland Barthes, *Image, Music, Text,* ed. and trans. Stephen Heath (London: Fontana, 1977), 142–48.

Stéphane Mallarmé: "Things exist, we do not need to create them; we only need to seize the relationships between them." ("Les choses existent, nous n'avons pas à les créer, nous n'avons qu'à en saisir les rapports.") Cited in Laurie Edson, *Reading Relationally: Postmodern Perspectives on Literature and Art* (Ann Arbor: University of Michigan Press, 2000), 63; with reference to Stéphane Mallarmé, "Réponse à Jules Huret," in *Oeuvres complètes,* eds. Henri Mondor and Georges Jean-Aubry (Paris: Éditions Gallimard, 1961), 871. First published as Stéphane Mallarmé, "Réponse à Jules Huret [Enquête sur l'évolution littéraire]," *L'Écho de Paris* (March 14, 1891). In response to Jules Huret, *Enquête sur l'évolution littéraire: Conversations avec MM. Renan, de Goncourt, Émile Zola, Guy de Maupassant, Huysmans, Anatole France, Maurice Barrès [...] etc.* (Paris: Bibliothèque-Charpentier, 1891).

II. The Game Continues...

> Contemporary art, no matter how much it has defined itself by a taste for negation, can still be analyzed as a set of assertions, of a formal kind.[2]
>
> — Susan Sontag

There are slight shifts in tonality and tense between the 1967 *Aspen* 5–6 version of "The Aesthetics of Silence" and the 1969

---

2   Ibid., 31.

anthologized version. Sontag has either re-written the text or an editor has taken liberties with the 1967 version. There is also the "problem" of the situated and commissioned work (the 1967 version) versus its conversion to autonomous "literary essay" (the 1969 version). "The Aesthetics of Silence" was effectively a continuation of Sontag's *Against Interpretation and Other Essays* (New York: Farrar, Straus and Giroux, 1966).

"Silence is the artist's ultimate other-worldly gesture: by silence, he frees himself from servile bondage to the world, which appears as patron, client, consumer, antagonist, arbiter, and distorter of his work." Sontag, "The Aesthetics of Silence," in *Styles of Radical Will,* 6.

"Most valuable art in our time has been experienced by audiences as a move into silence (or unintelligibility or invisibility or inaudibility); a dismantling of the artist's competence, his responsible sense of vocation — and therefore as an aggression against them" (ibid., 7).

"Art conceived as a spiritual project is no exception. As an abstracted and fragmented replica of the positive nihilism expounded by the radical religious myths, the serious art of our time has moved increasingly toward the most excruciating inflections of consciousness. Conceivably, irony is the only feasible counterweight to this grave use of art as the arena for the ordeal of consciousness. The present prospect is that artists will go on abolishing art, only to resurrect it in a more retracted version. As long as art bears up under the pressure of chronic interrogation, it would seem desirable that some of the questions have a certain playful quality" (ibid., 33).

"The avowal of agnosticism on the artist's part may look like frivolity or contempt for the audience. Antonioni enraged many people by saying that he didn't know himself what happened to the missing girl in *L'Avventura* — whether she had, for instance, committed suicide or run away. But this attitude should be taken with the utmost seriousness. When the artist declares that he 'knows' no more than the audience does, he is saying that all the meaning resides in the work itself, that there is nothing 'behind' it. Such works seem to lack sense or meaning only to the extent that entrenched critical attitudes have established as a dictum for the narrative arts (cinema as well as prose literature) that meaning resides solely in this surplus of 'reference' outside the work — to the 'real world' or to the artist's 'intention.'" Susan Sontag, "Bergman's Persona" (1967), in *Styles of Radical Will,* 134.

"Godard's films are simply what they are and also events that push their audience to reconsider the meaning and scope of the art form of which they are instances; they're not only works of art, but meta-artistic activities aimed at reorganizing the audience's entire sensibility. Far from deploring the tendency, I believe that the most promising future of films as an art lies in this direction." Susan Sontag, "Godard" (1968), in *Styles of Radical Will,* 152. With reference to Godard's "literary" intentions, even if these intentions are then deconstructed and problematized across the life-work of his films. "Indeed, from the numerous references to books, mentions of writers' names, and quotations and longer excerpts from literary texts scattered throughout his films, Godard gives the impression of being engaged in an unending agon with the very fact of literature — which he attempts to settle partially by incorporating literature and literary identities into his films" (ibid., 153).

III. The Game Shifts...

> Up to a point, the community and historicity of the artist's means are implicit in the very fact of intersubjectivity: each person is a being-in-a-world. But today, particularly in the

arts using language, this normal state of affairs is felt as an extraordinary, wearying problem.[3]

— Susan Sontag

Jacques Derrida, *De la grammatologie* (Paris: Éditions de Minuit, 1967). Jacques Derrida, *Of Grammatology,* trans. Gayatri Chakravorty Spivak (Baltimore: Johns Hopkins University Press, 1976). Failed doctoral thesis: *De la grammatologie: Essai sur la permanence de concepts platonicien, aristotélicien et scolastique de signe écrit* (*Of Grammatology: Essay on the Permanence of Platonic, Aristotelian and Scholastic Concepts of the Written Sign*).

Original PhD thesis title: "The Ideality of the Literary Object" (1957). See also "The Time of a Thesis" (Sorbonne doctoral defense, 1980), and "The Time of a Thesis: Punctuations," trans. Kathleen McLaughlin, in *Philosophy in France Today,* ed. Alan Montefiore (Cambridge: Cambridge University Press, 1983), 34–50.

"*De la grammatologie* is one of three books which Jacques Derrida published in 1967. The other two are *La voix et le phénomène* and *L'écriture et la différence. De la grammatologie* (Paris: Éditions de Minuit) was translated into English as *Of Grammatology* by Gayatri Chakravorty Spivak and first published in 1976 by Johns Hopkins University Press. A corrected edition of the translation appeared in 1997. Since its translation into English a number of commentators have tried to explain and discuss the philosophical issues the book presents." Zeynep Direk, "Review of *Reading Derrida's 'Of Grammatology'*," *Notre Dame Philosophical Reviews,* May 13, 2015, https://ndpr.nd.edu/news/reading-derrida-s-of-grammatology/. Review of Sean Gaston and Ian Maclachlan, eds., *Reading Derrida's "Of Grammatology"* (London: Continuum, 2011).

---

3   Ibid., 15.

Speech and Phenomenon: And Other Essays on Husserl's Theory of Signs, trans. David B. Allison (Evanston: Northwestern University Press, 1973). Or, *Voice and Phenomenon: Introduction to the Problem of the Sign in Husserl's Phenomenology,* trans. Leonard Lawlor (Evanston: Northwestern University Press, 2011). First published as *La voix et le phénomène* (Paris: Presses Universitaires de France, 1967).

Contents: 1. "Sign and Signs"; 2. "The Reduction of Indication"; 3. "Meaning as Soliloquy"; 4. "Meaning and Representation"; 5. "Signs and the Blink of an Eye"; 6. "The Voice that Keeps Silence"; 7. "The Supplement of Origin"

La voix et le phénomène (1967) was based on Derrida's 1953–1954 master's thesis (diplôme d'études supérieures, École Normale Supérieure), *The Problem of Genesis in Husserl's Phenomenology,* by way of the essay, "'Genesis and Structure' and Phenomenology" (written in 1959, first published in *L'écriture et la différence*).

Jacques Derrida, *The Problem of Genesis in Husserl's Phenomenology,* trans. Marian Hobson (Chicago: University of Chicago Press, 2003). First published as *Le problème de la genèse dans la philosophie de Husserl* (Paris: Presses Universitaires de France, 1990).

Jacques Derrida, *Writing and Difference,* trans. Alan Bass (Chicago: University of Chicago Press, 1978). First published as *L'écriture et la différence* (Paris: Éditions du Seuil, 1967). Collected lectures and essays.

Contents: 1. "Force and Signification"; 2. "Cogito and the History of Madness"; 3. "Edmond Jabès and the Question of the Book"; 4. "Violence and Metaphysics: An Essay on the Thought of Emmanuel Levinas"; 5. "'Genesis and Structure' and Phenomenology"; 6. "Parole soufflée"; 7. "Freud and the Scene of Writing"; 8. "The Theater of Cruelty and the Closure of Representation"; 9. "From Restricted to General Economy:

A Hegelianism without Reserve"; 10. "Structure, Sign, and Play in the Discourse of the Human Sciences"; 11. "Ellipsis"

"Is it not possible to invert all of Levinas's statements on this point? By showing, for example, that writing can assist itself, for it has time and freedom, escaping better than speech from empirical urgencies." Derrida, *Writing and Difference,* 102. See Jacques Derrida, "Violence and Metaphysics: An Essay on the Thought of Emmanuel Levinas" (1964), in *Writing and Difference,* 79–153.

"*Of Grammatology* is one of the texts to which people turn in order to make sense of 'post-structuralism.' It was Derrida's doctorat d'état, and appears in 1967 as nothing less than a breakthrough into a discursive field dominated by structuralism. As the early essay 'Structure, Sign, and Play' makes clear, structuralism presupposes the totality of the sense of the system it studies and conceives it as structured by laws. In the structure as *structuralism* 'fantasizes' *about it* there is a center that remains constant despite the permutation or the substitution of elements. Challenging the structuralist thesis, Derrida not only proposed a new conception of structure as de-centered, but also a new way of conceiving that which remains the same in the structure. Sameness no longer meant the identity of structural laws, but reiteration of writing, repetition productive of difference." Direk, "Review of *Reading Derrida's 'Of Grammatology'*."

"As is well known, *Of Grammatology* claims that in the history of metaphysics writing is read as threat, dead, exterior, and fallen. He argues that the privilege given through logocentric and phonocentric assumptions has always been undermined, haunted, supplemented by 'the signifier of the signifier.' He used the expression 'the signifier of the signifier' as another name for that iterable origin, a matrix of play that precedes presence and absence of the signified world of things and of concepts, meanings as of the sensible and the intelligible realms. At times Derrida speaks of the 'appearance' of this play. *Différance* can be taken as hinting at the equiprimordiality of the concealment and the unconcealment of this play. Derrida often speaks of play as apparent because the play is that of a non-dialectizable 'radical materiality' or historicity; and yet its movement could be taken as negligible or dispensable by the history of metaphysics in the face of what it produces, i.e., sense. The play of writing is the movement of this radical materiality that is the condition of both the possibility and the impossibility of all infinitisation. That is Derrida's way of inscribing finitude or death, at the origin of temporality, in terms of which the Heideggerian meaning of *Being* is articulated. What are the hermeneutical implications of this thesis? Derrida suggests that reading should free itself from the classical categories of history, 'and perhaps above all, from the categories of the history of philosophy' (*Of Grammatology*, lxxxix)" (ibid.).

"As Royle rightly notes, *Of Grammatology* is polyphonous; it has multiple voices: On the one hand, it is dry and formal. It is a thesis written for the French Academia, dominated on occasion by an authoritarian I and the most inclusive we. Avowedly, it respects classical norms, the constitutive protocols of what it studies. Thus it requires from the reader the most normative attentiveness and traditional respect for grammar, syntax, argument and demonstration. On the other hand, it involves a notoriously delirious tone and calls our attention to that which is 'bizarre' as it goes on between the lines, in hidden spaces. This polyphony of rational order and delirium is perhaps the underlying reason why we have found Derrida's philosophy so attractive" (ibid).

"Derrida became famous at the end of the 1960s, with the publication of three books in 1967. At this time, other great books appear: Foucault's *Les mots et les choses* (*The Order of Things* is the English language title) in 1966; Deleuze's *Difference and Repetition* in 1968. It is hard to deny that the philosophy publications of this epoch indicate that we have before us a kind of philosophical moment (a moment perhaps comparable to the moment of German Idealism at the beginning of the 19th century).

Hélène Cixous calls this generation of French philosophers 'the incorruptibles.' In the last interview Derrida gave (to *Le Monde* on August 19, 2004), he provided an interpretation of 'the incorruptibles': 'By means of metonymy, I call this approach [of "the incorruptibles"] an intransigent, even incorruptible, *ethos* of writing and thinking …, without concession even to philosophy, and not letting public opinion, the media, or the phantasm of an intimidating readership frighten or force us into simplifying or repressing. Hence the strict taste for refinement, paradox, and aporia.' Derrida proclaims that today, more than ever, 'this predilection [for paradox and aporia] remains a requirement.'" Leonard Lawlor, "Jacques Derrida," *Stanford Encyclopedia of Philosophy,* ed. Edward N. Zalta, Fall 2019, https://plato.stanford.edu/archives/fall2019/entries/derrida/.

"No one will ever know from what secret I am writing *and the fact that I say so changes nothing.*" Jacques Derrida, "Circumfession," 3–315, in Jacques Derrida and Geoffrey Bennington, *Jacques Derrida,* trans. Geoffrey Bennington (Chicago: University of Chicago Press, 1993), 207. Italics added. First published as "Circonfession," in Jacques Derrida and Geoffrey Bennington, *Jacques Derrida* (Paris: Éditions du Seuil, 1991). Written in 1990. See the appearance of Derrida's statement regarding this "secret" in Stanley Corngold, "A Contempt for Popularity: The Faith of a Heretic," in *Walter Kaufmann: Philosopher, Humanist, Heretic* (Princeton: Princeton University Press, 2019), 186. There is an implication here of a "messianic silence," or a silence that constitutes the basis for subjectivity proper. The perhaps ironic enjoinder, "the fact that I say so changes nothing," would appear to confirm a sense of the apophatic (and the relation of silence to language, enforced or otherwise). In this manner, and in the context of auto-biography, the basis of self-justification (writing) is "no justification" (silence). Perhaps it is Derrida's hope that in this Zen koan-like statement by Derrida (resembling "What is the sound of one hand clapping?") that some will see the distance between language and its other — silence.

IV. The Game Intensifies...

> This dual character of language — its abstractness, and
> its 'fallenness' in history — serves as a microcosm of the
> unhappy character of the arts today. Art is so far along the
> labyrinthine pathways of the project of transcendence that
> one can hardly conceive of it turning back, short of the most
> drastic and punitive 'cultural revolution.' Yet at the same time,
> art is foundering in the debilitating tide of what once seemed
> the crowning achievement of European thought: secular
> historical consciousness. In little more than two centuries,
> the consciousness of history has transformed itself from a
> liberation, an opening of doors, blessed enlightenment, into an
> almost insupportable burden of self-consciousness. It's scarcely
> possible for the artist to write a word (or render an image or
> make a gesture) that doesn't remind him of something already
> achieved.[4]
>
> — Susan Sontag

Giorgio Agamben, *Homo Sacer: Sovereign Power and Bare Life*,
trans. Daniel Heller-Roazen (Stanford: Stanford University
Press, 1998). First published as *Il potere sovrano e la nuda vita*,
Homo sacer, vol. 1 (Turin: Giulio Einaudi Editore, 1995).

Agamben's Homo Sacer publications project (1995–2014)
includes: 1. *Homo Sacer: Sovereign Power and Bare Life*; 2.1.
State of Exception; 2.2. *Stasis: Civil War as a Political Paradigm*; 2.3. *The Sacrament of Language: An Archeology of the
Oath*; 2.4. *The Kingdom and the Glory: For a Theological Ge-
nealogy of Economy and Glory*; 2.5. *Opus Dei: An Archeology
of Duty*; 3. *Remnants of Auschwitz: The Witness and the Archive*; 4.1. *The Highest Poverty: Monastic Rules and Form-of-
Life*; 4.2. *The Use of Bodies*

---

4   Ibid., 14.

See Adam Kotsko, "The Order of the Homo Sacer Series," *An und für sich,* August 26, 2015, https://itself.blog/2015/08/26/the-order-of-the-homo-sacer-series/.

See Giorgio Agamben, *The Omnibus "Homo Sacer"* (Stanford: Stanford University Press, 2017).

Giorgio Agamben, *Potentialities: Collected Essays in Philosophy,* ed. and trans. Daniel Heller-Roazen (Stanford: Stanford University Press, 1999).

Leland de la Durantaye, *Giorgio Agamben: A Critical Introduction* (Stanford: Stanford University Press, 2009).

Kevin Attell, *Beyond the Threshold of Deconstruction* (New York: Fordham University Press, 2014).

Giorgio Agamben, *What Is Philosophy?,* trans. Lorenzo Chiesa (Stanford: Stanford University Press, 2017).

Arthur Willemse, *The Motif of the Messianic: Law, Life, and Writing in Agamben's Reading of Derrida* (Lanham: Lexington Books, 2017).

Adam Kotsko and Carlo Salzani, eds., *Agamben's Philosophical Lineage* (Edinburgh: Edinburgh University Press, 2017). Derrida appears in the third section, subsumed under "Submerged Influences," which also includes Theodor Adorno, Sigmund Freud, Jacques Lacan, Karl Marx, Antonio Negri, Gershom Scholem, and Simone Weil.

Peter Goodrich and Michel Rosenfeld, eds. *Administering Interpretation: Derrida, Agamben, and the Political Theology of Law* (New York: Fordham University Press, 2019).

Contents: 1. Peter Goodrich and Michel Rosenfeld, "Introduction"; 2. Bernhard Schlink, "Interpretations as Hypotheses"; Stanley Fish, "Antonin Scalia, Bernhard Schlink, and Lancelot Andrewes: Reading Heller"; 3. Jeanne L. Schroeder, "The Interpreter, the Analyst, and the Scientist"; 4. Michel Rosenfeld, "Law against Justice and Solidarity: Rereading Derrida and Agamben at the Margins of the One and the Many"; 5. Pierre Legrand, "Jacques Derrida Never Wrote about Law"; 6. Bernadette Meyler, "Derrida's Legal Times: Decision, Declaration, Deferral, and Event"; 7. Katrin Trüstedt, "Derrida's Shylock: The Letter and the Life of Law"; 8. Marinos Diamantides, "A Postmodern Hetoimasia: Feigning Sovereignty during the State of Exception"; 9. Laurent de Sutter, "Contra iurem: Giorgio Agamben's Two Ontologies"; 10. Giovanna Borradori, "Cities of Refuge, Rebel Cities, and the City to Come"; 11. Marco Wan, "A Ghost Story: Electoral Reform and Hong Kong Popular Theater"; 12. Allen Feldman, "Appearing under Erasure: Of War, Disappearance, and the Contretemps"

See Derrida's late critique of Agamben (plus Foucault and others regarding the discourse of "animality" "biopolitics," and "sovereignty"), in *The Beast and the Sovereign.* Jacques Derrida, *The Beast and the Sovereign,* trans. Geoffrey Bennington, 2 vols. (Chicago: University of Chicago Press, 2009–2011). Derrida's "final seminar" at École des Hautes Études en Sciences Sociales (School of Advanced Studies in the Social Sciences), Paris (Vol. 1, 2001–2002; Vol. 2, 2002–2003). First published as Séminaire: *La bête et le souverain,* eds. Michel Lisse, Marie-Louise Mallet, and Ginette Michaud, 2 vols. (Paris: Éditions Galilée, 2008–2010).

David Farrell Krell, *Derrida and Our Animal Others: Derrida's Final Seminar, "The Beast and the Sovereign"* (Bloomington: Indiana University Press, 2013).

Michael Naas, *The End of the World and Other Teachable Moments: Jacques Derrida's Final Seminar* (New York: Fordham University Press, 2015).

See also Giorgio Agamben, "Friendship," *Contretemps: An On-line Journal of Philosophy* 5 (December 2004): 2–7.

For Agamben's supposed "rejection" of Derrida, see Lorenzo Fabbri's interview with Jean-Luc Nancy, "Philosophy as Chance," *Critical Inquiry* 33, no. 2 (2007): 427–40.

"Another familiarity of the 'Experimentum Vocis,' in a gloss on the implications of his argument, is the reference to Jacques Derrida. While works like *Language and Death, What Is an Apparatus?*, and 'Pardes' have seen Agamben address Derrida in the past, the dialogue between the two thinkers has been most often in subtext. This changes in *What Is Philosophy?* with the direct accusation that one of Derrida's most celebrated works, *On Grammatology,* and with it 'the Derridean critique of metaphysics is therefore founded on an insufficient reading of Aristotle, which fails to question precisely the original status of the *gramma* in *On Interpretation.*' Derrida's grammatology is thus hardly a liberating insight, because 'metaphysics is always already a grammatology' since 'Western metaphysics sets in its original place the gramma and not the voice'. The recent attention to the dialogue between Agamben and Derrida, in the work of Kevin Attell and Virgil Brower, receives an important contribution as Agamben offers a brief but acidic polemic against one of the fundamental works of Derrida's oeuvre. This point, as well as the 'Experimentum Vocis' as a whole, will prove provocative, not only for Derridean readers, but for theorists of language more broadly, in both human and posthuman frames." Michael P.A. Murphy, "Review of Giorgio Agamben, *What Is Philosophy?,*" *Philosophy in Review* 38, no. 3 (August 2018): 86. See Attell, *Beyond the Threshold of Deconstruction,* and Virgil W. Brower, "Jacques Derrida," 230–41, in Kotsko and Salzani, eds., *Agamben's Philosophical Lineage.* The latter text by Brower is a semi-sarcastic rendering of Agamben's supposed crimes against Derrida. While sarcastic (and Brower is a Derridean, as is Kotsko, editor of the book in which this forensic report appears), the comments are illustrative of the struggle between Derrida and Agamben to define what, if anything, "lies on the other side" of — or "lies on behalf" of — language and law.

Excerpt One: "A *sovereignty of surpassing* is perhaps detectable in the 'essential claim of sovereignty' that Derrida discerns in Agamben's style: that 'most irrepressible gesture' repeated throughout *Homo Sacer* (and not only there) to be 'the first to say who *will have been first*'. Worse, he 'wants to be first twice, the first to see and announce [...] and also the first to recall that [...] it's always been like that.'" Brower, "Jacques Derrida," 231, with reference to Derrida, *The Beast and the Sovereign,* 92, 330. All ellipses and italics belong to Brower's text.

Excerpt Two: "Despite his thresholds and zones of indifferences, Agamben remains an oppositional thinker; as if never 'truly' testing (or losing) that 'fundamental belief of metaphysicians' vilified by Nietzsche as '*the belief in oppositions of values*'. The oppositional ideality on which his project grounds itself seems automatically, even unconsciously, determined by compulsive repetition to develop only ever within the binary confines of one canonical opposition after another, even doubling-down on a dialectics. Even in his more mature breakthrough text, Derrida finds him 'putting his money on the concept of "bare life," which he identifies with *zoè,* in opposition to *bios*.'" Brower, "Jacques Derrida," 232, with reference to Derrida, *The Beast and the Sovereign,* 92–93, 328. All italics belong to Brower's text.

Excerpt Three: "If 'thwarted messianism' is 'a suspension of the messianic', then would not the 'suspended *Aufhebung*' of trace be, at the same time, a thwarted opposition? It is as if messianism, alone, must be thwarted in order to secure oppositionality itself. Perhaps nothing less than a messiah could possibly thwart dialectics. Could an unthwarted messianism ever become messianic, anyway? Especially in any Pauline valence? (At times, Derrida seems to play a role in Agamben's works much like Paul does in those of Nietzsche.) If thwarting the messianic entails opening it to a future coming of justice (or finding it opening

itself, as such), yet doing so 'without horizon of expectation [...
nor ...] prophetic prefiguration', then Derrida perhaps thwarts
it into a 'messianicity without messianism' ... but a messianicity,
nonetheless." Brower, "Jacques Derrida," 233, with reference to
Jacques Derrida, "Faith and Knowledge," trans. Samuel Weber,
in *Acts of Religion,* ed. Gil Anidjar (New York: Routledge, 2002),
56 and passim, and Jacques Derrida, *Rogues: Two Essays on Reason,* trans. Pascale-Anne Brault and Michael Naas (Stanford:
Stanford University Press, 2005), 110, 153. All ellipses and italics
belong to Brower's text.

Excerpt Four: "The sovereign state of exception seems ever to
suspend innumerable zones of indistinction, leaving Agamben — barely alive — to determine what it accomplishes by its
so-called suspension ... so that he may solve, resolve and sur-
pass it." Brower, "Jacques Derrida," 234. The ellipses belong to
Brower's text.

Excerpt Five: "If the most important aspect of Agamben's reading of Derrida is 'trace', then the most significant facet of 'trace' is
its *self-referentiality*. Trace is exceptional self-reference. This will
develop throughout Agamben's works into a form of auto-affection that is perhaps his most primal — even inventive — lesson
learned from Derrida. It sets the stage for later investigations:
mode, modification and self-modification; affect, affection and
auto-affection; suspense, suspension, 'autosuspension'; constitu-
ency, constitution and 'autoconstitution'" (ibid., 234), with reference to Agamben's *Language and Death,* "Pardes," *Remnants of
Auschwitz,* and the concluding book in the Homo Sacer series,
The Use of Bodies. The italics belong to Brower's text. Derrida
develops the concept of "trace" across his earliest works, from
Of Grammatology to *Margins of Philosophy.* Jacques Derrida,
Margins of Philosophy, trans. Alan Bass (Chicago: University of
Chicago Press, 1972). First published as *Marges de la philosophie*
(Paris: Éditions de Minuit, 1972). Brower states that Agamben
was most influenced by *Of Grammatology, Voice and Phenom-*

ena, and *Margins of Philosophy,* insofar as those are the works by Derrida most often cited or *not* cited.

On this difference of the role of the gramma, plus the dialectical struggles between the concept of "ban" and "secret," between Agamben and Derrida, see Arthur Willemse, *The Motif of the Messianic: Law, Life, and Writing in Agamben's Reading of Derrida,* 30–34. Willemse states that Derrida's "weak messianism" comes from his desire to maintain the "ban" (the "secret" of what language covers up) while Agamben's "strong messianism" comes from his desire to ban banishment — to violate the ban and expose what language covers up (hypostatized in Agamben's *Potentialities* as "self-destining without destiny," 131). The ban or secret concerns the role language plays in constitutive practices at the expense of what appears to be reducible to truth (Plato's "thing itself" or Being). Willemse also rightly notes that, despite good intentions, Agamben's hermeneutic nonetheless fails to overturn the ban imposed by language (per Aristotle's *gramma*). Willemse considers the key essay for Agamben regarding the ban to be Jean-Luc Nancy's essay "Abandoned Being" (1981), in *The Birth to Presence,* trans. Brian Holmes et al, (Stanford: Stanford University Press, 1993), 36–47. First published as "L'être abandonné," *Argile* 23–24 (Spring 1981): 193–217. Subsequently re-published as "L'être abandonné," in *L'impératif catégorique* (Paris: Flammarion, 1983), 139–53.

Agamben: "Only if it is possible to think the Being of abandonment beyond every idea of the law (even that of the empty form of laws being in force without significance) will we have moved out of the paradox of sovereignty towards a politics freed from every ban." Willemse, *The Motif of the Messianic,* 33, with reference to Giorgio Agamben, "Form of Law," in *Homo Sacer: Sovereign Power and Bare Life,* 38. Nancy and Agamben also differ on the implied, imagined, or real unsurpassable limit of *gramma* — viz., on the possibility of recovering the name crossed out by the iterative and fallen nature of language (and speech) itself.

In full: "Only if it is possible to think the Being of abandonment beyond every idea of law (even that of the empty form of laws being in force without significance) will we have moved out of the paradox of sovereignty toward a politics freed from every ban. *A pure form of law is only the empty form of relation. Yet the empty form of relation is no longer a law but a zone of indistinguishability between law and life, which is to say, a state of exception*" (ibid., italics added).

Giorgio Agamben, *Pilate and Jesus,* trans. Adam Kotsko (Stanford: Stanford University Press, 2015). "Here is the cross; here is history" (ibid., 45). First published as *Pilato e Gesù* (Rome: Nottetempo, 2013). See also the silence in "The Grand Inquisitor," in Dostoevsky's *The Brothers Karamazov.*

Thus, "History" and "No History," and the time of an artistic scholarship to come is a peculiar instance of "the time that remains…" — as exception and as exemplary form of "bare life."

A Short History of the Project

The following is a short history of the Works for Works project, showing origins, working papers, events, etc., as forms of "prior art" embedded in the research and publications project. OOI is Out of India, an informal collective that developed from transmedia projects at CEPT University, Ahmedabad, India, in early 2017. (See "Acknowledgments.") OOI-MTA is the successor collective. The MTA (Metropolitan Transmedia Authority) was formed in late 2019. The hybrid acronym connotes the presence of the OOI archive in MTA projects.

I. Fellowships and Residencies: 2017–2018

Teaching Fellow, Transmedia Projects (performance-based media projects), Center for Environmental Planning and Technology (CEPT University), Faculty of Architecture, Ahmedabad, Gujarat, India, July 2016–July 2017

Visiting Research Fellow, "The Moral Rights of Authors in the Age of Cognitive Capitalism," Birkbeck Institute for the Humanities (co-sponsored by the School of Arts and School of Law), Birkbeck, University of London, London, England, June 2017

Vittore Branca Center for the Study of Italian Culture Co-funded Research Residency, "The Moral Rights of Authors in the Venetian Renaissance," Giorgio Cini Foundation, Venice, Italy, May 15–30/July 21–28, 2017

II. Lectures and Performance-based Projects: 2017–2019

"Emptiness within Emptiness" (performance, exhibition, spectacle), Gavin Keeney, w/ Owen O'Carroll, Harsh Bhavsar, Ishita Jain, Anne Feenstra, and Gauri Wagenaar, w/ C'est la CEPT Troupe (Callan Green, Alexandre Guerin, Aniket Ahuja, Vishal Mehta, Mansi Shah, Marta Agueda Carlero, Juan Gutierrez Sanchez, Antonin Lenglen, Matteo Farina, Mihir Jagdish et al.), Archiprix+++/C'est la CEPT + NID, Faculty of Architecture, CEPT University, Ahmedabad, India, in association w/ Archiprix International 2017 (January-February 2017)

"Representation as Research?" (symposium presentation), "Creative Encounters with Science and Technology: Legacies, Imaginaries and Futures," Kochi-Muziris Biennale, Kochi, India (February 2017)

"Seeing and Hearing Things Again" (cinétracts/three-screen presentation/performance of "Library of Tears," "Will It Cry?," "Emptiness within Emptiness," and "The End of CEPT as Viewed by Archangel St. Michael"), presented by Gavin Keeney and the C'est la CEPT Troupe, GIDC Bhavan, CEPT University, Ahmedabad, India (April 2017)

CEPT University Summer School, "Media, Transmedia, and the Multiple Arts," Ljubljana, Slovenia, and Venice, Italy (May 2017)

"Works for Works" (lecture), Deakin University, School of Architecture and Built Environment, Geelong, Victoria, Australia (May 2018)

"Transmedia + Lived Law" (cinétracts/master class), International Graduate Centre for the Study of Culture (GCSC), Justus Liebig University, Giessen, Hesse, Germany (February 2019)

"What's Next? Works for Works" (cinétracts/performative lecture), Academy of Visual Arts, Ljubljana, Slovenia (February 2019)

"Transmedia + The Transcendental Object" (cinétract/performative lecture), ZRC-SAZU, Ljubljana, Slovenia (February 2019)

"Resting Place" (performance-based transmedia project), OOI Collective (Gavin Keeney, Ishita Jain, Harsh Bhavsar et al.), Abhivyakti City Arts Project, Ahmedabad, India (April-May 2019)

"The Icons of IRWIN: First Sessions" (performance-based transmedia project), Gavin Keeney et al., in association w/ Academy of Visual Arts, w/ the assistance of IRWIN, Ljubljana, Slovenia (May 2019)

"Doshi's Other Legacy" (cinétract/symposium presentation), Frascari Symposium IV, "The Secret Lives of the Architectural Drawings and Models: From Translating to Archiving, Collecting and Displaying," Session: "The Afterlife of Drawings and Models: Archiving, Collecting, Exhibiting and Teaching," Kingston School of Art, London, England (June 2019)

"Works for Works" (cinétract/performative lecture), Arts, Letters and Numbers, Averill Park, New York, USA (July 2019)

III. Cinétracts and Film-essays: OOI-MTA – 2017–2019

Emptiness within Emptiness (2017) w/ Harsh Bhavsar, Owen O'Carroll, Ishita Jain et al. – 1.29 GB (MP4) – 9:22

Video record of an investigation of "institutional memory" and its repressions through the projection and interception of 18 archival images of The School of Architecture in the mid-1960s – Produced in a semi-abandoned badminton building designed by B.V. Doshi in the early 1960s and one of several temporary homes for The School of Architecture prior to build-out of the current CEPT University campus – Faculty of Architecture, CEPT University, Ahmedabad, India

The End of CEPT as Viewed by the Archangel Saint Michael (2017), w/ Harsh Bhavsar, Owen O'Carroll, Ishita Jain – 244.8 MB (MP4) – 4:01

Video record of semi-toxic outtake of the "C'est la CEPT" project, produced following a visit to the Kochi Biennale and a brief exchange with B.V. Doshi to request an image of his shadow – Follows upon "Emptiness within Emptiness" as summary statement of CEPT University's suppression of its own past – Faculty of Architecture, CEPT University, Ahmedabad, India

Will it Cry? (2017), w/ Harsh Bhavsar, Owen O'Carroll, Ishita Jain – 292.2 MB (MP4) – 1:56

Video record of the trial session for establishing the minimal *mise-en-scène* for the "Library of Tears" performative design-competition project – Faculty of Architecture, CEPT University, Ahmedabad, India

Library of Tears (2017), w/ Harsh Bhavsar, Owen O'Carroll, Ishita Jain – 2.17 GB (MP4) – 14:50

Video record of student sessions associated with the performative design-competition project, "Library of Tears" – Faculty of Architecture, CEPT University, Ahmedabad, India

Semaforo Trailer (2017), w/ Harsh Bhavsar et al. – 332.5 MB (MP4) – 5:50

> Trailer for a video record of a "forced march" through archives and exhibitions in Ljubljana, Slovenia, and Venice, Italy, in search of forms of transmedia resulting in a bespoke set of divination cards (edition of 1) subsequently denoted to the library of the Giorgio Cini Foundation, Venice – Full video and associated ephemera donated to CEPT Archives – Faculty of Architecture, CEPT University, Ahmedabad, India

"Fragments of Khi + Ordo" (2019), w/ Ishita Jain, Harsh Bhavsar, Owen O'Carroll – 1.12 GB + 720.3 MB (MP4) – 7:21 + 4:52

> "Room A-702" and "The Dying Mermaid" – Cinétracts associated with the 15-day performance, "Resting Place," Abhivyakti City Arts Project, Ahmedabad, India, April-May 2019 – Ocean-Archive, TBA21 Academy, Thyssen-Bornemisza Art Contemporary, Venice, Italy

IV. Archived Projects and Editioned Works: OOI-MTA – 2017–2019

"C'est la La-la Land" (CEPT University, 2017) – "Emptiness within Emptiness" and "Library of Tears" – Media dossiers (still photography, video files, documentation of experimental, theatrical-cinematic design seminars), Faculty of Architecture, CEPT University, January–March 2017, in association w/ National Institute of Design, Ahmedabad, India, Archiprix International 2017, and "Empty Pr(oe)mises" design competition, EMST, Athens, Greece, Museum of Contemporary Cuts, and *Leonardo Electronic Journal* – C'est la CEPT Troupe (Gavin Keeney, Owen O'Carroll, Harsh Bhavsar, Ishita Jain et al.) – CEPT Archives, CEPT University, Ahmedabad, India

"C'est la CEPT" (CEPT University, 2017) – Limited-edition DVD (stop-motion video and "liner notes") – "Emptiness within

Emptiness," "The End of CEPT as Viewed by Archangel St. Michael," and "Library of Tears" – C'est la CEPT Troupe (Gavin Keeney, Owen O'Carroll, Harsh Bhavsar, Ishita Jain et al.) – Media dossier of performance-based works, CEPT University, January–February 2017, in association with Archiprix International 2017 – Graphic design by the Fingerprint Collective – Edition of 24 – Faculty of Architecture, CEPT University, Ahmedabad, India

"Addenda to 'C'est la La-la Land'" – CEPT University Summer School: "Media, Transmedia, and the Multiple Arts," Ljubljana, Slovenia, and Venice Italy, May 2017 – SWS media files: "Semaforo" (video), ephemera (booklets and pamphlets from the Venice Art Biennale 2017) – CEPT Archives, CEPT University, Ahmedabad, India

"Semaforo: Divination Cards" – CEPT University Summer School: "Media, Transmedia, and the Multiple Arts," Ljubljana, Slovenia, and Venice, Italy, May 2017 – Editioned set of 26 double-sided, black-and-white and color cards designed by Harsh Bhavsar, Gavin Keeney – Alpha numerical system by Gavin Keeney, Jullo da Costa – Photography by SWS students and Harsh Bhavsar – Based on *Triompho di Fortuna di Sigismondo Fanti Ferrarese* (Venezia, 1526) – 24 x 8 cm – Laser printed by Al Canal, Venice, Italy + Grace ICT, Venice, Italy, 300gm off-white card stock – "7 + 1 = 0" letterpress stamp by 3B Press Tipografia, Venice, Italy, 300gm Magnani watercolor paper – Edition of 1 – Giorgio Cini Foundation, Venice, Italy

"Fragments of Khi + Ordo" (OOI Collective/MTA, 2019), w/ Ishita Jain, Harsh Bhavsar, Owen O'Carroll – "Room A-702" and "The Dying Mermaid" – Cinétracts associated with the 15-day performance, "Resting Place," Abhivyakti City Arts Project, Ahmedabad, India, April-May 2019 – Ocean-Archive, TBA21 Academy, Thyssen-Bornemisza Art Contemporary, Venice, Italy

"MTA Scriptoria: Preliminary Exegesis" (MTA, 2019), w/ Ishita Jain, Harsh Bhavsar, and Owen O'Carroll – Multimedia dossier – Proposal for scriptoria for the networked production of transmedia projects – Future Architecture Platform, Ljubljana, Slovenia

V. Working Papers: OOI-MTA – 2017–2020

A Brief Sketch of *Privilegio* in the Venetian Renaissance

July 2017; "A Brief Sketch of *Privilegio* in the Venetian Renaissance," *Intellectual Property Watch* (February 7, 2018); this essay was part of an intended study of the Early Modern book in relation to editioning strategies and copyright law subsequently abandoned in favor of a more or less "transhistorical" treatment of author rights en route to a collective, non-proprietary rights regime in the works-for-works idiom

Dogma

September 2017; Four-point statement regarding "Event, Fall, Return"; included in "Texts for Artist–Scholars," Abhivyakti City Arts Project, April-May 2019; "Texts for Artist–Scholars" was a set of informally editioned texts (numbered and stamped with the OOI ideogram) distributed during performance sessions associated with the Abhivyakti City Arts Project; the "Event, Fall, Return" trinitarian analytic was first applied to the early 2017 transmedia events associated with OOI projects as generative and iterative foundation for the production of perpetually curated, performance-based works

In Search of Benevolent Capital

September 2017; "In Search of Benevolent Capital: Part I," *P2P Foundation* (February 14, 2018); "In Search of Benevolent Capital: Part II," *P2P Foundation* (February 21, 2018);

this essay accompanied the 001 submissions campaign to find institutional and other support for ongoing transmedia projects

Vector of Transmedia

October 2017; "Library of Tears," w/ Owen O'Carroll and Harsh Bhavsar, *Keep It Dirty, vol. "a": Filth* (November 2017); included in "Texts for Artist–Scholars," Abhivyakti City Arts Project, April-May 2019; the multimedia dossier published by the online journal *Keep It Dirty* subsequently vanished (was de-published) in early 2019

Event, Fall – Harvest

October 2017; "Event, Fall – Harvest," *MediaCommons Field Guide: Erasure* (November 2017); variation on the theme of "Event, Fall, Return"; in this case, the premise is that at certain times it is necessary to close a project and "archive" it, for later use and/or as record

Symbolic Capital – Bibliography

January 2018; Notes on Bourdieu's concept of symbolic capital; folded into aspects of the thematic of "editioning works"

A Few Points about Author Rights

January 2018; "A Few Points about Author Rights," *P2P Foundation* (February 6, 2018) https://blog.p2pfoundation.net/a-few-points-about-author-rights/2018/02/06; written in response to the European Commission's Digital Single Market Strategy and intended enforcement of so-called "neighboring rights" in the digital marketplace

Agent Intellect and Black Zones

March 2018; "Agent Intellect and Black Zones," *P2P Foundation* (March 8, 2018); based on an essay from *Not-I/Thou: The Other Subject of Art and Architecture* (Newcastle upon Tyne: Cambridge Scholars Publishing, 2014), part and parcel of the PhD project, "Visual Agency in Art and Architecture"

Universal Rights and Authors

April 2018; Advisory on the rights of authors regarding Open Access, collecting societies, etc.; subsequently incorporated into arguments for a new exception for works without concern for proprietary rights as such; as with moral rights of authors, universal rights – as inextricably caught up in statutory law concerning monetary rights – require re-calibration at another level before they have any demonstrative agency for works

Out of India Prospectus

May 2018; OOI prospectus featuring four projects; "Emptiness within Emptiness," "Library of Tears," "Semaforo," "Khi + Ordo"; circulated in association with OOI submissions, as "portfolio"

Doshi's Other Legacy

May 2018; Essay describing the "Emptiness within Emptiness" ("C'est la CEPT") performance-based project, CEPT University, Ahmedabad, India, February 2017; associated media presented at Kingston School of Art, Kingston, UK, June 2019; published in 2019 to Research Gate as test of the efficacy of online, pre-publication repositories

Report on Quantum Submissions

June 2018; Summary of 74 OOI submissions ("an eight-month series of submissions for open-call exhibitions, design competitions, art residencies, teaching and research fellowships, conferences, and publications") from October 2017 to June 2018; 65-page version included as prop in "Resting Place," Abhivyakti City Arts Project, April–May 2019; includes a July 2017 reading of the divination cards produced as part of the CEPT Summer School project, "Media, Transmedia, and the Multiple Arts"; the question asked of the cards was, "Where to take 'Lived Law'?" – precursor project to Works for Works

The Law of Quantum Submissions

June 2018; Satirical summary of possible outcomes of the quantum submissions process

The Spilled Cup

July 2018; written in direct response to the eight-month 001 submissions project documented in "Report on Quantum Submissions"; included in "Texts for Artist–Scholars," Abhivyakti City Arts Project, April–May 2019

Lessons for Artist–scholars

July 2018; "Executive Summary" of "Report on Quantum Submissions"; included in "Texts for Artist–scholars," Abhivyakti City Arts Project, April–May 2019

Real Subsummation

October 2018; subsequently re-titled "(Ir)real Subsumma-tion" to distance the terms of the short essay from Marxist theories of real subsumption; this early text summarized the developing presentiment that it is all but impossible to escape the mechanisms of appropriation and expropriation of works in both academia and the art world without re-defining the foundational terms of engagement

The Artist–scholar

October 2018; brief text privileging specularity in works of artistic scholarship; connects the concept of avant-garde artistic scholarship to the Romantic quest for the literary work of art; elements of this thematic are to be found in *"Elsewhere": Essays in Art, Architecture, and Cultural Production 2002–2011* (Newcastle upon Tyne: Cambridge Scholars Publishing, 2011)

White Cube-Black Box

November 2018; document utilized in applications for several research fellowships or artist residencies; included in "Texts for Artist–Scholars," Abhivyakti City Arts Project, April–May 2019; this document is also the basis for the physical design of the set for "Resting Place," Abhivyakti City Arts Project – a black-box theater inside a white cube

8 Maxims for Academics

November 2018; included in "Texts for Artist–Scholars," Abhivyakti City Arts Project, April-May 2019

Notes on Moral Rights

November 2018; a transitional summary of elements of research on the moral rights of authors as developed in *Knowledge, Spirit, Law: Book 1, Radical Scholarship* (Brooklyn: punctum books, 2015), and *Knowledge, Spirit, Law: Book 2, The Anti-capitalist Sublime* (Earth: punctum books, 2017); the intention to anthologize the Knowledge, Spirit, Law publications, by issuing updated editions, was subsequently abandoned when the defense of author rights shifted to an elective "right to have no rights"; the first texts in the Works for Works project were, therefore, evocations of a de facto exit from an analysis of publication ecosystems and a focus, instead, on ways of circumventing the appropriations given to such ecosystems; in the same manner, the privileging of the Enlightenment-era exception for works associated with Diderot et al., of early texts, was de-privileged and became the basis for a new exception devoid of author rights per se and favoring the transfer of moral rights to works

The Venusians Return

April 2019; photo-essay prepared during and for the performance-based project, "Resting Place," Abhivyakti City Arts Project, Ahmedabad, India; included in "Texts for Artist–Scholars," Abhivyakti City Arts Project, April–May 2019; the text describes an imaginary conversation held in a garden in Ahmedabad on Good Friday 2019 between two Venusian storytellers regarding St. Paul and the "end of the Law"

Ideational Franciscanism – Bibliography

July 2019; utilized in several post-doctoral research fellowship applications; working bibliography for "Ideational Franciscanism," an essay originally intended for Book One of the Works for Works project but subsequently deferred; traceable to Part II of *Not-I/Thou: The Other Subject of Art and Architecture* (Newcastle upon Tyne: Cambridge Scholars Publishing, 2014), "What Is Franciscan Ontology?"

Speculative Presentism and the Icons of IRWIN

November 2019; notes on forms of presentism to be found in the performance-based project, "The Icons of IRWIN," Ljubljana, Slovenia, May 2019

The Editioning of Works

November–December 2019; first return to the Situationist International and the development of the "History" and "No

History" dialectic of Works for Works; subsequently expanded with reference to the work of T.J. Clark and arguments to be found in *New Left Review* regarding "left defeatism"; early instance of the footnotes sponsoring a second narrative in excess of the structuralist-inspired argumentation of the main text; the supplemental narrative of the footnotes imparts a generative and iterative ambiance to the overall argument on behalf of works for works

Coda: Jarman's *Blue*

December 2019; based on preliminary research conducted in London, in June 2017, in association with the research fellowship, "The Moral Rights of Authors in the Age of Cognitive Capitalism," Birkbeck, University London; folded into the essay "Lived Law and Works for Works" and the preliminary discussion of "scriptoria" as milieux

Paralogisms for Scriptoria

December 2019; folded into the essay "Lived Law and Works for Works" and the discussion of "scriptoria" as milieux

Preposterous Presentism

December 2019; Three-part poem as illustration of time-senses and verb tenses; intentionally "Yeatsian"; the coastline invoked as atmospheric affect is northwest Wales

Icons of IRWIN

January 2020; discursive "post-rationalization" of performance-based research conducted in Ljubljana, Slovenia, in May 2019

Ontic and De-ontic

January 2020; folded into "The Editioning of Works"; second major dialectic within the Works for Works "structuralist" analytic; key passage in the justification for the transfer of moral rights to works proper

Prior Art and Things Given

January 2020; privileging of prior art as justification for the elective negation of proprietary rights; first instance for the re-introduction of themes from post-phenomenology by way of "things given"

Metaphysic of Prior Art

February 2020; folded into "Prior Art and Things Given"; primary instantiation of the abstract or universal precepts required to prevent the collapse of Works for Works back into the fold of situated critique and historical-materialist readings of art and scholarship

The Law Disappears…

January-February 2020; conclusion and escape route from situated critique and circular arguments regarding what constitutes an exception to over-determination for works; recurring motif across the various essays, and drawn primarily from the "silence" to be found in Veronese's *The Wedding at Cana*

Language and Its Other

February 2020; a "fifty-year" sampling of texts and positions across the arc of conceptual art, post-structuralism, and post-phenomenology; originating in an extensive footnote on the subject and historical context of Sontag's "Aesthetics of Silence" and later removed, re-formatted, and expanded as "Appendix B: Notes on Language and Its Other," in this volume

Bibliography

Adams, Thomas Jessen. "The Theater of Inequality." *Non-site,*
    August 12, 2014. https://nonsite.org/feature/the-theater-of-
    inequality.

Adorno, Theodor W. *Critical Models: Interventions and
    Catchwords.* Translated by Henry W. Pickford. New York:
    Columbia University Press, 2005.

———. *Minima Moralia: Reflections from Damaged Life.*
    Translated by E.F.N. Jephcott. London: Verso, 1974. First
    published as *Minima Moralia: Reflexionen aus dem
    beschädigten Leben,* ed. Rolf Tiedemann (Frankfurt:
    Suhrkamp Verlag, 1951).

———. *Negative Dialectics.* Translated by E.B. Ashton. New
    York: Seabury Press, 1973. First published as *Negative
    Dialektik* (Frankfurt am Main: Suhrkamp, 1966).

———. *The Culture Industry: Selected Essays on Mass Culture.*
    Edited by J.M. Bernstein. London: Routledge, 1991.

Adorno, Theodor W., and Max Horkheimer. *Dialectic of
    Enlightenment: Philosophical Fragments.* Edited by Gunzelin
    Schmid Noerr. Translated by Edmund Jephcott. Stanford:
    Stanford University Press, 2002. First published as *Dialektik
    der Aufklärung: Philosophische Fragmente* (Amsterdam:
    Querido, 1947).

Agamben, Giorgio. *The Adventure.* Translated by Lorenzo
Chiesa. Cambridge: MIT Press, 2018. First published as
L'avventura (Rome: Nottetempo, 2015).

———. *The Highest Poverty: Monastic Rules and Form-of-Life.*
Translated by Adam Kotsko. Stanford: Stanford University
Press, 2013. First published as *Altissima povertà: Regole
monastiche e forma di vita* (Vicenza: Neri Pozza, 2011).

———. *The Signature of All Things: On Method.* Translated
by Luca D'Isanto and Kevin Attell. New York: Zone Books,
2009. First published as *Signatura rerum: Sul metodo*
(Turin: Bollati Boringhieri, 2008).

———. *The Time That Remains: A Commentary on the Letter
to the Romans.* Translated by Patricia Dailey. Stanford:
Stanford University Press, 2005. First published as *Il tempo
che resta* (Turin: Bollati Boringhieri, 2000).

Agamben, Giorgio, and Peppe Savà. "'God Didn't Die, He
Was Transformed into Money': An Interview with Giorgio
Agamben." *Libcom,* February 10, 2014. https://libcom.
org/article/god-didnt-die-he-was-transformed-money-
interview-giorgio-agamben-peppe-sava.

Ali, Tariq. *The Idea of Communism.* London: Seagull, 2009.

Anderson, Perry. "Origins of the Present Crisis." *New Left
Review* 1, no. 23 (January–February 1964): 26–53. https://
newleftreview.org/issues/i23/articles/perry-anderson-
origins-of-the-present-crisis.

———. *The Origins of Postmodernity.* London: Verso, 1998.

Anon. [Jochmann, Carl Gustav]. *Über die Sprache.* Heidelberg:
C.F. Winter, 1828.

Avicenna [Abū-ʿAlī al-Ḥusayn ibn-ʿAbdallāh Ibn-Sīnā]. *Liber
de anima, seu sextus de naturalibus.* Edited by Simone van
Riet. 2 vols. Louvain and Leiden: Peeters and E.J. Brill, 1968-
1972.

Bachelard, Gaston. *The Psychoanalysis of Fire.* Translated by
Alan C.M. Ross. Preface by Northrop Frye. Boston: Beacon
Press, 1964. First published as *La psychanalyse du feu* (Paris:
Éditions Gallimard, 1938).

Badiou, Alain. *Being and Event.* Translated by Oliver Feltham. London: Continuum, 2005. First published as *L'être et l'événement* (Paris: Éditions du Seuil, 1988).

———. *Saint Paul: The Foundation of Universalism.* Translated by Ray Brassier. Stanford: Stanford University Press, 2003.

———. *The Communist Hypothesis.* Translated by David Macey and Steve Corcoran. London: Verso, 2010. First published as *L'hypothèse communiste* (Paris: Nouvelles Éditions Lignes, 2009).

Badovinac, Zdenka, Eda Čufer, and Anthony Gardner, eds. NSK *from Kapital to Capital: Neue Slowenische Kunst – An Event of the Final Decade of Yugoslavia.* Cambridge: MIT Press, 2015. Exh. cat.

Balfour, Ian. *The Rhetoric of Romantic Prophecy.* Stanford: Stanford University Press, 2002.

Barthes, Roland. *Writing Degree Zero.* Translated by Annette Lavers and Colin Smith. London: Jonathan Cape, 1967. First published as *Le degré zéro de l'écriture* (Paris: Éditions du Seuil, 1953).

Bastani, Aaron. *Fully Automated Luxury Communism: A Manifesto.* London: Verso, 2019.

Bates, David W. *Enlightenment Aberrations: Error and Revolution in France.* Ithaca: Cornell University Press, 2002.

Becker, Carl L. *The Heavenly City of the Eighteenth-century Philosophers.* New Haven: Yale University Press, 1932.

Beistegui, Miguel de. *Heidegger and the Political: Dystopias.* London: Routledge, 1998.

Benjamin, Walter. "Die Rückschritte der Poesie bei Carl Gustav Jochmann." *Zeitschrift für Sozialforschung* 8 (1939–1940): 92–114.

———. *Gesammelten Schriften.* 7 vols. Edited by Rolf Tiedemann and Hermann Schweppenhäuser. Frankfurt am Main: Suhrkamp Verlag, 1972–1989.

———. *Illuminations: Essays and Reflections.* Edited by Hannah Arendt. Translated by Harry Zohn. New York: Schocken, 1969.

————. "On the Concept of History." Translated by Dennis Redmond. "Walter Benjamin Archive," *Marxists.org,* 2005. https://www.marxists.org/reference/archive/benjamin/1940/history.htm.

————. *One-way Street and Other Writings.* Translated by J.A. Underwood. London: Penguin, 2009.

————. *The Arcades Project.* Translated by Howard Eiland and Kevin McLaughlin. Cambridge: Belknap Press, 1999. First published as *Das Passagen-Werk,* ed. Rolf Tiedemann (Frankfurt am Main: Suhrkamp, 1982).

————. *Walter Benjamin: Selected Writings.* Edited by Marcus Bullock and Michael W. Jennings. 4 vols. Cambridge: Belknap Press, 1996-2003.

Berger, John. *Hold Everything Dear: Dispatches on Survival and Resistance.* New York: Knopf Doubleday, 2009.

Berman, Morris. *Why America Failed: The Roots of Imperial Decline.* Hoboken: John Wiley and Sons, 2012.

Bonaventure (Giovanni di Fidanza). *Saint Bonaventure's De reductione atrium ad theologiam: A Commentary.* Edited and translated by Emma Thérèse Healy. 2nd edn. Saint Bonaventure: Franciscan Institute, Saint Bonaventure University, 1955.

————. *The Works of Bonaventure.* Translated by José de Vinck. 5 vols. Paterson: St. Anthony Guild Press, 1960-1970.

Bourdieu, Pierre. *Homo academicus.* Translated by Peter Collier. Stanford: Stanford University Press, 1988. First published as *Homo academicus* (Paris: Éditions de Minuit, 1984).

————. *The Field of Cultural Production: Essays on Art and Literature.* Edited by Randal Johnson. New York: Columbia University Press, 1993.

Bourriaud, Nicolas. *Relational Aesthetics.* Translated by Simon Pleasance and Fronza Woods, with Mathieu Copeland. Dijon: Les Presses du Réel, 2002. First published as *Esthétique relationnelle* (Dijon: Les Presses du Réel, 1998).

Breton, André. *Free Rein (La clé des champs).* Translated by Michel Parmentier and Jacqueline d'Amboise. Lincoln:

University of Nebraska Press, 1995. First published as *La clé des champs* (Paris: Éditions du Sagittaire, 1953).

Brown, Gregory S. *A Field of Honor: Writers, Court Culture and Public Theater in the French Intellectual Field from Racine to the Revolution.* New York: Columbia University Press, 2005.

Brown, Horatio F. *The Venetian Printing Press: An Historical Study Based Upon Documents for the Most Part Hitherto Unpublished.* London: John C. Nimmo, 1891.

Buchloh, Benjamin H.D. *Neo-avantgarde and Culture Industry: Essays on European and American Art from 1955 to 1975.* Cambridge: MIT Press, 2000.

Cacciari, Massimo. *Posthumous People: Vienna at the Turning Point.* Translated by Rodger Friedman. Stanford: Stanford University Press, 1996. First published as *Dallo Steinhof: Prospettive viennesi del primo Novecento* (Milan: Adelphi, 1980).

———. *The Withholding Power: An Essay on Political Theology.* Translated by Edi Pucci. London: Bloomsbury, 2018. First published as *Il potere che frena* (Milan: Adelphi Edizioni, 2014).

Callinicos, Alex. "The Radical Left and the Crisis – A Tale of Two Journals." *Europe Solidaire Sans Frontières,* March 14, 2010. http://europe-solidaire.org/spip.php?article26129#nb4.

Canguilhem, Georges. "The Living and Its Milieu." Translated by John Savage. *Grey Room* 3 (Spring 2001): 7–31. First published in Georges Canguilhem, *La connaissance de la vie* (Paris: Librairie Hachette, 1952).

Carretto, Carlo. *I, Francis: The Spirit of St. Francis of Assisi.* London: Collins, 1982. First published as *Io, Francesco* (Assisi: Cittadella Editrice, 1980).

Castellani, Carlo. *I privilegi di stampa e la proprietà letteraria en Venezia dalla introduzione della stampa nella città fin verso la fine del secolo XVIII.* Venice: Fratelli Visentini, 1888.

Chartier, Roger. *The Cultural Origins of the French Revolution.* Translated by Lydia G. Cochrane. Durham: Duke University Press, 1991. First published as *Les origines culturelles de la Révolution française* (Paris: Éditions du Seuil, 1990).

Chateaubriand, François-René Vicomte de. *Memoirs of Chateaubriand: From His Birth in 1768, Till His Return to France.* London: Henry Colburn, 1849.

Chesterton, G.K. *The Everlasting Man.* Mineola: Dover, 2007.

Clark, T.J. *Farewell to an Idea: Episodes from a History of Modernism.* New Haven: Yale University Press, 1999.

———. "For a Left with No Future." *New Left Review* 2, no. 74 (March–April 2012): 53–75. https://newleftreview.org/issues/ii74/articles/t-j-clark-for-a-left-with-no-future.

———. "Origins of the Present Crisis." *New Left Review* 2, no. 2 (March–April 2000): 85–96. https://newleftreview.org/issues/i23/articles/perry-anderson-origins-of-the-present-crisis.

———. "Reinstall the Footlights." *London Review of Books* 39, no. 22 (November 16, 2017): 10–12. https://www.lrb.co.uk/the-paper/v39/n22/t.j.-clark/reinstall-the-footlights.

Clark, T.J., and Donald Nicholson-Smith. "Why Art Can't Kill the Situationist International." *October* 79 (Winter 1997): 15–31. http://www.jstor.org/stable/778836.

Coetzee, J.M. "The Man Who Went Shopping for Truth." *The Guardian,* January 20, 2001. https://www.theguardian.com/books/2001/jan/20/history.society.

Collini, Stefan. "A Life in Politics: *New Left Review* at 50." *The Guardian,* February 13, 2010. https://www.theguardian.com/books/2010/feb/13/new-left-review-stefan-collini.

———. "In Real Sound Stupidity the English Are Unrivalled." *London Review of Books* 42, no. 3 (February 6, 2020). https://www.lrb.co.uk/the-paper/v42/n03/stefan-collini/in-real-sound-stupidity-the-english-are-unrivalled.

———. *Speaking of Universities.* London: Verso, 2017.

———. *What Are Universities For?* London: Penguin, 2012.

Courtine, Jean-François, et al. *Of the Sublime: Presence in Question.* Translated by Jeffrey S. Librett. Albany: State University of New York Press, 1993. First published as *Du sublime* (Paris: Belin, 1988).

Day, Gail. *Dialectical Passions: Negation in Postwar Art Theory.* New York: Columbia University Press, 2010.

Dean, Jodi. *The Communist Horizon.* London: Verso, 2012.

Debord, Guy. *Correspondence: The Foundation of the Situationist International (June 1957–August 1960).* Translated by Stuart Kendall and John McHale. Los Angeles: Semiotext(e), 2009.

Debray, Régis. "Remarks on the Spectacle." *New Left Review* 214 (November-December 1995): 134–41. https://newleftreview. org/issues/i214/articles/regis-debray-remarks-on-the-spectacle. First published as "A propos du spectacle: Réponse à un jeune chercheur," *Le débat* 85 (May-August 1995): 3–15. [The NLR translation is an abridged version of the *Le débat* version.]

———. *Revolution within the Revolution? Armed Struggle and Political Struggle in Latin America.* Translated by Bobbye Ortiz and Gregory Elliott. London: Verso, 2017. First published as *Révolution dans la révolution* (Paris: Maspéro, 1967).

Deleuze, Gilles. *Pure Immanence: Essays on a Life.* Translated by Anne Boyman. New York: Zone Books, 2001.

Derrida, Jacques. S*pecters of Marx: The State of the Debt, the Work of Mourning, and the New International.* Translated by Peggy Kamuf. New York: Routledge, 1994. First published as *Spectres de Marx: L'état de la dette, le travail du deuil et la nouvelle Internationale* (Paris: Éditions Galilée, 1993).

Derrida, Jacques, and Paule Thévenin. *The Secret Art of Antonin Artaud.* Translated by Mary Ann Caws. Cambridge: MIT Press, 1998. Abridged translation of *Antonin Artaud: Dessins et portraits* (Paris: Éditions Gallimard, 1986).

Diderot, Denis. *Œuvres complètes.* Edited by Roger Lewinter. 15 vols. Paris: Le Club Français du Livre, 1969-1973.

Dostoevsky, Fyodor. *The Brothers Karamazov.* Translated by Constance Garnett. New York: Macmillan, 1922.

———. *The Brothers Karamazov.* Translated by Constance Garnett. New York: Modern Library, 1996. First published in book form as *Brat'ia Karamazovy. Roman v chetyrekh chastiakh s epilogom* (St. Petersburg: Tipografiia brat, 1880).

Douzinas, Costas, and Slavoj Žižek, eds. *The Idea of Communism.* London: Verso, 2010.

Dvořák, Max. "Über Greco und den Manierismus." *Wiener Jahrbuch für Kunstgeschichte* 1 (1921–1922): 22–42.

Eagleton, Terry. "The Slow Death of the University." *Chronicle of Higher Education,* April 6, 2015. http://chronicle.com/article/The-Slow-Death-of-the/228991/.

Eve, Martin Paul. "Open Access and Neoliberalism." *Social Epistemology Review and Reply Collective* 9, no. 1 (2020): 22–26. https://wp.me/p1Bfg0-4Lv.

Fausto di Riez [Saint Faustus of Riez]. "Discorso 5 sull' Epifania" (c.440). In *Patrologiae Latinae,* Supplementum 3, 560–62. Paris: Jacques-Paul Migne, 1841–1855.

Fellows, Jay. *Ruskin's Maze: Mastery and Madness in His Art.* Princeton: Princeton University Press, 1981.

———. *The Failing Distance: The Autobiographical Impulse in John Ruskin.* Baltimore: Johns Hopkins University Press, 1975.

Flash Art 329 (February–March 2020), "Post-copyright." https://flash---art.com/issue/329-february-march-2020/.

Focillon, Henri. *The Life of Forms in Art.* Translated by Charles Beecher Hogan and George Kubler. New York: Zone Books, 1989. First published as *Vie des formes* (Paris: E. Leroux, 1934).

Freedberg, Hannah, ed. *Thomas Ruff: Nature Morte.* London: Gagosian Gallery, 2015. Exh. cat.

Fuchs, Christian. "Introduction." *tripleC* 18, no. 1, Special Issue: "Communicative Socialism/Digital Socialism" (2020): 1–31. https://doi.org/10.31269/triplec.v18i1.1144.

Gagliardi, Pasquale, Bruno Latour, and Pedro Memelsdorff, eds. *Coping with the Past: Conservation and Restoration.* Florence: Leo S. Olschki, 2010.

Gagliardi, Pasquale, ed. *The Miracle of Cana: The Originality of the Re-production — The Wedding at Cana by Paolo Veronese: The Biography of a Painting, the Creation of a*

Facsimile and Its Theoretical Implications. Venice/Verona: Fondazione Giorgio Cini/Cierre Edizioni, 2011.

Gerulaitus, Leonardas Vytautas. *Printing and Publishing in Fifteenth-century Venice.* Chicago: American Library Association, 1976.

Gilson, Étienne. *La philosophie de Saint Bonaventure.* Paris: J. Vrin, 1924.

———. *Peinture et réalité.* Paris: J. Vrin, 1958. French edition of *Painting and Reality* (New York: Pantheon, 1957).

Giroux, Henry A. *Against the Terror of Neoliberalism.* Boulder: Paradigm Publishers, 2008.

———. "Culture of Cruelty: The Age of Neoliberal Authoritarianism." *CounterPunch,* October 23, 2015. http://www.counterpunch.org/2015/10/23/culture-of-cruelty-the-age-of-neoliberal-authoritarianism/.

Godard, Jean-Luc, dir. *Film socialisme* (2010). Kino Lorber, 2012. DVD.

Godard, Jean-Luc, and Anne-Marie Miéville, dirs. *Four Short Films: De l'origine du XXIᵉ siècle* (2000); *The Old Place* (1999); *Liberté et patrie* (2002); *and Je vous salue, Sarajevo* (1993). ECM, 2006. DVD.

Gogol, Nikolai. *Dead Souls.* Translated by Richard Pevear and Larissa Volokhonsky. New York: Pantheon, 1996. First published as *Mertvye dushi, poema* (Moscow: Universitetskaia tipografiia, 1842).

———. *Dead Souls.* Translated by Constance Garnett. New York: Barnes and Noble, 2005.

———. *"Dead Souls": The Reavey Translation, Backgrounds and Sources, Essays in Criticism.* Edited by George Gibian. New York: W.W. Norton, 1985.

Goldmann, Lucien. *The Hidden God: A Study of Tragic Vision in the "Pensées" of Pascal and the Tragedies of Racine.* Translated by Philip Thody. London: Routledge and Kegan Paul, 1964. First published as *Le dieu caché: Étude sur la vision tragique dans les Pensées de Pascal et dans le théâtre de Racine* (Paris: Éditions Gallimard, 1955).

Gramsci, Antonio. *Selections from Political Writings*, Vol. 1: *1910–1920*. Edited by Quintin Hoare. Translated by John Mathews. London: Lawrence and Wishart, 1977.

Gray, John. *Black Mass*. New York: Farrar, Straus and Giroux, 2007.

Greenaway, Peter. *Veronese, The Wedding at Cana: A Vision by Peter Greenaway*. Milan: Charta, 2010.

Greenberger, Alex. "Jean-Luc Godard to Stage Exhibition Version of His Latest Film, 'The Image Book.'" *Artnews*, May 11, 2018. http://www.artnews.com/2018/05/11/jean-luc-godard-stage-exhibition-version-latest-film-image-book/.

Griffero, Tonino, and Marco Tedeschini, eds. *Atmosphere and Aesthetics: A Plural Perspective*. Cham: Palgrave Macmillan, 2019.

Hall, Gary. "Anti-bourgeois Theory." *Media Theory*, February 3, 2020. http://mediatheoryjournal.org/gary-hall-anti-bourgeois-theory/.

Hall, Stuart. "The Neo-liberal Revolution." *Cultural Studies* 25, no. 6 (November 2011): 705–28. DOI: 10.1080/09502386.2011.619886.

Hallyn, Fernand. *The Poetic Structure of the World: Copernicus and Kepler*. Translated by Donald M. Leslie. New York: Zone Books, 1990. First published as *La structure poétique du monde: Copernic, Kepler* (Paris: Éditions du Seuil, 1987).

Hardt, Michael, and Antonio Negri. *Commonwealth*. Cambridge: Belknap Press, 2009.

Harris, Malcolm. *Kids These Days: Human Capital and the Making of Millennials*. New York: Little, Brown and Company, 2017.

Harvey, David. *A Brief History of Neoliberalism*. Oxford: Oxford University Press, 2005.

Hauser, Arnold. *Mannerism: The Crisis of the Renaissance and the Origin of Modern Art*. Translated by Eric Mosbacher. London: Routledge and Kegan Paul, 1965. First published as *Der Manierismus: Die Krise der Renaissance und der Ursprung der modernen Kunst* (Munich: Beck, 1964).

———. *Sozialgeschichte der Kunst und Literatur.* 2 vols. Munich: Beck, 1953. First published as *The Social History of Art,* trans. Arnold Hauser and Stanley Godman, 2 vols. (London: Routledge and Kegan Paul, 1951).

Hesse, Carla. "Enlightenment Epistemologies and the Laws of Authorship in Revolutionary France, 1777–1793." *Representations* 30 (1990): 114–16. DOI: 10.2307/2928448.

Hewison, Robert, ed. *Ruskin's Artists: Studies in the Victorian Visual Economy.* Aldershot: Ashgate, 2000.

Hissette, Roland, ed. *Enquête sur les 219 articles condamnés à Paris le 7 Mars 1277.* Philosophes Médiévaux, XXII. Louvain and Paris: Publications Universitaires and Vander-Oyez, 1977.

Hobsbawm, Eric. *Behind the Times: The Decline and Fall of the Twentieth-century Avant-gardes.* New York: Thames and Hudson, 1998.

Holmwood, John. "Commercial Enclosure: Whatever Happened to Open Access?" *Radical Philosophy* 181 (2018): 2–5. https://www.radicalphilosophy.com/commentary/commercial-enclosure.

Holmwood, John, and Chaime Marcuello Servós. "Challenges to Public Universities: Digitalisation, Commodification and Precarity." *Social Epistemology* 33, no. 4 (2019): 309–20. DOI: 10.1080/02691728.2019.1638986.

Hudson, Cheryl, and Joanna Williams, eds. *Why Academic Freedom Matters: A Response to Current Challenges.* London: Civitas, 2016.

Hugenholtz, P. Bernt. "The Great Copyright Robbery: Rights Allocation in a Digital Environment." Institute for Information Law, *University of Amsterdam,* 2000. https://www.ivir.nl/publicaties/download/thegreatcopyrightrobbery.pdf.

Hugh of Digne. "De finibus paupertatis." *Archivum Franciscanum Historicum* 5 (1912): 277–90.

Ingarden, Roman. *The Literary Work of Art: An Investigation on the Borderlines of Ontology, Logic, and Theory of Literature.* Translated by George G. Grabowicz. Evanston:

Northwestern University Press, 1973. First published as *Das literarische Kunstwerk: Eine Untesuchung aus dem Grenzgebiet der Ontologie, Logik und Literaturwissenschaft* (Halle/Saale: M. Niemeyer, 1931).

International Journal of Žižek Studies 4, no. 4 (2010). Special issue: "Žižek's Theology." http://oajournals.blogspot.com/2011/02/international-journal-of-zizek-studies.html.

Jablonka, Ivan, and Roger Chartier. "The Book: Its Past, Its Future." Translated by Eric Rosencrantz. *Books and Ideas,* October 14, 2013, http://www.booksandideas.net/The-Book-Its-Past-Its-Future.html.

Janicaud, Dominique, Jean-François Courtine, Jean-Louis Chrétien, Michel Henry, and Jean-Luc Marion. *Phenomenology and the "Theological Turn": The French Debate.* New York: Fordham University Press, 2000.

Jarman, Derek. *Chroma: A Book of Colour – June '93.* London: Century/Random House, 1994.

———. *Modern Nature: The Journals of Derek Jarman.* London: Vintage, 1991.

Jarman, Derek, dir. *Blue* (1993). Kino Lorber, 2019. DVD.

———. *Blue: Text of a Film by Derek Jarman.* London: Channel 4 Television/BBC Radio 3, 1993.

"Jean-Luc Godard: Le Studio d'Orphée," *Prada Group,* December 2019. https://www.pradagroup.com/en/news-media/news-section/jean-luc-godard-le-studio-orphee.html.

Jensen, Robert. *Arguing for Our Lives: A User's Guide to Constructive Dialog.* San Francisco: City Lights Books, 2013.

Jones, Caroline A. "In Praise of Wetware." *MIT School of Humanities, Arts and Social Sciences,* February 18, 2019. https://shass.mit.edu/news/news-2019-ethics-and-ai-praise-wetware-caroline-jones.

Juergensmeyer, Erik, Anthony J. Nocella II, and Mark Seis, eds. *Neoliberalism and Academic Repression: The Fall of Academic Freedom in the Era of Trump.* Leiden: Brill, 2020.

Karatzogianni, Athina, and Andrew Robinson. "Virilio's Parting Song: The Administration of Fear and the

Privatisation of Communism through the Communism of Affect." *Media Theory* 3, no. 2 (December 2, 2019): 161–78. http://mediatheoryjournal.org/karatzogianni-robinson-virilios-parting-song/.

Keeney, Gavin. "A Brief Sketch of Privilegio in the Venetian Renaissance." *Intellectual Property Watch,* February 7, 2018. https://www.ip-watch.org/2018/02/07/brief-sketch-privilegio-venetian-renaissance/.

———. *Art as "Night": An Art-theological Treatise.* Newcastle upon Tyne: Cambridge Scholars Publishing, 2010.

———. *Dossier Chris Marker: The Suffering Image.* Newcastle upon Tyne: Cambridge Scholars Publishing, 2012.

———. *"Else-where": Essays in Art, Architecture, and Cultural Production, 2002–2011.* Newcastle upon Tyne: Cambridge Scholars Publishing, 2011.

———. *Knowledge, Spirit, Law: Book 1, Radical Scholarship.* Brooklyn: punctum books, 2015.

———. *Knowledge, Spirit, Law: Book 2, The Anti-capitalist Sublime.* Earth: punctum books, 2017.

Khlebnikov, Velimir. *Collected Works of Velimir Khlebnikov.* Edited by Charlotte Douglas. Translated by Paul Schmidt. 3 vols. Cambridge: Harvard University Press, 1987-1997.

———. *The King of Time: Selected Writings of the Russian Futurian.* Edited by Charlotte Douglas. Translated by Paul Schmidt. Cambridge: Harvard University Press, 1990.

Kioupkiolis, Alexandros. *Freedom after the Critique of Foundations: Marx, Liberalism, Castoriades and Agonistic Autonomy.* New York: Palgrave Macmillan, 2012.

Kleist, Heinrich von. "On the Marionette Theatre." Translated by Thomas G. Neumiller. *The Drama Review: TDR* 16, no. 3, Special issue: "Puppet" (September 1972): 22–26. DOI: 10.2307/1144768.

"Knowledge Entanglements." *KfW Stiftung and DAAD Artists-in-Berlin Program,* 2018. http://www.berliner-kuenstlerprogramm.de/en/veranstalt_detail.php?id=2061.

Kreckel, Reinhard, ed. *Soziale Ungleichheiten.* Göttingen: Otto Schwartz, 1983.

Lanier, Jaron. "The Gory Antigora: Illusions of Capitalism and Computers." *Cato Unbound,* January 8, 2006. https://www.cato-unbound.org/2006/01/08/jaron-lanier/gory-antigora-illusions-capitalism-computers.

Laswell, Bill. *Hashisheen: The End of Law.* Brussels: Sub Rosa, 1999. Audio CD.

Laycock, Henry. *Words without Objects: Semantics, Ontology, and Logic for Non-singularity.* Oxford: Clarendon Press, 2006.

Leaver-Yap, Mason. "Film without Film: Derek Jarman's *Blue.*" *Walker Art Center,* October 23, 2014. https://walkerart.org/magazine/film-without-film-derek-jarmans-blue.

Le Chapelier, Isaac-René-Guy. *Rapport fait par M. Le Chapelier, au nom du Comité de Constitution, sur la pétition des auteurs dramatiques, dans la séance du jeudi 13 janvier 1791, avec le décret rendu dans cette séance.* Paris: De l'Imprimerie Nationale, 1791.

Léger, Marc James. *Don't Network: The Avant-garde after Networks.* Brooklyn: Minor Compositions/Autonomedia, 2018.

Levinas, Emmanuel. *On Escape: De l'évasion.* Translated by Bettina Bergo. Stanford: Stanford University Press, 2003. First published in *Recherches philosophiques* 5 (1935–1936): 373–92. Re-published as *De l'évasion* (Montpellier: Éditions Fata Morgana, 1982).

———. *The Levinas Reader.* Edited by Séan Hand. Transalated by Alfonso Lingis. Oxford: Blackwell, 1989.

———. "La réalité et son ombre." *Les temps modernes* 38 (November 1948): 771–89.

———. "Reality and Its Shadow." In *Collected Philosophical Papers,* edited and translated by Alphonso Lingis, 1–13. Dordrecht: Martinus Nijhoff, 1987.

———. "Reality and Its Shadow." In *The Levinas Reader,* edited by Séan Hand, translated by Alphonso Lingis, 129–43. Oxford: Blackwell, 1989.

Lodder, Christina. "In Search of 0,10 – The Last Futurist Exhibition of Painting." *Burlington Magazine* 158, no. 1354

(2016): 61–63. https://www.burlington.org.uk/archive/back-issues/201601.

Lodder, Christina, ed. *Celebrating Suprematism: New Approaches to the Art of Kazimir Malevich*. Leiden: Brill, 2019.

Logie, John. "1967: The Birth of 'The Death of the Author.'" *College English* 75, no. 5 (May 2013): 493–512. https://www.jstor.org/stable/24238249.

Lordon, Frédéric. "Capitalism in the 21st Century Short on Capital: Why Piketty Isn't Marx." *Le monde diplomatique,* May 2015. http://mondediplo.com/2015/05/12piketty.

Lovnik, Geert. "Hermes on the Hudson: Notes on Media Theory after Snowden." *e-flux journal* 54, April 2014. https://www.e-flux.com/journal/54/59854/hermes-on-the-hudson-notes-on-media-theory-after-snowden/.

Lukács, György. *The Theory of the Novel: A Historico-philosophical Essay on the Forms of Great Epic Literature*. Translated by Anna Bostock. Cambridge: MIT Press, 1971. First published as *Die Theorie des Romans: Ein geschichtsphilosophischer Versuch über die Formen der großen Epik* (Berlin: P. Cassirer, 1920).

Malraux, André. *Les voix du silence*. Collection La Galerie de la Pléiade. Paris: Éditions Gallimard, 1951.

———. *The Voices of Silence*, trans. Stuart Gilbert. Garden City: Doubleday, 1953.

Marion, Jean-Luc. *Being Given: Toward a Phenomenology of Givenness.* Translated by Jeffrey L. Kosky. Stanford: Stanford University Press, 2002. First published as *Étant donné: Essai d'une phénoménologie de la donation* (Paris: Presses Universitaires de France, 1997).

———. *The Crossing of the Visible*. Translated by James K.A. Smith. Stanford: Stanford University Press, 2004. First published as *La croisée du visible* (Paris: Éditions de la Différence, 1991).

Maritain, Jacques. *Creative Intuition in Art and Poetry*. A.W. Mellon Lectures in the Fine Arts. Cleveland: Meridian Books, 1954.

Marker, Chris, dir. *La jetée* (1962)/*Sans soleil* (1982). Criterion Collection, 2007. DVD.

———. *Le fond de l'air est rouge* (*A Grin without a Cat*) (1993). Icarus Films, 2008. DVD.

Maurer, Armand A., CSB. *Medieval Philosophy*. Rev. edn. Toronto: Pontifical Institute of Mediaeval Studies, Toronto, 1962.

McCarraher, Eugene. *The Enchantments of Mammon: How Capitalism Became the Religion of Modernity*. Cambridge: Harvard University Press, 2019.

McDonough, Tom, ed. *Guy Debord and the Situationist International: Texts and Documents*. Cambridge: MIT Press, 2002.

Meltzer, David. "Interview with Kenneth Rexroth." *Bureau of Public Secrets*, n.d. http://www.bopsecrets.org/rexroth/meltzer.htm.

Meltzer, David, ed. *The San Francisco Poets*. New York: Ballantine, 1971.

Moulier Boutang, Yann. *Cognitive Capitalism*. Translated by Ed Emery. Cambridge: Polity, 2011. First published as *Le capitalisme cognitif: La nouvelle grande transformation* (Amsterdam: Éditions Amsterdam, 2007).

Nancy, Jean-Luc. *The Inoperative Community*. Edited by Peter Connor. Translated by Peter Connor, Lisa Garbus, Michael Holland, and Simona Sawhney. Minneapolis: University of Minnesota Press, 1991. First published as *La communauté désœuvrée* (Paris: Christian Bourgois, 1986).

Nejeschleba, Tomáš. "Thomas Aquinas and the Early Franciscan School on the Agent Intellect." *Verbum* 6, no. 1 (2004): 67–78. https://verbum.ppke.hu/index.php/verbum/article/view/193.

Nietzsche, Friedrich. *The Birth of Tragedy, and The Case of Wagner*. Translated by Walter Kaufmann. New York: Vintage, 1967. First published as *Die Geburt der Tragödie aus dem Geiste der Musik* (Leipzig: Fritzsch, 1872).

Novalis [Friedrich von Hardenberg]. *Novalis Schriften: Die Werke Friedrich von Hardenbergs*. Edited by Richard Samuel and Paul Kluckhohn. 5 vols. Stuttgart: W. Kohlhammer, 1960–1988.

O'Doherty, Brian. *Inside the White Cube: The Ideology of the Gallery Space.* San Francisco: Lapis Press, 1986.

O'Doherty, Brian, ed. *Aspen* 5–6 (Fall–Winter 1967).

Orwicz, Michael R. "Critical Discourse in the Formation of a Social History of Art: Anglo-American Response to Arnold Hauser." *Oxford Art Journal* 8, no. 2 (1985): 52–62. DOI: 10.1093/oxartj/8.2.52.

Osborne, Peter, ed. *Walter Benjamin: Critical Evaluations in Cultural Theory,* Vol. 2: *Modernity.* London: Routledge, 2005.

Parisi, Luciana. "Reprogramming Decisionism." *e-flux journal* 85, October 2017. http://www.e-flux.com/journal/85/155472/reprogramming-decisionism/.

Peake, Tony. *Derek Jarman: A Biography.* London: Little, Brown, 1999.

Petersen, Charles. "Serfs of Academe." *New York Review of Books,* March 12, 2020. https://www.nybooks.com/articles/2020/03/12/adjuncts-serfs-of-academe/.

Piedmont, Susan Carty. "Operative Criticism." *Journal of Architectural Education* 40, no. 1 (Fall 1986): 8–13. DOI: 10.1080/10464883.1986.11102649.

Piketty, Thomas. *Capital in the Twenty-first Century.* Translated by Arthur Goldhammer. Cambridge: Belknap Press, 2014. First published as *Le capital au XXIe siècle* (Paris: Éditions du Seuil, 2013).

———. *Capitalism and Ideology.* Translated by Arthur Goldhammer. Cambridge: Belknap Press, 2020. First published as *Capital et idéologie* (Paris: Éditions du Seuil, 2019).

Pistor, Katharina. *The Code of Capital: How the Law Creates Wealth and Inequality.* Princeton: Princeton University Press, 2019.

Pozza, Neri, et al., eds. *La Stampa degli incunaboli nel Veneto.* 2nd edn. Vicenza: Neri Pozza, 1984.

Proust, Marcel. *Remembrance of Things Past*, Vol. 1: *Swann's Way, Within a Budding Grove*. Translated by C.K. Scott Moncrieff and Terence Kilmartin. New York: Vintage, 1982. *Swann's Way* first published as *Du côté de chez Swann* (Paris: Éditions Grasset, 1913). *Within a Budding Grove* first published as *À l'ombre des jeunes filles en fleurs* (Paris: Éditions Gallimard, 1919).

"QS: Lessons for Artist–Scholars." Unpublished manuscript. 001 Archive, 2018.

Quinn, John Francis. *The Historical Constitution of St. Bonaventure's Philosophy*. Toronto: Pontifical Institute of Mediaeval Studies, 1973.

Rancière, Jacques. *The Politics of Aesthetics: The Distribution of the Sensible*. Translated with an introduction by Gabriel Rockhill. London: Continuum, 2004. First published as *Le partage du sensible: Esthétique et politique* (Paris: Fabrique: Diffusion Les Belles Lettres, 2000).

Richardson, John G., ed. *Handbook of Theory and Research for the Sociology of Education*. New York: Greenwood Press, 1986.

Ruskin, John. *Diaries*. Edited by Joan Evans and John Howard Whitehouse. 3 vols. Oxford: Clarendon Press, 1956–.

———. *The Stones of Venice*. 3 vols. London: George Allen and Unwin, 1925.

Schonfeld, Roger C. "Elsevier Acquires Bepress." *Scholarly Kitchen,* August 2, 2017. https://scholarlykitchen.sspnet. org/2017/08/02/elsevier-acquires-bepress/.

Schwab, Michael, and Henk Borgdorff, eds. *Artistic Research Expositions: Publishing Art in Academia*. Leiden: Leiden University Press, 2014.

Severino, Emanuele. *The Essence of Nihilism*. Edited by Ines Testoni and Alessandro Carrera. Translated by Giacomo Donis. London: Verso, 2016. First published as *Essenza del nichilismo: Saggi* (Brescia: Paideia, 1972).

Shabistarī, Saʿd Ud Din Mahmūd [Maḥmūd ibn ʿAbd al-Karīm Shabistarī]. *The Secret Rose Garden*. Translated by Florence

Lederer. London: J. Murray, 1920. [*Gulshan i Rāz* dates to c.1311.]

Shelley, Percy Bysshe. *Prometheus Unbound: A Lyrical Drama in Four Acts with Other Poems*. London: C. and J. Ollier, 1820.

Strasser, Sabine, Georgeta Stoica, and David Loher, eds. *Social Anthropology* 27, no. 52, Special issue: "Politics of Precarity: Neoliberal Academia under Austerity Measures and Authoritarianism Threat" (December 2019). DOI: 10.1111/1469-8676.12697.

Solovyov, Vladimir. *The Justification of the Good: An Essay on Moral Philosophy*. Translated by Nathalie A. Doddington. Grand Rapids: Eerdmans, 2005. First published as *Opravdanie dobra: Nravstvennaya filosofia* (St. Petersburg: Stasjulevič, 1897).

Sontag, Susan. *Styles of Radical Will*. New York: Farrar, Straus and Giroux, 1969.

Sousa Santos, Boaventura de. "Beyond Abyssal Thinking: From Global Lines to Ecologies of Knowledges." *Eurozine,* June 29, 2007. https://www.eurozine.com/beyond-abyssal-thinking/.

Standing, Guy. *Plunder of the Commons: A Manifesto for Sharing Public Wealth*. London: Pelican, 2019.

Steinberg, Leo. *The Sexuality of Christ in Renaissance Art and in Modern Oblivion*. New York: Pantheon Books, 1983. First published in *October* 25 (Summer 1983).

Stirner, Max [Johann Kaspar Schmidt]. *The Ego and Its Own.* Edited by David Leopold. Translated by Steven T. Byington. Cambridge: Cambridge University Press, 1995. First published as *Der Einzige und sein Eigentum* (Leipzig: Otto Wigand, 1844).

Svetina, Ivo. "Ivo Svetina: In the Name of the Mother." *Slovenian National Theatre,* n.d. https://www.drama.si/en/event/in-the-name-of-the-mother/.

Therborn, Göran. *From Marxism to Post-Marxism?* London: Verso, 2008.

Tönnies, Ferdinand. *Gemeinschaft und Gesellschaft: Abhandlung des Communismus und des Socialismus als empirischer Culturformen Attribution von Ferdinand Tönnies*. Leipzig: Fues, 1887.

Tooze, Adam. "How 'Big Law' Makes Big Money." *New York Review of Books,* February 13, 2020. https://www.nybooks.com/articles/2020/02/13/how-big-law-makes-big-money/.

Turgot, Anne-Robert-Jacques. *Œuvres de Turgot*. Edited by Eugène Daine and Hippolyte Dussard. 2 vols. Paris: Guillaumin, 1844.

Turnovsky, Geoffrey. "Modern Authorship and the Rise of the Market: Evolution of the Literary Field in France, 1750–1789." PhD diss., Columbia University, 2000.

Valéry, Paul. *The Collected Works of Paul Valéry,* Vol. 13: *Aesthetics*. Translated by Ralph Mannheim. New York: Pantheon, 1964.

Veblen, Thorstein. *The Theory of the Leisure Class: An Economic Study in the Evolution of Institutions*. New York: Macmillan, 1899.

Wark, McKenzie. "A Hacker Manifesto (version 4.0)." Edited by Joanne Richardson. *Subsol,* n.d. http://subsol.c3.hu/subsol_2/contributors0/warktext.html.

Watkins, Susan. "Presentism? A Reply to T J Clark." *New Left Review* 2, no. 74 (March–April 2012): 77–102.

———. "Shifting Sands." *New Left Review* 2, no. 61 (January–February 2010): 5–27.

Weber, Max. *Readings and Commentary on Modernity*. Edited by Stephen Kalberg. Malden: Blackwell, 2005.

Williams, Raymond. *Communications*. Harmondsworth: Penguin, 1976.

Witcombe, Christopher L.C.E. *Copyright in the Renaissance: Prints and the "Privilegio" in Sixteenth-century Venice*. Leiden: Brill, 2004.

Wolff, Robert Paul, Barrington Moore, Jr., and Herbert Marcuse. *A Critique of Pure Tolerance*. Boston: Beacon Press, 1965.

Woodward, James B. *Gogol's "Dead Souls."* Princeton: Princeton University Press, 1978.

Zevin, Alexander. *Liberalism at Large: The World According to the "Economist."* London: Verso, 2019.

Ziarek, Krzysztof. *The Force of Art.* Stanford: Stanford University Press, 2004.

Žižek, Slavoj. *Event: Philosophy in Transit.* London: Penguin, 2014.

———. *Tarrying with the Negative: Kant, Hegel, and the Critique of Ideology.* Durham: Duke University Press, 1993.

———. *The Puppet and the Dwarf: The Perverse Core of Christianity.* Cambridge: MIT Press, 2003.

———. "The Thing from Inner Space." *Angelaki* 4, no. 3 (1999): 221–31. DOI: 10.1080/09697259908572073.

———. *The Universal Exception.* London: Continuum, 2005.

Žižek, Slavoj, ed. *The Idea of Communism 2.* London: Verso, 2013.

Žižek, Slavoj, and Alex Taek-Gwang Lee, eds. *The Idea of Communism 3.* London: Verso, 2016.

Zupančič, Alenka. *The Shortest Shadow: Nietzsche's Philosophy of the Two.* Cambridge: MIT Press, 2003.